A Face to Meet the Faces

A Face to Meet the Faces

An Anthology of Contemporary Persona Poetry

Edited by Stacey Lynn Brown and Oliver de la Paz

The University of Akron Press
Akron, Ohio

16   15   14   13   12   5   4   3   2   1

LIBRARY OF CONGRESS CATALOGING-IN-PUBLICATION DATA
A face to meet the faces : an anthology of contemporary persona poetry / edited by Stacey Lynn Brown and Oliver de la Paz. — First edition.
p. cm.
Includes index.
ISBN 978-1-937378-12-7 (pbk.)
1. American poetry—21st century. 2. Persona (Literature)—Poetry. I. Brown, Stacey Lynn. II. De la Paz, Oliver, 1972–
PS617.F33 2012
811.608—DC23

2011050855

Cover image: *Dalmation* by Pamela Klaffke, copyright © 2010. Used with permission. Cover design by Amy Freels.

A Face to Meet the Faces was designed and typeset by Amy Freels. The typeface, Stone Print, was designed by Sumner Stone. The display type, Futura, was designed by Paul Renner. *A Face to Meet the Faces* was printed on sixty-pound natural and bound by BookMasters of Ashland, Ohio.

Contents

Releasing the Kraken: Mortals, Beasts, and Gods from Folklore and Mythology

Fifteen Easy Minutes: Pop Culture and Celebrity

It Kept on Burning: The Fires of Social and Political Consciousness

As It Was Written: Saints, Sinners, and Holy Figures from Sacred Texts

After *Happily Ever After:* Fairy Tales, Creatures, and Other Imaginings

From the Page to the Pen: Authors, Their Characters, and Everything in Between

The Muse Talks Back: Artists and Their Subjects

Not the Poet, Not Me: The Other Faces That You Meet

Introduction
Speaking of Masks

The ability of writers to imagine what is not the self, to familiarize the strange and mystify the familiar, is the test of their power.
—Toni Morrison

Like many things, it began with a need, an absence, a lack. A noticeable omission from the spines on our bookshelves. Somewhere between The New Anthology of This and The Modern Anthology of That, there should be an anthology of persona poetry. Not the definitive anything. Not a comprehensive, historical collection, with "My Last Duchess" as its centerpiece, but one that reflects both the literary tradition of persona poetry as well as its current manifestations, the ways in which this generation of poets practices it. Where was this anthology? Why didn't it already exist?

As educators, we know the value of having such a resource at our fingertips. Students learn best by example, by seeing the ways in which concepts are enacted in practice. And we know the value of persona as a teaching tool, as a way of gently guiding students away from the "write what you know" directive, prying them loose from their own stories, and encouraging them to experience the world from a different point of view. As teachers, we needed it. And as poets, we knew this was the kind of book we'd want to read. So we set about making it.

The term *persona* is derived from the Latin and was used to describe the masks that ancient Greek actors wore to exaggerate their features, allowing their characters to be more fully known and understood by their audience. The psychologist Carl Jung further adapted the definition of persona to refer to the public mask one presents to others. It is the version of ourselves we want other people to see, one that does not necessarily reflect the inner-life of the wearer. (Not coincidentally, "persona" is also the basis of the word "personality.") The persona poem is a self-contained conversation, or *dramatic monologue*, in which the subject matter is filtered through the perspective of a speaker who is distinctly different from the poet-author. The persona poem bridges the various definitions by both amplifying the features of the created character while also revealing a good deal about the poet who wrote it.

Persona has a wide-ranging and far-reaching role in the literary tradition. Early in its history, poetry operated as an oral chronicle of important cultural and historical events, a way of both "knowing" and "remembering," of handing down stories to future generations. Because the subject matter largely consisted of vainglorious accounts of battles and defeats, the point of view of the story-teller was one of witness, or scribe, and poems were very rarely written in the first-person narrative "I." In the fourteenth century, Geoffrey Chaucer's *The Canterbury Tales* introduced a series of poetic monologues in the voices of very different characters, pilgrims on their way to Canterbury. These types of mono-logues and varied personae remained contextualized within epic poetry, but in the mid-nineteenth century, the dramatic monologue as a stand-alone poem was popularized by Robert Browning, which is why "My Last Duchess" is so widely studied and anthologized as representative of the form.

More modernist versions of persona emerged in the twentieth century, with poets such as Ezra Pound and T. S. Eliot utilizing personae as both poetic alter-egos and foils to their own narrative perspectives. Eliot's "The Love Song of J. Alfred Prufrock," from which this anthology takes its title, is an excellent example of persona as alter-ego, allowing the poet to voice the unspeakable and think the unthinkable without direct ownership, consequence, or reproach. In this way, the idea of "hiding behind a mask" can be utterly revealing and liberating. The playful aspect of persona is also apparent in the work of more contemporary poets like Norman Dubie and Ai, who, in their careers, broke the genre wide open by trying on a number of outfits, perspectives, and characters, and creating a rich body of work that cemented the importance—and limitless possibili-ties—of writing beyond one's self.

The poets in this anthology were chosen because their work best repre-sented, in our opinion, the intersection of tradition and possibility. They range in age and accolade and draw their inspiration from sources that are as disparate as the ways in which information is disseminated in our multimedia world. From ancient mythology to popular culture, from fairy tales to tabloids, the voices in these poems address a wide range of issues that are historical, contemporary, and ultimately timeless.

In curating the submissions, we were struck by how many poets chose to occupy the voices of "minor" characters from more major, well-known narratives—perspectives that were, until now, largely unspoken or unsung. Since our overarching sense of history comes primarily from the major narratives, from the "official versions" that are often politically motivated and subsequently biased, it has long been held that a more reliable way of "knowing" can come from the diaries, letters, and writings of everyday people living their lives during a given time. This certainly seems to be an alluring prospect for poetry, as many poets were led to imagine what the lives of unknown, "unimportant" characters might have been like—and what they might have to tell us about our own.

We were also struck by how truly disparate the subject matter was. Our goal in constructing this anthology was to make it as intuitive and user-friendly as possible so that it is easy to access as a teaching tool and also as a text. To that end, we divided the poems and arranged them into categories by subject, content, and theme. Some of these divisions were easier than others. Some poets seemed naturally drawn toward writing about certain subjects, like mythology or religion; other poems could have easily fit into more than one category. The end result is nine sections that cover thousands of years and demonstrate a range of expression and understanding about our histories, our lives today, and our futures.

Our story begins with the stories, people, and events that have come before. In the first section, "That Was Then," some major and minor characters from history reappear, with well-known figures like Calamity Jane sharing the pages with Galileo, Frederick Douglass, bootleggers, and physicists. The second section, "Releasing the Kraken," is based on the varied characters from mythology and folklore, including recognizable names like Penelope, Leda, Prometheus, and Icarus, as well as more esoteric characters like the wives of *The Odyssey*'s lotus-eaters, hybrid "carriers" (part ancient Greek Muse, part Christian angel), and the chimera.

The third section, "Fifteen Easy Minutes," contains characters from popular culture, an expansive category that holds Dorothy from *The Wizard of Oz*, Anna

Nicole Smith, Beetle Bailey, and bluegrass legend Bill Monroe in the first four poems alone. This section is followed by "It Kept on Burning," which takes its title from "He Kept on Burning" by Ai and contains poems of heightened social and political consciousness. While many of the anthology's poems could have fit into this category, as the motion of speaking from another's perspective is often a socio-political move, we found that these particular poems held these issues at their core, with personae that included political prisoners and protestors, soldiers and their casualties, and abolitionists and segregationists.

The fifth section is entitled "As It Was Written" and contains poems inspired by the Bible and other religious texts. This section includes the perspectives of more minor Biblical characters, like the wives of Noah, Abraham, and Pilate, who shed a different kind of light on the familiar stories and lessons. In "After *Happily Ever After*," well-known fairy tales, and their characters, are re-envisioned: Little Red Riding Hood tries on the perspective of her predator, Pinocchio elegizes his former life, and werewolves retract their claws long enough to ruminate about their anger issues.

In the seventh section, "From the Page to the Pen," poets take their place in the ongoing literary conversation by responding to the authors and characters of other literary texts. In these pages, you'll find a love poem from *Beloved*'s Paul D, afterthoughts by Hamlet and Ophelia, and musings from Walt Whitman and Li Po. The poems in the eighth section, "The Muse Talks Back," give voice to famous artists and their equally famous subjects, with narratives from the perspectives of Frida Kahlo, Picasso's immortalized models and lovers, and "His Coy Mistress," to name a few.

The final section, "Not the Poet, Not Me," takes its title from John Berryman's preface to his collection *The Dream Songs*, in which he emphatically identified the speaker of the poems as someone distinctly different from himself. This final category consists of poems that largely defy categorization and is a kind of catch-all for "everything else." Ever wonder what a knife might think about the violence it enacts? What about the inner lives of misogynistic kings? The characters in these poems continually surprise by virtue of the varied nature of their voices and the perspectives they engender.

As disparate as these poems and poets are, they all share one thing in common: the desire to step outside of oneself and imaginatively inhabit the world of someone, or something, else. In a world that is so saturated by, and obsessed with, "reality" and the minutiae of private lives, the motion away from the limitations and constraints of literal truth can be exhilarating and fruitful for a poet. And in the post-confessional landscape of contemporary poetics, where the modern audience tends to read for the (auto)biographical in a poem, these poems are equally refreshing for the reader in their clear-cut boundaries of assumed identity.

Because these poems reference both real and imaginary characters and span thousands of years, and because there are as many reasons to write in persona as there are poets who practice it, we have asked each author to provide a contextual note that will help identify the speaker of each poem, as well as the reasons why that poet was moved to write from that perspective. These contextual notes appear in addition to the biographical notes of the poets themselves and are placed at the end of the volume so as not to interfere with or impede the reader's experience of the actual poem on the page. It is our hope that these notes will function as windows into both the world of the poem as well as the process of the poet who crafted it.

In all of these poems, we were struck by how well the poets navigated and maximized the potential inherent in using masks. Playful and political, practical and polemical, there is a certain freedom of expression that is unhindered by direct ownership or consequence and a kind of joyful exuberance in divorcing oneself from one's *self*. From the moment we are children pretending to be our parents, to shamans pretending to inhabit elements of the natural world, to actors and actresses assuming the roles of the famous and infamous, there is something primal about the act of donning the mask, an urgent connection that demands to be made. And in the world of literature, this urgency makes persona a vital poetic act because of a poem's emotional immediacy and its ability to articulate the nature of the "other" in economical and profound measures.

This project may have begun with our need, as teachers, to fill a perceived absence and address our questions about persona poems and how or why poets write them, but the anthology itself became a whole lot more. What rose to our consciousness as we collected and assembled these poems was the understanding that persona poetry is, at its heart, an act of empathy, of walking that mile in someone else's shoes to determine not only what the view is like from there, but what those shoes, and that body, *feel* like. Truly inhabiting the consciousness of someone else heightens our own and makes us more aware of our own predispositions, prejudices, and predilections. And in this world of fracture and fragmentation, where ignorance and prejudice and bigotry and hatred threaten to rip apart the very fabric of our humanity, empathy remains one of the most important tools we have to help us realign ourselves with each other and rediscover what it is we have in common, what binds us together rather than what separates.

Our hope is that you'll find a place for this anthology among the spines on your shelves and that the stories being told will remind you again and again of the value of empathy—and the ways in which imagining the world through someone else's eyes can show us what it means to be both human and humane.

Stacey Lynn Brown
Edwardsville, IL

Oliver de la Paz
Bellingham, WA

That Was Then
· ·
Voices from Our Historical Pasts

Aubuchon Creek
Angie Macri

When the violets walked
the forest floor with birdsfeet,
I left my sons.

Céledon cut the bars
of the room, the chains
the Widow Aubuchon bought
to keep me there.

Louis, Baptiste—I could
only take one of them
with me, and the older
wouldn't leave the younger.

I will come back, I promised,
with every one of our tribe
to set you free. I took
their faces in my hands.

When they were babies, I drew
my fingertips across their eyes
to help them fall asleep. I kissed
their feet as if they were kings

or the fathers, and they laughed
and held their feet back up
to me again. I didn't know
the tribes were gone.

The otters we trap and skin,
the furs we sleep in at night
and trade by day, Céledon's
musket and the oil for traps,

the way the ducks raise
off the water and fly, reaching
forward in violet as the dawn—
I can't go back. The Widow

has sold one of my sons
to her brother. We were worth
two thousand livres.
The coureurs de bois won't

surrender us, although they speak
of my sadness. Hunters and trappers
relay my message: my sons must pray
to our mother who held her son

one last time against her, to the son
bound in thorns. We feel the free circles
of the rain even when water bears their name.

Calamity Jane Informs Wild Bill of His Faults while Visiting His Grave
Sarah Grieve

I used to think there was no better smell than gun powder
        searing flesh, but turns out leather smeared with dirt
and sweat beats it, and you and me, we smelled a lot of it
      on each other briaring our way through the territory. I'm sure
you would've liked to see me strip out of a corset and bloomers,
        let the ribbon in my hair dust our foreplay, but I'm a two gun
woman and there's no place for a holster over calicos or ginghams—
      but dammit, Bill, if I can't still feel the calluses of your hands
hitching their way under my belt, your mustache blackberrying
        my neck and no one here believes me. They don't think I can
be all teacups and hatpins, and maybe I can't, but there's a place

    for spitting and cursing and carrying on, and it isn't
when you're Colt-pistol-crazy for a man. If you could,
        you'd tell them those letters to that woman in Ohio
were penned while knee deep in my saddle bags, tell them
      you loved the hoof-beaten trails of my torso, stream-stroked
trench of back—licking dirt, tinny and coarse, from between
        my breasts, but you ain't here to do the telling. I don't care
what people say, not my concern if their minds don't think
      about the world in colors, but I can't stop seeing it in the reds
that spilled with your brains on that poker table or the orange
        of vomit McCall retched when I went after him with a cleaver.

They won't see the purple of the dress I'll wear dead,
      but they'll dig me a grave next to yours and they'll have to swear
and spit to it, and then they'll believe me, they'll have to believe
        you loved me loosey tooth and tumbley all the way to the day

you got shot. I'd shoot myself now just to get near you again,
        mingle my rot with yours as we sour, but then they'd think
the only way I could land you was you forked and me begging
                and there's no truth to that, so I'll stay here near your marker,
wait them out watching the row of pines, the way they sway
        as if playing the last hand with a stacked deck, knowing it's all
going to fall my way so I'll take a long swig of whiskey and nod.

Constantinople, Plague Summer
Sarah Lindsay

Wind out of the north today, with the stench
from the towers across the Horn, where the emperor's men
have packed the dead. I danced for a man last night
with black peas all over his arms. When I placed my hands
on the floor, reaching over my head, he began to scream.
Spilled red fish sauce, I think, ran over the table.
I took all the food I could carry.

Those the plague passes over are starving.
I dreamt of ortolans in a pastry nest,
woke to another slave bolting to drown his fever.
They say plum pickle wards it off, or lemons;
they say God sends it. I think it's part of the world
that strikes and spares and never gives us the pattern.
Tertia, our best, went first.

They say the emperor prays all day.
Some say he is dying. He's sent for me, nonetheless.
No chin, like a rat, and his small hands are never still,
but if any wine is left in the city he'll have it,
olives and figs to push between my breasts,
perhaps little birds in a pie with fruit in their beaks
or spitted with their eyes open.

Courting Mary Ann Cotton

R. Elena Prieto

When Mary Ann Cotton died on 24 March 1873,
she had been accused of killing four of her husbands
and almost three times as many children.

—from Mary Ann Cotton: The Black Widow,
  The Most Evil Women in History

I walk on men like glass.
Bouquets of flowers might win me,
bouquets of flowers won't save you.
I'll bring them back graveside,
dried petals to kiss the turned earth,
back to husbands I walked on
like parlor floors or dried bones:
powdered marrow slick and soft
on the point of my heel.

Inheritance powder—
        arsenic oxide, rat poison.
I spill children like milk.

Convenience is acquiring a new life
at will: new husbands snared
by the smudge of life growing within.
Sign here, dear. Your future—
a swarm of black umbrellas,
little boxes for little children who
might have parted their hair like you.
Might have worn red ribbons or bowties,
small hourglasses waiting to be tipped.

Dr. Balmis
Peter Pereira

—March 17th, 1804: at sea between Puerto Rico and Puerto Cabello

Our first stop, Puerto Rico—a disaster.
Oller (that charlatan) had already infected the populace
with his inferior vaccine.

I tried to convince the townspeople my vaccine
was superior, *proven* effective *and* safe. So safe,
I would infect my own son—if I had one.

Still, not one person stepped forward,
or bared an arm. And now, of our Expedition's
last two foundlings, only one has taken.

The other I hear was discovered playing
with a cow below deck *two weeks* before his injection.
Contaminated—the idiot! Why did nobody tell me?

We are in danger of losing everything.
At least the other boy is safe for now.
As in nature, having two of a thing

preserves us: Two eyes, two ears, two legs,
two lungs. (Why only one heart?) I've
brought him to my room, the good boy.

He will stay by my side
until his vesicle has matured.
No matter what his governess says.

Ah—what a beautiful boil he is making.
Red and swollen as a rosebud,
exquisitely tender to the touch.

He moans and whimpers in pain,
his forehead warm and beaded with sweat.
To prevent him from spoiling it

I've bound his wrists
to the bedpost with a scarf.
I lie awake in the night and watch him sleep.

I kneel at his side and softly stroke his good shoulder,
run my fingers through his wispy hair. His face
is like an angel's, and his lovely arm

with its swollen blossom fills me with joy.
Such a beautiful boy. If he were my own son
I could not love him more.

Drifting towards the bottom, Jacques Piccard recalls the sky

R. A. Villanueva

Hour #4, Hadal zone—*Forgive
me. I can only think of chainmaille for
a fitting match to this die-cast shade of
black outside our porthole. It is far more
deep a nothingness than that. So pure a
cold that our floodlights appear to burn as
stars do. What words can render void, this nova
of mercury bulbs through the clear abyss?*

*Our descent was marked by medusae, clouds
of shrimp, luminescent matter adrift
on ambient currents. No such flares and
flashes at these fathoms. Don says we passed
the basement of twilight hours ago,
likens the dark to a murder of crows.*

*

Bathyscaphe Trieste, Mariana Trench,
23 Jan.—*I have heard how Iceland's
sunlight trickles away by minutes each
fall so that, by the solstice, darkness spans
8/10 of the day. I cannot divine
living without sight of the sky for so
long and here must admit relief that fine
fissures now run the face of our window.
It means we must cut our stay at the Deep
to minutes in case the pressures decide*

*to gnaw at the hull itself. It means we
should thank the Good Lord for lime-hydroxide,
for Father's gondola lifted miles above
Augsberg, breaching the air, buoyant as doves.*

*

13:06, gauges mark seven miles
deep—*To settle here atop the trench floor
is to kick up grackles from their perches,
to run headlong into rooks on the tor
and to watch their wings overcome the sky.*

*All around us seems an empire at the
height of its forces, a tuber of night
and ooze, bone fog and soot we come to love
because we can. Don and I lack the room
to embrace. We arrive without cornet
or flag. There is something like an anthem
in my marrow so let us sound this last
fathom out with it. Let us trawl the dark
for whale fall, sing of our ballast like larks.*

Elvie Comes Home to Rosetta
Randall Horton

Elvie come home from that straw pallet
with dust and red clay stuck to his body.
I soak him in the wash-tub for an hour,
scrub loneliness from his arms with lye soap
before he lay on our cotton mattress. The firmness
of his muscles brings me to those hallelujah
eyes, and my insides moan like I'm testifying
for the Lord. Wrapped in safeness, I forget
the lonely nights that held him from me while
he streams a creek of salt-water tears. My hand
grazes up and down his washboard chest, I erase
the stripes that once labeled my man animal.
I take his lips in mine, where his tongue held
grits and coffee—now it holds the aching of
my womanhood. In his heartbeat, I hear
twenty inch iron chains, rustling, as he shuffle-steps
to the center of my sweet spot to be whole again.

The Empress Dreams after a Poisoned Meal
Tina Chang

Once the guards sprayed me down unclothed
I left my veil in a pool of my own waking
A pomegranate ruptured in my sleep, stains
under my fingernails and on my ghost gown
when I rose my maid played the music of my tragic
birth   I miss my husband's summoning harmony
swirling   Yesterday I met the ruler of Turkey
and all the pitiful people at the party The only
vantage point is me   I am always alone Documents
confirm I had many different names and official
stamps that said I was born   I exhale smoke
signals through a haze A throat raw from yawning
feet bruised from tripping through the green maze
Soon the mechanical toys and windup clocks
will be smashed and shot in the Summer Palace
Oh the jewels   hairpin of plum blossoms
ring of dragonfly circling above this chipped crown
Bring the gems into my room on someone's back
Let me model all my bracelets that anchor me
to this empire   In the courtyard I am a cat mewing
with my collar on   fed with imperial poison I sleep
curled at the center filled with lion dogs sniffing
as if I were historical food   I never minded   My
kingdom one world beneath me   My sleeping sound

Extant Diary of Amanda Elizabeth McKenzy [Mistress of Hopewell Plantation, Four Forks, Marswell County]

Carolyn Beard Whitlow

March 5, 1864

Fife and drum. This infernal war goes on, on, on.
Cannon balls and muskets do not stop. Rattle plates
in the breakfront and thrum the carpet on the floor,
noise thick like a dust cloud. I cannot breathe
without quiet. My nerves on edge.
Why can everything not become as before?
I was not happy but had no cares.
Now I am blighted with every care.

*

March 19

Clephus and Zolene slippt away during the night.
Wretched beasts. I told myself I would not sleep
as to be watchful. Dozed but for a moment
yet still the fault is mine. I needed a tincture
of spirits to ease my mind, must have overfilled.
My nerves so ruffled who could blame me.
I try to ration as my store dwindles sorely.
What does this bondage hold for me?
Keys to the cupboard, the pace from storehouse
to smokehouse to cellar. I must ever be watchful
of their herb and plant gardens, the cooking, blends
of medicines, dipping candles, spinning thread,

weaving cloth, knitting socks, sewing clothes,
do this do that. I am ever worn. I am but one woman.
Flies, mosquitoes, the overbearing summer heat.
Nurse the cholera, influenza, yellow fever.
'Tis I must mete the punishment out
even when I have no strength. Follow the rules.
John was never here even before the war.
'Tis I who suffer without Zolene to care.
I have but Margaret Rose for comfort now.

*

April 6

The rain pellets down like bullets,
each drop harsh with searing cold.
Even the crocuses will not lift their heads
from their cellar of earth. God knows
we are in need of warmth and cheer.
Margaret Rose prattles her best to soothe
but my irritability grows. Of late
without John everything has fallen in disarray
though he stayed abroad at Charleston talking
secesh before the war. At least I do not more
have to suffer his wenches and whelps.

Always then I felt alone.

*

May 30

I trample in the garden grubbing
like a mudsill for meager food and fear
any sighting of blue, even the sky.

*

June 25

Margaret Rose just must do more.
I've pampered and spoilt her so.
She frets when even I ask her to fan
my face and bring a cooling cloth, my beneficence
unrewarded. Does she not know
of any mistress she could have I am most kind.
Of her ilk and by her age she should gather kindling,
sweep the grounds, collect eggs from the barnyard
if any hen is left to lay. I cannot afford to keep her
now as would I my own. She must care for me.
She does not know that her wretched father John
has fallen near Chancellorsville and lays there
in the ground. So I may do with her as I please.
I could have sold her, did not have to keep her
and certainly not in my own house
to call me Mama, my own babe shriveled
in the cold corridors of my womb.
But Doll will never again rock my cradle,
nor will she see the blush of Margaret's rose.
And brutish John never will know.

*

July 12

I stole onto the old Stone Plantation
to raid their garden, Priscilla having fled
in a one-horse trap in sulky weather.
Tho' I pray God knows how she has fared.
Among the scattered stalks found shells, a severed
foot and near, a bright red sash. Frighted, home
I staggered. Sacked without carrot, onion, radish.
There's no one left to know I'm here.

*

July 17

She screams and stomps and pouts.
No longer can I keep her like a doll.
She cries and cries but I can
break

*

Galileo to Maria Celeste

Gregory Fraser

Don't, you kept repeating, *you'll regret it,*
but that was why I planned to go ahead.
I needed to be able to say, in the end,
I lived, even if that meant a shattered past.

I'd had enough of careful calculations—
dead light ricocheting between stars, streets
of Florence whorled like a thumbprint.
It was time to damage something, someone,

first of all myself. All the signs agreed:
the late autumn wind, forcing trees to undress
like inmates or drafted soldiers being processed,
the morning's racket of grackles, so cacophonous

it made a laughing stock of sense. *Don't,*
you said again, but I could tell what had
to be done—by the widow bent with mourning,
clouds of dingy sheep's wool, then a hard,

seed-like rain on the window glass. It ticked
like the small explosive fashioned in my mind
in boyhood—wired with my mother's quiet
rage (the red), my father's mire (the black)—

to detonate at the proper time. This time.
Couldn't you tell, from the start, how oddly
I stuck out, like a silo on a family farm,
or a water tower in a prairie town? *Promise me*

you won't, you insisted. Sheets of newsprint
roamed the streets like tramps. *Very well,*
I promised, studying the bands of grime around
the children's wrists. Forgive me, dear. I lied.

The Given Account
Blas Falconer

—Puerto Rico, 1510

They said they were gods, and we believed—
they crossed uncrossable seas after all

in ships with sails like wings—but Salcedo
is dead. Pacing river shallows, turning rocks,

sifting sand for flecks of gold, he cut his foot
on stone or shell, sending braids of blood

downstream. Overhead, wind shook trees
so leaves and light spilled in, catching a school

of fish, a silver shimmer. I was there.
Kneeling on the bank, I dressed his wound

pressing strips of cloth to stop the flood
but red spots seeped through the weave,

my fingers wet with blood, his blood,
no different from mine. He winced, his face

paled by pain, but nothing, nothing changed,
no dove, no cloud, no beam of light, and he

a god or son of god? I, who came to drink,
struck dumb by one thought—they bleed, they die—

led him back into the pool and pushed
his head below. His arms thrashed, legs kicked,

lungs inhaled mouths of water. He stopped.
Three days I stayed to see him stir, but he,

not strongest, weakest or cruelest of them,
did not move. I pulled him out. He hung

wet and limp and heavy in my arms—
this man, this man, almost too much to bear.

A Great Physicist Recalls the Manhattan Project

Kathleen Flenniken

—John A. Wheeler (1911–2008)

Think of our little group with a map spread out in front of us—
great expanses of the empty west—as if we were new Columbuses.

Think of it—a *desert* in Washington State. Along the icy blue Columbia.
Think of the caravan of laborers, several hundred a night, unloading at Pasco.

Immense mess halls accommodating thousands. Big band dances.
Beer joints with ground-level windows for tear gas. Constant construction.

When the chain reaction at B-Reactor died that first night,
the mood was excitement and puzzlement. As for whether

I solved the poisoning riddle, let no man be his own judge.
Fermi was there. A marvelous person. One scorching Sunday afternoon,

our group hiked along a rushing irrigation canal. If we jumped in,
how would we get out? Fermi thought our ropes were sissy. The water

dragged him downstream clambering, until he reappeared,
roughed up, shins bleeding. That was Fermi. That's how he got things done.

I recall a Sunday with the children hiking in the Horse Heaven Hills.
I watched my youngest climb as the sun blazed behind her golden hair

and realized that halos were not a painter's invention,
but a consequence of nature. Have you ever held plutonium

in your hand? Someone once gave me a piece shaped and nickel-plated
so alpha particles couldn't reach the skin. It was the temperature, you see,

the element producing heat to keep itself warm—not for ten
or a hundred years, but thousands of years. This is the energy contained

in Hanford's fuel. I think of that place as a song not properly sung.
A romantic song. And not one person in a hundred knows the tune.

The Hangman Recalls a Dream to His Son, Abbot
Nik De Dominic

—Arkansas, 1875

Listen:

A room of Geissler tubes: there's a mulatto girl bent over the green
        felt of the uptown bunco parlor, manned
                by me and a northwand'ring Mex'can
       woman; out the mullatta's body, tubes. The Mex'can
works a lever system, so my seed
        runs through the elbow joints out the mule's knees to
            a basin—a furnace below heats white.
None of this bothers me: the syphilis
     rot around her thighs; the worms once
        in her mind, I see squirm through the glass vein
works that glow, phosphorize the room. She
         being purged, vindicated by God
            and His love; by my hand, the Hangman's,
courses water and lye. Cleanse.

       Then, odd thing, Abbot, I ask Him why?

     And what did He say, oldman?
He said, nothing, but in the dream—
     the works collapse. Glass breaks, shreds our faces,
        our hands, my member wriggles on the floor. I, eunuch,
ask why?   *And what did He say, oldman—?*
     I told you boy, *he says* nothing.
       But we are all—
         we are enveloped all
          in white, white heat

Here You Are
Stephanie M. Pruitt

—June 1849

And here you are riding my wind,
meeting me around each corner. I turn
away and away and sigh you out. But you seep
back and back and into my air where you reside
when not on top and behind and inside. Out I climb
from under your weight, bundling knots of nights
into small corners of memory: my side-room cot,
the curing barn, creek banks, stables, the east field.
At night, I may rise and come, but in my workday, there is no space
for your breath on my neck. And yet, here, with my arms full
in the parlor, at the spring house, I feel you
gripping my cornsilk hair (glory, you say), wrapping
it across your palm, wrist and knuckles, pulling
me into your smell—earth and talcum and leather. You waft
in boiled clothes I wring and hang on the line, the embers
I fan for a kitchen fire. You are here, here within
each breath and I am without my own space. Outside
is no better. Every breeze returns me. I carry you on my shoulders.
You are all about my head, surrounding my ears. The wind
tosses my hair across my face. I inhale and there, there, here—
your smell drapes each strand flowing down my back. It is carrying
you. My hair smells of you. You. My hair—black like my mother's,
silken straight like your father's. Even my hair is another's. And it is all in your hands.
The wind – memory – my neck – you – hair – your palm – my hair – you –
in my hair – wrapping – your hands – this smell – gripping – my hair.

History
M. Nzadi Keita

*It was no unusual occurrence for mother to be called up
at all hours of the night, cold and hot as the case may be,
to prepare supper for a hungry lot of fleeing humanity.*

—Rosetta Douglass Sprague

We will be something more than we
are now. Our crumbled days and nights,
our saddest parts will mix like ash
and dirt, kept secret, pounded down

by traveling feet. Some later man
will cry some rugged song in praise
to Douglass. Write the sun up as
he used to do, then walk

awhile with God (but never knowing),
walk in the leaves, trampling afternoon.
His thoughts will tumble. Words
all dressed in flags and velvet. Swelling up

like boils. Jumping to his feet,
pretending he is Douglass, struck
by Covey, spitting fire. And when
the writer turns to me, what shape

will fill his mouth?
How many pages will he need
for laundry, heaping plates and croup
that breaks at dawn, to heed the mark

of my accounts? Will it
be said that I could speak? Seal cracks?

And years from now who will remember bread
and stew that set those bound to Canada on their feet?

Four hundred buried shackles
in my garden. Will he paint across my truth
one hundred years from now or hush
me silent on a page that reads: *the wife of an important man*

I am the Real Jesse James
Sarah Messer

It took four men with big heavy hands to hold the horse down. The horse kicked its stomach, collapsed like an ironing board and rolled over, pinning the legs of the men beneath it. One man sat on its neck while the other administered the needle—Bute and Demerol in the night paddock. The horse's eyes were like stoplights in the headlights of the men's trucks parked in a circle around the animal. I have faced this animal in a paddock when it was too late to run. I was young but I was no girl when my hand came down hard on the muzzle of the horse that charged, half a ton of meat and muscle thrown my way.

*

I am the real Jesse James. I have stared down that stampede, that rage he thinks belongs only to him. I heard it took four men to hold him down when his mouth frothed and he swore and spit and bit people, had to be held down against the smashed furniture. This rumor follows him like a legend, like a bad smell. An animal that can be held down by four grown men. But what kind of animal is that? A horse that kicks its own stomach. A thought that eats away at men's guts when they are already trapped, already tamed. The one last thing that she should have told him but didn't; the one time he reached for her and she turned away. I am the real Jesse James. Not the man you may have heard of held down by four men, his friends who ran after him when he drank too much as usual and was off like a horse out of the bar and down the street and into the forest of buildings, the forest of his own thoughts, all the things he should have told her.

*

Perhaps you have heard about my legend? The one that follows me like a hang-over, a bad smell. It was rage that held the big animal down in the paddock, not the heavy hands of the men who pinned it there in the dirt that wasn't a paddock really, just the circle of their trucks parked and running. This happened when I was just a girl, so it is hard to remember. I watched as it took two of them to hold the neck down and administer the needle—Bute and Demerol. One man sat on the horse's neck and said: this is one sick horse, fucking bastard. The men were angry, standing in front of their trucks after chasing the horse across the field, through a forest of trees and I wasn't supposed to follow.

*

I am the real Jesse James. I know you have heard of me. That was what I was supposed to say, the last thought before I turned my head away from him and he flew into a rage. I am the real Jesse James. But I have drunk far too much tonight. And I am just a girl. Perhaps you have heard of his legend? It took four men to hold him down in the paddock after he ran out of the bar, four of his friends to hold him down because rumor has it that he smashed some furniture. I have seen this man naked and I can tell you that he is no Jesse James. I am the real thing. I mean, I am telling you the real story now. But I have drunk far too much tonight. And I am just a girl.

*

What is known about the doctor who helped the outlaw Jesse James when he was wounded, rolling in a frothy rage and held down by four men in a paddock: He brought his doctor's bag with him. Needles, Bute, Demerol. The doctor did not know he was helping an outlaw. When he entered the circle of trucks the men had parked with the engines running, the air smelled like horses let loose from barns. The outlaw Jesse James was a small girl held down by four men. She was in a rage—having smashed furniture and split a man's lip, kicked him in the stomach. Why had the men been holding her down, the doctor asked, couldn't they see she was just a girl? The air smelled like outlaws and the girl said, I am the real Jesse James, you aren't gonna tell on me, are ya, doc?

*

The doctor lived in a red house that burned light from the inside. When he walked out the red door, the air smelled like a legend. Somewhere out in a field, four men were holding a girl down by the legs, they were kneeling on her neck. Her eyes were stop lights in the air that smelled like the men's breath, like the inside of whiskey glasses. They said they were looking for a friend who ran away and they talked about him as if he were some sort of outlaw, as if he were the real Jesse James.

*

The horse, the girl said, the horse has escaped its stall, is running out in the night, has broken out of the barn. I am no girl. And I am no doctor, the doctor thought, I am a thief. I steal from medicine cabinets. The girl rides the horse to all her private robberies. Who has stolen her horse? The doctor placed a hand on the girl's neck where the boot had been. He felt a vein pulse. A red house that burned light from the inside. Isn't it always rage, the doctor thought, that makes one body hold another to the ground like some sort of legend? The men are all outlaws. They are all little girls who need to be held down and given medicine. She needed this medicine, the men told the doctor. Her mouth was a red house that burned light from the inside. I am no girl, she said, I am the real Jesse James. The men drank too much tonight and could not find their friend. The doctor placed his bag down in a circle of dirt, in the air that smelled like whiskey. I am no doctor, he said.

*

When I was a girl, my father was a doctor who lived in a house that caught fire and burned red from the inside. He was always falling asleep with a needle in his arm, burning things down. He was always running away from his four friends, those men with heavy hands who used to chase him out of bars and down the street through a forest of buildings, his own thoughts that were filled with the smell of burned houses, horses and the outlaw Jesse James. That night I watched the men driving their trucks across the fields. The trucks stopped with their headlights in a circle, the engines running. I was riding my horse through the forest until he sweated with rage, his mouth foaming, his red coat burning from the inside against my legs. I was just a girl and I was not supposed to follow the men when they drove their trucks across the field looking for my father with his doctor's bag caught in the circle of light, his eyes burning red stop lights when he said where is my girl? And the men's hands were on him.

*

But the men were not outlaws. They held themselves down with their own hands. The doctor came with his bag and gave them clean needles. The air carried the smell of horse on its back. The men talked to each other as if they were creating a legend. Each of them said I am the outlaw, I am the real thing, the one who ran out of the bar and into the streets and give me your hands, go ahead put your hands on me and try to hold me down now that my veins burn red from the inside. I am a horse that rolls over on your legs and pins you down. And what do you think I am? Do you think I am a girl? I am no girl. Did I tell you that before I left she let four men put their hands on her? She let them hold her down to the ground.

*

There was a girl I loved who was a legend among her friends. They said that she was prone to fly into rages and sometimes just ran out of bars and into the streets. I was no doctor, but I could tell this girl needed help. Rumor had it she smashed some furniture, burned letters, and split the lip of her friend, all because a man turned himself away from her at the wrong time. I loved her, yes, but there is no point in making a legend of it. Jesse James was shot by a friend in his own home. But in his photo, they crossed his hands over his chest in a restful pose.

Ishi Speaks
Kelly Madigan Erlandson

Later they will say I was starved
and though it is true I had grown thin
this did not compel me. I knew scarcity
as a brother and a guide.

Did you think I didn't anticipate
the mockery? How could I be anything
but foolish? I knew they would smell
my breath, that they would press
the ends of my fingers into ink.

Of course many had died
in the canyon and I had said words
above them. Though I moved
into a high crevice, I came down
to visit the bones. Sometimes I spoke
in the old way to the beautiful
hoop of ribs, but eventually
they each fell inward. One whole
day I laid in the stream. The clouds
moved their dark shapes across
my skin and I learned to forget.

You may think it is my duty
to remember, but I do not value
recollection. It is work
that is never done, and serves no one.

You want my stories, my ways.
These things are cached in rock.

I came down not for food,
your slimy gruel with its foreign flavor.

I came because your odd speech,
which I still cannot comprehend,
called me down, the voices especially
of your children, the way
they yawn and sing. I came to listen
to the sounds that rise from your throats
that had left the canyon deafening.

from *The Lost Letters of Frederick Douglass*
Evie Shockley

June 5, 1892

Dear Daughter,
         Can you be fifty-three this
month? I still look for you to peek around
my door as if you'd discovered a toy
you thought gone for good, ready at my smile
to run up and press your fist into my
broken palm. But your own girls have outgrown
such games, and I cannot pilfer back time
I spent pursuing Freedom. Fair to you,
to your brothers, your mother? Hardly.

But

what other choice did I have? What sham,
what shabby love could I offer you, so
long as Thomas Auld held the law over
my head? And when the personal threat was
ended, whose eyes could mine enter without
shame, if turning toward my wife and children
meant turning my back?

Your mother's eyes stare

out at me through yours, of late. You think I
didn't love her, that my quick remarriage
makes a Gertrude of me, a corseted
Hamlet of you. You're as wrong as you are
lucky. Had Anna Murray had your
education as a girl, my love for
her would have been as passionate as it

was grateful. But she died illiterate,
when I had risked my life to master language.
The pleasures of book and pen retain
the thrill of danger even now, and you
may understand why Ottilie Assing,
come into our house to translate me into
German, could command so many hours,
years, of my time—or, as you would likely
say, of your mother's time.

                        Forgive me,
Rosetta, for broaching such indelicate
subjects, but as my eldest child and
only living daughter, I want you to
feel certain that Helen became the new
Mrs. Douglass because of what we shared
in sheaves of my papers: let no one
persuade you I coveted her skin.
I am not proud of how I husbanded
your mother all those years, but marriage,
too, is a peculiar institution.
I could not have stayed so unequally yoked
so long, without a kind of Freedom in
it. Anna accepted this, and I don't
have to tell you that her lot was better
and she, happier, than if she'd squatted
with some other man in a mutual
ignorance.

                  Perhaps I will post, rather
than burn, this letter, this time. I've written it
so often, right down to these closing lines,
in which I beg you to be kinder, much
kinder, to your step-mother. You two are
of an age to be sisters, and of like

temperament—under other circumstances,
you might have found Friendship in each other.

With regards to your husband—I am, as
ever, your loving father—

Frederick Douglass

History is
preserved through
Art

Manatee
Eliot Khalil Wilson

—from the unwritten diaries of Francisco Vázquez de Coronado

I hadn't been so turned on since
we sacked the leaping houses of Venice—
    that flotsam ghetto of hemorrhaging ditches—
and there was nothing mystical about any of that.

We had sailed to the mortal edge of the world
through mirror seas and squall,
    following the breath of whale and the rumor of spice
for two raw and womanless years.

The touch of the sun on the deck grew carnal,
the lowered jib sails puddled the prow like wedding dresses,
and the sirens hiding in the soft valleys of waves
whispered obscenities under the dizzy stars.

A few could tar-patch some forbearance together, but still,
callipygian whale calves wrought despondency;
Sanchez and Manolo crossed swords over a pulchritudinous cloud.
The ship's goat hid itself.

After Father Alonzo, with his delicate thighs,
was caught tupping the figurehead,
I feared we were not far from the baboon lunacy.

Then, ten fathoms to port, fairly perched
on a sunlit sandbar was she.
She beckoned us with her scalloped hand
and tossed her long sea-grass hair coquettishly
before this rapture, this orchid of the waves, was overcome
by maidenly shyness, and parted the sea before her.

Even had the waves been the teeth of flames
who would have not leapt in to reach her?
And no volley of cannon fire ever left that ship as fast
as all of us—from cook to captain—with only Valdez,
twisted in the rigging, left aboard—
though the glimmering maiden had long since vanished
under a sequined wave.

As we stood on the crumbling sandbar,
some dared question her charms—*Una mujeruca* said Machado
*An aborted elephant or perhaps
a finned eastern European,* opined Estremera.

But I saw her mythical beauty as certain
as I saw our ship sailing away without us,
with only prone Valdez still tangled upside-down
in the mainmast rigging, and at the stern,
the goat.

A Medium Rehearses the Square Order Shuffle
Mary Kaiser

How unlikely to rotate at noon, how baffling,
after pearl-headed stickpins and amber parquet,

to come undone on plain oak boards, trip and snag
among the saints like a dangling hook, stray eye.

Bowing and twisting while the brethren drill,
I mean to follow their order, but the shuffle's

hobnail thunder drives too quick through Isaac's
grate: wrist-heel-turn-away, palm-toe-back-again;

fold-weep-put-away, greet-bow-kiss and turn away.
Panting through this figure, spun round to face

the road, I see a wonder striding in jangling beads
and fringes: Sook, the Cherokee control, keeping

his own time. Oh, I have turned too late; I never
did believe this shuffle could be charmed. Sisters,

brothers, bend me head to ankle, hands together—
what mountain is like to—prod me, lead, drum me

to victory or topple me now, a rocking, spun-off
rim, ringing *Mother, Mother, what can I do to be saved?*

Memory
Sally Ball

*If memory be done by characters in the brain yet the soul
remembers too, for She must remember those characters.*

—Isaac Newton

Messala Corvinus forgot his own name.
One, by a blow with a stone, forgot all his learning.
Another, by a fall from a horse,
forgot his mother's name and kinfolk.
A young student of Montpellier, by a wound,
lost his memory, so that he was fain to be taught
the letters of the alphabet again.
The like befell a Franciscan friar after a fever.

Messala, the soul—
she knows the faces of your friends,
Barrow's face, and your mother's.
The difficulty lies in believing her.
She does not bother with evidence.

She bears in her pockets notation
and also all the human qualities.

We do not experiment with her:

She must be trusted, followed,
a path in a dark wood, where the trees
are inscribed with faces, with letters,
the imperfect curve of C,
the depth of O
an R like new foliage, the V of a forked elm.

Trusted and pursued.

Nadya to Stalin, 1925
Shelley Puhak

Otherwise, I will tell the world who was really Lenin's wife—
—Stalin's attempt to blackmail Nadya Krupskaya, Lenin's widow

But you need a widow, no? for that pickled
pear in your marble mausoleum. Like he needed
me. Needed both of us. It can still be done, I know,

but isn't it easier to keep me? And I will go kicking,
Soso, you must know by now. The not being in love, the always
almost—he did need both of us, the tug and the pull.

But in those days, I needed nothing.
Bellies soft, jaws slack, lashes beating—
I got to hear her three young ones snuffle in their sleep.

Our children, I thought of them then. Oh, if only I'd had my own.
I'd stay behind with the children, Inessa's children,
in the window, waving, watching.

Her cheeks flamed and still I'd stay.
Heads tented, mouths making theory,
they would go striding off on those long walks,

not to be in love, but almost.
And he said no. He needed to work, he needed—
I offered, you know, to leave him, three times.

It had always been quiet between us.
But she made that go away.
Indeed, I may have loved her more than he did.

You may think we were pecking eyes the whole time. No.
True, she was thin and fair and *française,* and I was scorned.
But I wasn't always fat, Soso. You may think because I'm ugly—

but you only like your women green. As if I was never young—
your own wife was your typist first. She was barely sixteen, no?
and you already going gray. So what's a wife anyway?

Why else Inessa's direct line to the Kremlin, his white face,
his white wreath on her coffin? What of it?
Who, Soso, who will you tell? Everyone already knows—

The Naming of Peru

Juan J. Morales

I.

Hugging shores, drifting south, we did not find vacant coasts. Natives piloted barges along our course, responding to us with silent awe. We called out commands, lost in currents, and natives became lonely footprints on the land. Toward a river's mouth, we observed the lone fisherman, anchored in his fear. Out of view, we rowed our skiff to the bank.

II.

The large beast wandered through our calm waters like a dream. My sacked fish squirmed against the weaves. I gaped at the hulking form, too gripped to detect the gods nearing from behind. The net freed from my hands when they pulled gloom over my eyes, dragged me across water to their waiting beast, rocking with the waves.

III.

We coerced patience, manipulated hands to ask the land's name. We stroked our chins, phrased and pointed to ourselves, and described his new King and Queen perched in a land a stretched sea away. He baffled out words and we resisted our urges to cut him down. Syllables hung in the air.

IV.

They showed teeth, spoke lagging cues, and offered snarled questions in word strands. With a shining spear, they scraped a pattern like land near my feet. When they pointed, I said my name, Berú, and told them about the river, pelú. When they combined two words into one, it clung to tongues like celebration. After freeing me back on the shore, they muscled back to their beast, leaving me to imagine a return of greater numbers.

Notes from a Sodbuster's Wife, Kansas, 1868

Peter Ludwin

What really got us in the end—
we women who didn't make it,
who withered and blew away in the open—
was the wind. Space, yes, and distance,
too, from neighbors, a piano back in Boston.

But above all, the wind.

In our letters it shrieks hysteria from sod huts,
vomits women prematurely undone by loneliness,
boils up off the horizon to suck dry
their desire as it flattened the stubborn grasses.
Not convinced? Scan the photographs,
grainy and sepia-toned, like old leather.
Study our bony forms in plain black dresses,
our mouths drawn tight as a saddle cinch,
accusation leaking from rudderless eyes, betrayed.

I tried. Lord knows I tried.
Survived the locusts and even snakes
that fell from the ceiling at night,
slithering between us in bed.
I dreamed of water, chiffon, the smell
of dead leaves banked against a rotting log.
I heard opera, carriage wheels on cobblestone.
Cried and beat my fists raw into those earthen walls.

The wind. Even as it scoured
the skin it flayed the soul,

that raked, pitted shell.
And how like the Cheyenne,
appearing, disappearing,
no fixed location,

not even a purpose one could name.

Oswald, to His Father

Tony Trigilio

I hit Marina. Can't help it, the way
she holds the baby. When the pacifier falls
on the floor, she cleans it with her mouth—
she can't see the drift of microbes.

The floors are dirty and must be washed
every day. They tell me you sold
insurance, you know what I mean—
if you keep things clean, you don't need

to gamble with a premium, a briefcase,
some rickety box of soul we call
property. I could not tell Mother
about my plans because she could hardly

be expected to understand. Say something,
father, to give me back the moonlight
from the rafters. When they told me about
you, I was a burst tub gashed with an axe,

sweet beer sloshing. They said you died
two months before I was born.
A safe, virtuous desertion.
I'd spell out what I mean for you

if I could. Let me put it this way.
I'm supposed to believe this world
was made by a father who turned
one son against the other

over slaughtered sheep and bundle
of hay? No, we've made it here: at night
we watch the Svisloch River from the balcony,
grazing the green banks of Kalinina Street.

It's February in Minsk but I'm so sweaty
I'd like to grab a rocking chair
for a breeze. I feel like an old man.
Marina's eye is black. Junie's crying.

Rachel Carson

Iris A. Law

> *The sedge has withr'd from the lake,*
> *And no birds sing.*
>
> —John Keats

In this dream, the noise never ends.
The eagle cuts circles across the plane
of a brittle sky, trees scratch
the surface of the earth, a child cries,
clutching at the breasts of a woman
wearing tumors like a shriveled necklace.

When I wake, I see nothing but white.
The clatter of the typewriter stills the rushing
of some panicked river rising in me.
I imagine the shadow of a sparrow
stirring the tableau of my window,
but look out onto stillness,
white quiet, all snow.

The world is asleep, the blade
of its mind tucked neatly
under a pillow, thoughts stopped
by the rise and flux of slow breath.
It knows nothing of my nights,
the terror of waking alone.

The square of my window grows red
and I open the curtains to let the light in.
The neighborhood is beginning to stir.
A family of foxes leaves prints in the fresh snow.
The newspaper boy shuffles by with his bag.

Somewhere, a woman rises
to weep over a bowl of broken eggs.

Reputation

Laura Madeline Wiseman

—Hamburg, Iowa, 1882

My mind climbs up and down the sermon given without notes
at the pulpit of a Des Moines church by a minister only just widowed.
A man built like a skyscraper, each story balanced on the one before.

His feet and ankles in polished boots. His legs, pelvis, buttocks
in the loose fabric and tight stitches of ordered readymade slacks
from the Sears and Roebuck catalogue. Each well read page saved

as tissue to wipe the delicate blossom of the ass. Inside his pants
below the ironed button down, the imported ebony of his coat,
the hard white band sung around his neck, all of this, his mystery.

He didn't sweat or prance. Not the antics of Henry Ward Beecher
or the cool logic of Abraham. He kept still. No phrase swayed him.
He spoke. His lips moved, his tongue in the wet bath of his mouth.

His blue eyes hot flames in the container of his face. After his words,
I waited to shake his hand. He said, *Yes, I know who you are.*
I'm sure I held his palm and fingers too long for polite conversation.

The Resurrectionist's Wife

Jennifer Perrine

He always returns—some nights
        from the pub, his skin radiant with smoke

        and the sweat of other men,
his breath hot as judgment against my ear—

or else from the graves, trailing
        the fecund dirt behind him—and then, too,

        the smell of other bodies
in our bed, the dull worm of it pressing

up to me when he does. Can
        this be the way he touches them, one hand

        on the abdomen, groping
in the dark for rotted spots? Does he trace

all the points where the scalpel
        will dig in, the bone-strapped organs huddled

        in the chest? Do their faces
bloom with blue flowers where the blood's gathered,

their cheeks dragging against his
        as he hauls them up—the loll of their head

        like an assent to desire
newly awake, its wink of furtive light?

Robert Oppenheimer Near Los Alamos, October 1945
John Canaday

We lost the moon among mountains,
urging our horses forward, watching ribbons
of steam rise from their flanks as they climbed in the midnight cold.
We had left the trail. Crisis' steel shoes sang
on the sandstone outcrops. High slopes
barred the sky.

The moon was waiting down by the river
where the boatman slept in an old alder shack
between two palms. We pulled ourselves
across the wrinkled water. Slick, moon-silvered planks echoed
when our horses stamped. The wet ropes
chafed our hands.

On the far bank, soaptrees bloomed—pale, odorless.
We called farewell to the sleeping boatman. The salty breath
of desert tamarisks replied
as the moon set behind Los Alamos.
Their dry leaves flickered like candles
and went out.

Submariner
Liz Ahl

I am writing blindly. . .

—Lt. Dmitry Kolesnikov, in a final letter aboard
the Russian submarine *Kursk*, August 12, 2000

Dive, dive. Each command twice
for accuracy and double-confirmation
down in here, but not even redundancy
can save us now. For months I've lived
in this nuclear tube, suspended
in the ocean's dark feathers, shut in
by tons of the Atlantic. This slow
cylinder is crammed full with men
and the sleek fingers of missiles.
Where shall we point them?

The only private space I have
is between my ears, tight also,
and nuclear, and navigating by
the intuitive pings of sonar, of
blind man's bluff.
                              Down here,
with my only brothers, we defend
the hull, feel our way through
fathoms, imagine what the sonar
tries to paint for us as it listens.

Up top, I'm dizzy in the wide open spaces
of our bed, too big for two. That house
alone is deeper than the ocean.
I misunderstand the wind, the lightness
of air; I can't recall how to measure
distance between people. She touches me.

Eyes shut, I'm down again,
in the precise, square feet of my bunk.

Of course, I'll scrawl none of this
in the note she may never see.
First, the business of how we came
to be here, after the explosions killed
most of the others. Then, for her, private

words, the tender ones she will want
to hear. They come easily, even
as we lose the lights, two dozen of us
nestled into one compartment, some
quietly crying, and I fold the paper
blindly, press and fold, focusing
my fingertips on each crease, as if
I could force this message into
the future, and into my pocket they go,
those easy words.

The hard words are the ones I try
to cobble together, for myself alone:
last scraps of sense and consciousness,
final sips of this world as the air thins,
as water seeps in and holds us all
too tightly. To whom would I speak
them if I could? If I manage to fold
them into sentences, pocket them
deep and safe, would the gentle hand
of the one who finally finds me
comprehend? I pray he will unfold
me as a letter, understanding what
I cannot about this dark, ineffable
passage, these last, best moments.

War Wives at Tea Talk

Martin Galvin

and then there is the d-d prunes I have no means of making pieces
of them nothing to stew them in nor any thing to sweeten them with.

—One of a series of complaints in a Civil War letter from
a Union Army volunteer to his wife, 1862

Were he my man, I'd send him cankers, cess,
And a woman's curse—which we both know
Does twice the damage of a man's and more
Because, a man, he looks to us for sweetly words

That he can take to his cot and finger for his joy.
Oh, there's no doubt they finger, or worse,
Consort with those camp girls who follow armies
As floods follow snow. It's bad enough,

The soldiers coming home to pester us,
Bringing along muskitoes and wood ticks.
A man like him, complaining that the prunes
His wife sends are damned because he has no skill

At stewing them, I'd damn that man
To be stopped up a year and when he shat,
that it would bend him like a crackly hag
And keep him bent so he could scrub and sew

The way we've done our lives away.
"*No thing to sweeten them,*" Poor Dear.
Maybe some worms, fattened on molasses,
Would sweeten the fruit to fit his belly.

Won't you then have some more tea, Sister?
The leaves will get our bowels to move
And this Eastern tea has a sleep in its leaves
Will bring us peace in bed without our men.

Whaling Wives: Desire Hathaway (2)
Madeline DeFrees

2

I set up house in a timbered cranny of the ship's
cabin, my heart already
heavy with hope and his child. I would not yield
my body to his mother for delivery and answered
his every argument with wiles.
Some visitor must have reported I wear
bloomers on deck, as is my habit. The words
hung still in air when she dispatched,
posthaste, her frosty disapproval. If she were to
guess my condition, I should have little
peace. My husband insists that she must know
very soon or be unforgivably
offended. Across the wide sea, it appears, armed
truce continues, although she cannot
touch me here.

              The crew is another matter, the men
satisfied with nothing
meaner than my husband's undivided passion. I see
my true rival is the Arctic Ocean.
That, and his mother's cold blood.
The one standing watch calls him from our bed
at each imagined peril. I do not quarrel with duty
but have been already widowed four years and would
be shut of that. When sailors jest about the easy
women of Talcahuano, his eyes
freeze over like hers. Can a son alter his nature?

I feel the small mouth pulling
at my breast and can believe *my* blood enough to warm
another's. I do not need the ship's glass to show me
clearly rough seas ahead.

The Woods Behind General Walker's House
Elizabeth J. Colen

Ours was the splinter group, picking up rocks, pocketing, rocked red,
rode by on screen, on springs. Red to the one wonderland of leaves.

Our house was vacant, except for the lies mother told.
Flies ate butter off the counter. Bit by bit we stole the control.

Pennies from mother's purse, dimes when we were older.
Brother folded dollars under his tongue, *dirty, tastes like paper.*

For a share we let him in on our vision of a cold-free world.
One, have friends in high places, figurative and in elevation.

Two, get a P.O. box and a name change, an alias: be somebody new.
Three, have the guts to do it all; don't mind blood or jail or pain.

Four, follow your directions. Five, look surprised every time a gun
fires; wipe the powder from your hands.

Releasing the Kraken

Mortals, Beasts, and Gods from Folklore and Mythology

...and her severed head said to Perseus,

Corrina Bain

one.

The day I saw your ship
flyspeck on the horizon,
fear stormed in your heart
as you recognized
the stones that had been men

I know that you remember.
Try to brush it from your eyes
like a bad dream.
Telling Andromeda how you fought for her
whispering into the apricot nectar
of her hair, how brave you had been.

The sea was hammer dented steel—
you pulled yourself ashore,
the shield, one of the holy gifts
given you to conquer me
reflecting you back

shuffled toward me like a crab
sword stuck out behind you, ridiculous
I had to do it myself,
eyelashes crashing together like iron filings
I sunk my scaly neck into the blade
the hissing protest in my head finally stilled

I could see your reflection,
light pouring like blood out your face

dark, fallible flesh that you hide and flatter
so close, I could smell
the inside of your mouth like wet silk
sick with fear,
sweat beading your wide back
some hot bellows under the earth calling my name

two.

my corpse became your weapon
forced to watch it, eyes hung in the air,
the legions you turned to stone.
The girl you pried from her father's arms
using only the threat of my name

try to imagine, in the muscled sarcophagus
of your hero's body,
being so ugly that it petrifies.
To know in the glare of your gaze
what you destroy,
pink sponge of their lungs
sopping marrow of their long bones
transmuted into stone,

your terror, even now as you think of it.
When you see girls at the bazaar,
hieroglyphics made of meat, the trophy
proof of your worth
you think of me. Nights,
instead of blood rolling into your groin
like sobbing,
a hollowness in their painted faces
shocks you back. The fear that I will blossom
in the dark of your daughter's bodies

Home, curling yourself around your bride
you tell again, how hideous I was.
The things you had to do to my body to keep her safe
skeleton key unlocking her city's bright gate
and my head, gently rotting in your leather sack, laughs

The story you do not tell, Perseus,
do you even remember it
When you were born—
the fever they thought would kill you
How the physician found a second heart
asleep beside your heart

Removed it, cast the bloody scrap
behind your house, raw flesh hatching the snakes
that nearly poisoned you. And I grew eyes.
In the trash heap. In earshot
of your infant wailing.
I grew legs, the pulpy vise
of my new gums making a noise
that was nearly your name.

Arachne

Aimee Nezhukumatathil

The sweetest medium
is water. I envy the frog;
her mate holds her firm
in a wet embrace, then
the release—an egg froth
on her back and good-bye.
I cannot imagine a hunger
filled, a calm stretch of nerve.

My legs won't even break
the surface to let me dip
my body in. Perhaps a breeze,
perhaps a dew will come
to envelop me. In the branches
of this gum tree, I sigh. This air
is no good. Who knows
what god I will inhale.

Aunt Eloe Schools the Scarecrow
Matthew Hittinger

As the crow flies, you say? Come now you god
of the crossroads, I'm talking ravens here.
Corvids are corvids, yes, but like a dog

compared to a wolf you can't call a crow
a raven and have the word "nevermore"
mean the same thing. Now, two facts: ravens mate

for life, but this raven, let's call him Caw
the raven husband, he lived with the wolf
wife Howl. You didn't hear? It was the lead

post on "Fuck You Penguin" during inter-
species week. Anyway, Caw and Howl hunt
together: Caw scopes, Howl clamps, bloody beak

and talon after tooth and claw. They have
lived like this for ages: after the flood
it was not the dove but the white raven

(Apollo later turned his feathers black)
who found the wolf and helped found Rome. Go back
before these stories were writ before your

tar and straw and wood and you'll find Caw loved
Howl even then, there where their forms had yet
to settle into fur and feather. Why

do I tell you this? Next time you measure
say corn husk doppelgänger pumpkin shell
twin. Point left, howl. Right, caw. Sing tin, wind, spin.

The Calypso Diaries
Shaindel Beers

I.

I did not let him go because Zeus told me to,
nor because I had grown weary
of his love.
It's just that sometimes a girl's got to know
that a man is happier with a woman than with
a goddess, even a minor one.
If you promise him immortality on an island,
it just means you'll be walking the same beach,
century in and century out;
with Penelope, he'll have another thirty, forty years
tops. They'll watch Telemachus grow
into a man and laugh at the folly of all those suitors,
while I sit here, enjoying sunset
after sunset
after sunset
and all the quiet of the world.

II.

Sometimes you let him go because it is more cruel
than keeping him.
Sometimes you let him go because freedom
is the opposite of love.
Sometimes you let him go because freedom
is the only love.
Sometimes you let him go because there is only

one Penelope.
Sometimes you let him go because there is only one Calypso
and you know that he will think of her more often
from across the sea.

III.

Watching the raft disappear into the horizon
is bittersweet
because you wish him favorable winds
and send him with enough provisions
to know he'll look back on you kindly,
but you get to wondering if your heart was too big,
why you smoked and dried your fattest sow
and cross-cut your tallest cedars for the raft
to take him back to Ithaca
and Penelope
her pale arms
their oaken bed.

IV.

It's the same double-standard, always;
a god can sleep with as many
mortals as he wants
but a goddess takes a man as a lover
and Zeus must intervene.
I decried Zeus for his indiscretions
with Leda and Europa,
but, alas, he's Zeus, and there's no reasoning.
When I uttered Leda's name, I faltered,
because she's the reason for Helen
and this insipid war.

At the crack in my voice, Zeus
chuckled—I knew my case was lost
but tried every trick possible,
Odysseus isn't really a mortal—
he's almost a god, or why would Athena,
your daughter, from your own head sprung,
so adore him? Or
Odysseus is less than a mortal—
it was pity. He washed up on my shore,
more a half-drowned kitten than a man—
can I keep him?
But none of these worked.
Zeus, who must have Hera and Leda
and Europa and many others,
can't understand the curse
of being alone
and immortal
in paradise.

V.

Sometimes there are centuries between shipwrecks
and I picture ravaged vessels,
their crews scattered
on other islands
with Circe and Nausikaa,
and other goddesses I have never heard of
while I watch the sky pinken
and grey,
pinken and grey.
I scratch names of long-dead men
in the sand
with my palm frond
and watch the surf

erase the beach
the way time restores my mind
to peace,
the way Odysseus' back was healed from
Circe's fingernail welts by the time
he washed ashore.

The Carriers

Christopher Hennessy

The filament in my throat rattles,
a burnt-out bulb in a shaking fist.
At least, the hollowing sound has replaced
the electric hum of my asthma.
And my wings, how sore! pressed
deep into my spine. Each feather
feels like the wooden leaf
of a great desk I carry on my back.

At my age, I dread each sortie—
He lays on us two leaden words
instead of the usual one.
Take care: they easily flake
into pieces of brittle slate
if you hold them too tight.
I have little hands and must hug
the word precious to my chest,
keep my wings tamed.

On my last run, over the Azure Coast,
I felt a letter slipping from me.
In panic, I dropped the whole word.
Forgive me, I was distracted:
a naked young man singing to me,
his long fingers separating tangled
grape vines. He heard the rattle,
now in my lungs, or noticed
the shadow I laid across his chest
when I flew overhead, the sweat
suddenly cool on his skin.
A presence above him.

He looked up, frightened
and aroused; and the word I'd let slip
slid so easily down his throat....
What must it feel like, to swallow
a word fallen from the sky,
to choke on inspiration?
I hope it was a nice, rich noun.
Peach or *maelstrom.*

The Chimera Faces Extinction, Displacement
Susan Slaviero

What I am has something to do with teeth,
with stone gods who've forgotten my breath
should be volcanic, more yellow than the nucleus
of a sphinx's egg. I am portentous, luck-broken.

If you see me, you should find a shipwreck or something
skinned and shuddering. My body reminds you of poppies,
spiraling wasps in a windstorm. I will not take a stone
in my mouth, swallow doves or mice, strike anything

that occurs in threes. I go marauding in suburban yards,
my goatspine scraping beneath your swingsets, the limbs
of acacias and oaks. I slouch past your dwellings unnoticed,
like a housecat during dinner hour. I don't understand

your zygotes, your finely-tuned and matching cells.
Where are your manes, your udders? Even my plainest sister
had a bouquet of heads at birth. Even your dogs seem
unfinished, lacking in mosaic patterns. Today, I am watching

your bones, hoping to see them grow monstrous beneath
your too-bright skins. Maybe you will consume a cobra
and evolve more useful appendages. Maybe you will grow
mothwhite scales when the moon drops away, so beautiful.

Coma Berenices
Jory M. Mickelson

My husband took my head in one hand, his long knife in another, and cut. Cut. Cut the hair from my head. In praise to Her for the field of broken soldiers, my locks fell like spears, a harvest for the dead. He laid them on the white altar of Aphrodite, praising Her, with my black serpent-coils with their pulsing eyes of turquoise, garnet and malachite. Long weavings that flicked their linen tongues, flashed their markings in gold, and lay still.

During the night, my skull ticked and twitched at every breeze. At dawn, I went to see them again, but they were gone. The priests took my husband aside saying, "This will be resolved by nightfall." We returned and the old priest pointed saying, "Aphrodite was pleased with your offering and placed it among the stars. See how each stone shines along the length of sky." My hair embroidered to the sail of night.

At six this evening, I step down 5th and turn onto 17th. The garbage cans overflow onto the sidewalk. In one shop, bowls filled with a thousand bright constellations, hundreds of gleaming seeds. The flash of coins, the bleed of ribbon, and the dart of serpent-like stones. Beads of Paradise. Each dish an offering to the god of commerce. I turn again onto 5th and walk up 14th. Entering another shop, I am not the only woman with a shaved head. I pick the longest wig I can find. It is the color of ink across marble. I pour the beads onto the table, tell him to begin. Weave for me.

Hecuba
Gail Griffin

> . . .and Zeus destroyed me not but is still preserving my life,
> that I may witness in my misery fresh sorrows surpassing all before.
> —Euripides, Hecuba

A woman keening might mean anything.
Other things than men and children
may be lost, run over
by the gods' big truck, those eternally
drunken drivers. What has dropped
from me has fallen silent.

I almost asked what I did to deserve this.
That old song. Let's say I wanted
not too much but too little.
Let's say my special hubris grew
inward, like a navel. I have given birth
to nothing, I have tried to be a city.
And when the strangers sent their gift horse,
my gates swung wide like legs.

Now it starts—feet first, then the creeping gray
cold up the shins. It's not all that bad, really.
Next the crotch goes numb. There goes
the womb, that bag of old news.

So I am petrified. I might make a useful statue.
You can tell a tale by me. Oh, I edify.
In the wet slate cave of my chest,
the rattle of a small stone.

Icarus / Sinking
Kazim Ali

you became real to me father
when I saw you fly over me from beneath the waves

a bone-white door against the cloud-white ceiling
looking for me, flapping and furious

I watched you in the dark as you slept
knowing the edge of you only by the deeper darkness

below you now in the blue-black, a star
winking out, I am thinking I may wake up in the labyrinth

and not ever do this
not seek for the sun

oh father my storm-dark coast
nothing fills

I Live on Milk Street
Martha Silano

Via Lactea, to be exact. Once it was the path
to Zeus's palace, then a creamy cul-de-sac; now

they just keep widening and widening. Its origin?
On that the jury's still out. It could have been paved

by the Holy People who crawled to the surface
through a hollow reed, then formed my kind

from ears of white and yellow corn. Some say
it was born of Juno's wrath, wrath that tore

her breast from a suckling infant Hercules
(her no-good hubby once again knocking up

a mortal). What spurted up, they tell me,
begat this little avenue, this broad and ample road

where I merry-go-round with my 200–300
billion neighbors, give or take a billion or two.

(Then again, it might've all been cooked up
by Raven.) My street has the mass

of a trillion suns; my roundabout's a black hole.
My backyard abuts with my dear friend Io's.

She's always asking me to come on over,
but enduring speeds upward of 106,000 mph

usually means I'm waving from the porch.
(On the plus side, the ash from her many volcanoes

does wonders for my whispering bells.) I do wish
I could get to know the Leptons, though.

I invite them to my cookouts, but they're always off
to hither and yon. And I don't mean to be catty,

but it's high time Ms. Nuclear Bulge
ponied up for some high power Spanx.

I know there's a whole lot else out there—
starbursts, whirlpools, magellanic clouds—

but I'm busy enough keeping up
with the slugs attacking my pole beans,

making sure the garbage goes out. Truth be told, I'm happy
right here where I am, lulled by my own sweet byway's

hazy halo, its harmony of traffic.

Leda's Flashback

Maureen Alsop

Breadcrumbs in ash survive hunger. A crescent
of gray birds climb northward as I sift
through the clapboard house. The dead
were rooms I called through one daylight
to the next. I gaze at a sparrow
through the window. A pale
flickering over my one blind eye
as the other eye dreams of burning. The bird

is a wet thread. He wicks blackness out of juniper, de-thorns
branches, & tilts spirit from fruit. This incessant tremor
in my hand argues against the irregular sway of hip; up the stairs,
I clutch the rail, one foot rises. One foot another foot. *Who*

is this walking in miracles? Who is this crossing XXX
He is cancellation XXX *I do not see I do not see I do not see*
light dulls the mirror XXX *I am shadow passing over water* XXX
…bridge between worlds…XXX The heart doubts all song.   A lowing
wind that dull green summer with little rain,

sky as knife blade; salt thick inside me; dress torn. Choked
in the corner of the barn, I'd taken
his beard into my teeth, mouthfuls of feather between grain
& gristle. Who knows what

culled stains into the pine planks—clouded & throbbing.

I am not this body. I am not the one sleeping
alone in the reeds. This room is not safety—trespasser—
route of flies. *Leave me.* I opened my mouth. I opened
to God—Maybe

I was never there if I had not been there.
I better write this quietly as no one else
who listens continues to listen. Better keep wishbone
to the throat, better keep this bucket of cracked eggs under the bed.

The grass at dusk now is as tall as my shoulders
& the bird in my windpipe refuses to stir. Soundless thistle, I hear
the heat of his breath, a flammable wheeze. Calm sips
of air flutter.   I cough a black rasp—snowfall
through the lungs.   I speak
to the bird the softening murmur of bells, hoary
plumes on his crest smell of clover.

The night shimmers
over the hills. It is warm in the dark
the dark itself expands.

Lotus-Eater's Wife
Danielle Cadena Deulen

I understand why you might prefer it to remembering.

In the dusk you embarked, the water shuddered, turned away, and I could almost
    see the slow, constant rocking of the ship, the hard winds and western loneliness
        deepening the salt in your heart.

In your memory now, there is no wake.

There are no seagulls circling the slack, half-massed sails,
    no lime-water fetid in barrels, no woman crying, no woman
crying a ballad from the cliffs you lost in a fog and a poorly drawn map.

And it must be so easy for you now, eating and drinking and butchering
    cattle by the shore, the sometimes flashes of faces you can no longer name
emerging and ebbing and ebbing until everything erodes into sand, sky, water.

I wonder which tide pools your fractured memory lingers in.

What pieces are you surprised to find, roll around in your large palms?

    Which sighs do you keep in your sad, heavy pockets?

Which do you throw back to sea?

Medusa and Neptune

Susan Varnot

> *She was very lovely once, the hope of many*
> *An envious suitor, and of all her beauties*
> *Her hair most beautiful—*
>
> —Humphries' *Ovid*

The men are a diary of my days with stone:
one posed climbing from his boat,
one crouched against a boulder's shadow,
one hoisting blade. My sisters take turns looking
at what I've done, passing their one eye
like a child between them. Father,
I have trouble sleeping. Sometimes
it's the seaweed shifting along the shore or the vipers
in my hair—they glide and pull from the roots
without healing; some nights
I walk the island like a sentry
or like a woman again gleaning shapes
in the waves, searching the water
for scaled hips riding the crests.
All night, I hear flight, wings rustling
like a boat scraping sand.

Before my exile, I was down by the sea searching
for anemones and picking the chamomile
that knots the path to the shore. I selected
gaping sea roses, bundling them to take
to Minerva's shrine. The light
on the water was enormous. I was praying.
I smarted with the sea so near; I smelled
the acrid salt and scales, as fingers webbed
against my neck. Something wet
pushed me down. My lip caught

the edge of the altar and I tasted the tin of blood.
I washed beneath one wave and another.
I stared into that darkness, stammering
into its emptiness, its piteous lack of form; I
gave to it my body, my head turned towards
a fracture in the wall. I could not identify him
if you were to bring him before me,
but I would know the touch
of a god wet and dark
that flew straight through me
as though I were water or air broken into.

The flowers I had gathered scraped my wrists.
I could do nothing but look and keep on
looking at the wall, emptying myself of light.
A flicker of fire, metal sparked
against stone. When he was gone,
I tried to fold the blossoms
back onto their stems. Father, your daughter
who once drew an alabaster comb through hair
with the ease of sunlight slipping through trees
now listens to hissing that walks where she walks.
Do you know what it's like to stare
at the stone effigies of men
who have come to slay you.

When I bathe, my sisters keep watch.
I fear I will live this sea forever. Father,
I remember the pears ripening
beside the garden wall, the scent of thyme
and rosemary blurring, but it grows tiring, and how
I would mourn, for perhaps history or gods.
I am no longer even myself but what once was
a girl, back turned to the sea.

My Life as a Woman

Tomás Q. Morín

—Teiresias

Before I lived this lady's body
I struck snakes coiled in the brush
because I judged their entanglement dirty.

My punishment came dimly. Bit by bit,
I woke under the pasture of night
to new fingers, new legs, and then finned.

Flayed and popped I groped for an hour
like the blind then stopped and slept
under the black tree-line. Two showers

came and still I slept. Later, I wept
and even later still I found work
twisting the sweaty melodies of men.

Now, the sex is never the matter,
as many think. Men shed their diffidence
at the cool touch of my sheets. The fathers

and husbands at my doorstep come to tug
my braids, to snuggle their maws
against my nape and puff, not hug.

No, their false mugs are what annoy
me most when, the house empty,
I climb the hill to market and coy

men whose faces I've seen contort
and flush greet me with stiffness
and blanche when I smile at their tots.

I much prefer the crushing grins of wives
just before the volley of sticks and stones
because at least there is honesty in their lies.

Odysseus, on the Eve of Departure, Prepares His Wife

Kristine Uyeda

Be still and let me
tell you something:
the earth is flat.
In times like these,
what are we willing
to say we know for certain?
In the ache and expanse
of what has not yet
happened, do not dwell.
For though a man dreams
of the sea, who adrift
does not long for his lover,
his son, the linnet, the shore?
Each morning, within
the field of what the sea refuses,
among shell and stone,
listen for a sound
shaped like my name.

Penelope Blows Smoke Rings
Elizabeth Volpe

If it's true that men navigate by spatial relationships
and women by landmarks, then I can't say I'm lost.
For here is the bed he made from the olive trunk,
here my loom, copper basin, footstool, the new issue
of Vanity Fair. So wanderlust is simply his nature,
his birthright. Well, frankly, I'm tired of waiting
for word, sending couriers to this beach and that, watching
them run off in pairs. Sometimes they're gone for days.
My loom thumps along, drowns the sound of suitor-lutes.
At first my fingers lingered over each thread, as if taking
all the time in the world would mean he hadn't been gone
any time at all. That was the first ten years. Then word came:
the slut Helen was back home in Sparta, Menelaus oiling
her feet, wrapping her in softest goatskin, all forgiven.
She does yoga or lounges by the pool, cabana boys floating
at her feet, while I sort threads at this stupid loom,
chain smoking and weaving shrouds. I'm out of tricks, out of
sorts, out of my mind. The bard appears in my doorway with
soap operas of doomed voyages home, then the jester comes,
silly with antics and pranks, the bard weepy enough to make me
laugh, the other cheery enough to make me weep. I need
to get out more. But downstairs there's only my lazy,
drooling son and a bunch of fat fools with hairy hands.
Long past are the days of beardless chins and burnished
biceps, eager outstretched arms, nosegays, serenades. Now
the brutes slaughter my oxen and bed my maids, play blackjack
and hold thumb wars. It's been twenty years since my husband
held me. Even with our small son between us, I could feel his lust
for battle pulling him away, his eyes signaling to his men
even as he winked at me. There's something careless about

the way men live. Even now with his dog dying on the dung heap,
his son busy with identity issues, his kingdom ransomed by idiots,
as long as he has fair winds and muscles to flex, the world
as his chessboard, he's content. He's always had a soft spot
for honeyed tongues and caves, for sorceresses
and waitresses. So here I am, life passing by
like a slide show: in this shot she sits, in this shot
she stands, in this she sits. I find my way to the window
and watch the fat carp slug their way through
the fishpond. It's only far inside that I step out
of my widow's weeds, let the veils trail to the floor,
move outside my room into the wider, smaller world,
into the enigma of each lily's upturned mouth.
Out where the moon curls its thick red muscle.

Psyche
Joelle Biele

That I pushed too hard, that I did not
believe, that I lost you and did not hear
you leave, that all I wanted was to hear

your feet, know you felt the same stones
as me, that I wanted to see your face,
know more than your body going forward

and back that I find myself in these woods
looking for wool snagged on branches
or trapped under stray leaves. I did not accept

what my body told me. I listened to my sisters,
was only to ready to agree you weren't
who you made yourself out to be. I do not

know if I'll find you or if I'll cross that river
or get through the reeds or if I can tell you
I did not know you wanted night as much as me.

Still Bound

Dan Albergotti

Still here, and every morning it's almost a surprise
that the sun might come, that it could happen again.
This is how it is. The eagle arrives each day,
but not for my liver. Instead, she comes for my heart.
And it's still agony every time, although I have learned
by now how not to scream. Most days, she lights
on my shoulder, clenching her talons in the flesh,
and right away begins ripping down into my chest,
her head like a cold hammer, tail feathers brushing my nose.
She pulls the heart out in long, thin strips, and flies away,
and I imagine her feeding the dark flesh to her young.
Yet some days, she will light on the rock beside me
and step softly up onto my chest. She will pace along it, stop,
cock her head, and stare into my eyes. Her own dark eye
will bloom wide. She will slowly blink, then lower her beak
to my skin and begin a gentle tearing until her small tongue
is pushing at the shell of my heart. She cuts it out clean
those days and almost seems sorry to leave, to fly off
as my hollowed chest burns. But she does. She flies up
and disappears into the distance, though I can make out
the dwindling speck of her in the great sky for hours.
The day is long. The day is long when you're growing a heart.
Still, look at how the sun falls behind that far peak,
how it glows like one steady eye gazing only here,
how it makes those colors burn and emanate where soon
it will be purely black, how it can make a gift of fire.

What she could do, Medea did..."

Kathy Fagan

—*Ovid's* The Metamorphoses

When I cut
my blade was hardly red—
so little blood was in him.
Less spill than suck,
his wound worked like a mouth,
and mouth and wound alike drank
what I fed him,
my husband's father,
eyes fluttering like an infant's,
until I saw in them
the sated look that women
mistake for gratitude,
and saw too, beneath my hands,
a lustrous black returning to his beard,
a pleasing heft to thigh and shoulder.
What happened next
was strictly clientele—I'd always
been, as they say, in business,
exchanging life for life.
When Jason turned
us out to wed another,
it took no art of mine to kill
our sons. I'd loved
the magic for how it loved him.
I loved the anger for how it did not.

The Wife of Sisyphus
Laura P. Newton

I.
I threw your unconsecrated body into the town square at noon
when the sunlight off the Mediterranean would blind the living,

the sand would fill your pores with memories of heat,
and the gulls would carry your body to the underworld.

I prayed my last kiss would fire a fuse of want to bind you to me
and the yeast of midday bread would raise your tongue in a rage

even Pluto could not refuse. All during autumn your loss
was my consolation; I was as free as any widow in mourning.

II.
Ah, Sisyphus, by the time you convinced Pluto of my crime
and returned from the dead to chastise me, as we had planned,

I was beyond the reach of your memory. I saw how the glint
of sunlight off a villa wall lit your face, how the sea buoyed

your browning body in salty defiance. When Pluto
sent Mercury to seize you I had grown tired of pretending

my hand was your own, so I distracted him a while. After
you had fallen in love with your life again, I told him where

you were and watched him drag you by the hair, back
to the underworld where the rock of my heart waits for you.

Fifteen Easy Minutes

Pop Culture and Celebrity

After Oz
Charles Jensen

—Dorothy Gale

At dusk, I dug the dirt with clawed hands—
    I dreamed the gold was there,
        the path leading back to the other world.
    My fingernails blackened into talons, raw,

but I dug deeper, sweeping dirt into my lap,
    dusting my lips with the white taste of iron.
        I dreamed of children,
    I dreamed of shoes,

I dreamed a field of poppies pulling me back into sleep,
    nesting the dream where I woke up in Kansas
        brown and sullen, the light filtering through
    a shimmering veil of dirt.

The opposite of landscape is this
    dirt field, the shack, the gingham curtains
        that match my gingham dress.
    Kansas is the space surrounding an emptiness.

Take away the bedroom window
    and wood boards up the horizon. Take away light,
        take away its opposite, the evening and its dim stars.
    Peel back the earth

and see gold,
    see bricks there, see a path that leads
        toward where you can't see a thing.
    Peel back the layers of this dress—

the girl is buried there,
    wrapped in cloth and buttons and skin.

Anna's Ghost: (Prologue)

Denise Duhamel

Hey, y'all, thanks for the news blitz after my death.
I appreciate all of it, even the jokes.
Daniel and I sleep late in pink heaven. We just woke
Up. It feels a little like we're still on meth,
Doesn't it Danny? (laughter)

It's true that I ballooned to 224,
That I chowed down a bit more than a Guess? model should.
I tried to eat only pickles, but then I'd crave instant pud-
Ding. I hated those Trim Spa shakes—they went down like chalk.

Daniel says Hamlet's father's ghost opened
Act I, Scene IV. I'm so proud of my boy.
Hey, up here I can eat stacks of Chips Ahoy
Without gaining a pound. Dannielynn Hope,
Mama's blowing you a kiss!

Beetle Bailey Goes Home
Donald Illich

The sarge, irate, red-faced, looks
for me in the usual places—in the
wide hammock, forming letter Zs
in the air; behind the green barracks,
rolling lucky sevens in dice games
and taking bets from the officers;
in the kitchen, eating all the pizza
for the recruits' lunches, when all
they needed was a taste of home.

Sarge, I'm not loafing, but I'm also
not cutting your potatoes or toting
a machine gun in an oil-stained desert.
I'm on a bus home, chatting up
an ex-con with a dragon tattoo;
we'll buy shots at the Blue Mariner,
sleep in each other's muscled arms.

You missed your chance, Sarge. If
you'd stayed your fists for just one second,
all you had to say was, "Love me."

Bill Monroe
Chris Dombrowski

When a feller plays a banjo
so well like that that it begins
to make the cold chills run over you
he can be doing you some good there
I'm telling you and Lester here can strum
a November midnight with the big moon
lone as a thumbprint on a frosty window-pane
and make that G yelp like a yard dog porcupine-
quilled and left out to learn in deep snow he might
hold one note still as a bluebottle fly on a December
sill then tick his way through a scale like a right fevered
man he can make a bass chord seem hollow as a dilapidated
cabin procured by the wind as its instrument then fill you up
with the next one warm as whiskey chased down with cold water
straight from the spigot

Cammi Granato, Age Five: "I Hate Dorothy Hamill"
Erin Elizabeth Smith

My father gives me white skates
with a bread knife pick at the toe.

Like hers. My chubby legs taut
in beige tights. The hard round belly

swathed in pale taffeta. I'm taught
to keep my arms up like a scarecrow.

Like Dorothy, my father says, points
to her picture on the rink wall,

that fishing lure hair, leg bent
obscenely like a dog's. When he leaves

I watch the boys play—Tony slides
a puck beneath the goalie's right pad,

Don smacks his stick on the ice.
Who is anyone to tell me what girls love?

Camel spins. Pageboys. Tiny lips
on a bright medal. And her and I

from the same city, both too young to know
what we can't do. These skates so tight

my feet can't breathe, while Dorothy's eighteen
year old smile gets seared into her mouth.

Crossing the Street, Valentine's Day
James Caroline

—for Chet Baker

I did know better
that the window wasn't a doorway
but a mouth with heavy tongue.
I knew
but swear it grinned
lady-like
and the tumble
those notes of a free body
given to law.

Build the tribute over a woman
let their bodies pop and quiver
wet sounds
like cheap boots
daring Amsterdam's puddles.
Sing that lasso
my chiseled cards
fanning coffee tables
my rose bud throat positioning legs of ash
strobe and flick of innocence
disappearing with the wave of a hand.

I was rough
but pretty
slacked notes and bright wind
in my tour case.
I made mistakes.

So here
against the maw of God's digging
I tell you
this sick and shake in me
still
I wasn't a bad player.
I loved like shutters swing
open.

I gathered my sagging marble
my olive lungs and and milkless veins
put the shiny brass in its case
hoping to hear the smash
the break and pour of me.
I'd forgotten how I sound.

I remember the mouth
its cold silver warming in my hand
waiting for spit and breath.

Go Somewhere with Me
Collin Kelley

—for Betty/Diane on Mulholland Drive

I'd follow you until I split into
two smiles in my good girl purse
one for nights at home, riding you
on the couch, and another
for your Hitchcock fantasy
fitted gray suit, I'm spunky
and a little dangerous
I'm hearty Canadian stock
grown cold and in the dark
jitterbugging my way, no sweat
all the way to Los Angeles
starlet dreams put in a box
until I looked like someone else
unrecognizable making coffee
or embarrassing bit parts
You've got the key in your bag
all it takes is one twist, tell me
what this opens, what comes out
this is the girl I never dreamt I would be
so the night you take me clubbing
at 2 a.m. and the seizures come
shocking me out of this reverie
that you will never love me
will leave me . . . *llorando* . . .
I will disappear into blue light, but
we will never be done with each other
because you are the dream I made real
and in those dark Deep River nights
when no one else would listen
I told every little star.

How She Didn't Say It

Camille T. Dungy

It used to bother me when people I didn't know
called me Ella   they ain't been blue   no
they should say Miss Fitzgerald   somehow
they never do   you have to let them see
the sweat   just don't let them see the feeling
stealing down below the ground you walk   listen
to the voice Chick said   he said don't look
at her   their eyes close and I'm rising up
Sinatra at my feet like I'm his friend   his
wet nurse   Tormé calling me Ella   Ella   I'm called
into nights I don't recognize   my song
like a cashbox   no change in their hearts
but I'm up here already   have to do something
my voice passes through them   shining   a knife

Hulk Smash!

Greg Santos

> *I am the least difficult of men. All I want is boundless love.*
>
> —Frank O'Hara, *Meditations in an Emergency*

Hulk know. Hulk have a problem.
Hulk took break from Avengers after orphanage and tanker truck incident.
Hulk's therapist said it cry for help.
Hulk said "Hulk strong! Hulk self-reliant! Ugh!"
Who Hulk kidding? Hulk not really so incredible.
Hulk look in mirror every day and want to smash things.
Hulk never cut out to be superhero.
Hulk really just regular Joe.
Hulk got Hungry Hungry Hippos for birthday.
But no one want to play with Hulk. Everyone too busy saving world.
Hulk like watching Tennessee Titans with bowl of chips and dip.
Hulk like to go beachcombing for giant squid carcasses.
Hulk OK guy. Just misunderstood.
Hulk really just want to have normal 9 to 5 job.
But who would hire Hulk?
Hulk first tried 7-11 cashier job in Schertz, Texas.
Hulk wore stupid uniform even though it too small.
Hulk still want to smash Slurpee machine.
Hulk think it give too much ice, not enough syrup!
Captain America lecture Hulk. Captain America douche bag.
Hulk then tried work in office job.
Hulk carpool with Joan and Frank from accounting.
Hulk wear snappy tie and dress shirt.
Hulk even bought new purple pants!
Cubicles too small for Hulk, though.
Hulk hate paperwork!
Hulk smash paper shredder!
Hulk got yelled at by Shelley in cubicle next door.
Hulk hate Shelley! (Hulk think about Shelley every day.)

I am the Immaculate Conception

Hershman John

Wintertime, the stars fell like snow.
The moon with a halo tonight, one, two, three-
rings singing together just like Saturn's belts.
I channel flip, alone in the dark,
with the glow of the electric;
it was black and white outside. In black
and white, a girl Bernadette with
her doe eyes picks through garbage
with her sister. There, a vision of Holy Virgin
Mary with the red, red thorny rose at her feet.
Linda Darnell died in 1965 in a house fire,
burning alive. She was afraid of fire,
I am afraid of thunder. Bernadette
was a French peasant girl no different
than my Navajo upbringing in a BIA Boarding School.
Silent, I feel my pinions floating outside, a fallen
angel. I was always afraid of having visions,
in my teenage years, because of Jennifer Jones.
I'd pray to Jesus, *Oh Please I am not worthy*
for a vision, I don't want to go through Hell.
Please Lord, please. I'd shut my eyes
and sleep with the cover pulled over my head,
even in the summer heat. I'd sweat under my covers
not wanting to see Linda Darnell,
along with her sweet smelling feet—years later I find
The Virgin was the mistress of Darryl F. Zanuck.
With glassy eyes at 3 am, I watch Bernadette
reject life and love and even miracles to
show the truth of her visions.
The truth about visions, little did I know

I too would commit adultery, willingly
or not. I would live that "black and white"
Jennifer Jones lived, at the convent, alone. Unbelieved,
a circus act, a woman who
dug up a healing spring, eating mud
from the ground—almost a crazy woman.
I have always felt out of place living in two
worlds: in a white world and a red world.
Even the old nun, with the burning eyes, *like the holy
fires of Hell*, and with *hands gnarled from prayer*,
didn't believe and knew that we must be chosen—
even a peasant girl, even a 12-year-old Navajo boy
imagining a life outside my Rainbow Blessing,
living in sin. Even Bernadette, a mistress
to David O. Selznick, how could I ever watch
Bernadette's *Song* and see its holiness.
Our Lady or Lourdes, the 12 year Navajo, and the peasant,
all the same on this winter night, loss of wings.

In the Unlikely Event of a Water Landing
Don Colburn

—US Airways Flight 1549

When the pilot told us to, I couldn't
take my glasses off and put my head down
between my knees. I wanted to watch
to the last moment before smithereens.
Closing your eyes won't help, not like in music.
The eerie part wasn't death touching down early
but how quiet it was, how smooth. We were gliding,
the buzz and rumble of engines gone,
and I could hear everything—
the crying (less than you think), Hail Marys,
the man up front trying against the rules
to call home. An old woman many rows back
sang beautifully in Spanish, maybe to God,
I don't speak that language. I wish I had known
they called the captain Sully and how Sully
was a glider pilot too. We had no idea
why it was happening, no inkling
of geese or gulls, but we were losing
altitude and the quiet sounded terribly wrong.

After we banked left, Sully brought us down
easy onto the river. The trick is
to ride the thickening air down slow
and plow into the water, head up like a duck,
not to nosedive, jackknife, cartwheel, burn.
When we didn't die, some panicked.
Suddenly there was time, and ice water
sloshing at our ankles, our knees. How long
can a heavier-than-air machine float?

Someone named Josh knew to knock the door out
over the wing. I didn't notice the guy carrying
his garment bag or the lady screaming for her shoes.
I just remember getting pushed toward a hole
in the side of the plane and tumbling out
into the cold gray blinding afternoon
which held me. I came to my feet
on the submerged wing with the others
and we walked on water.

Jack Benny Plays the Carousel Club
Sebastian Matthews

—for Gerry LaFemina

They say Jack Benny played it in '55,
flew into a little landing strip
somewhere down highway 127
between Hicksville and Defiance,
with just his manager and that famous violin.
Blew in halfway through the first set,
persuaded the owner to let him on.
Think he'd turn him down?
Picture the master, lit like a steam liner
in harbor as he tries on the outfits
of his repertoire at a manic clip—
sawing the bow to punctuate the segues,
smothering the laughs. Then *Bam!*
into the next. Takes a while for the crowd
to catch on. *Damn, it really IS Benny!*
I believe the story, sort of. Maybe not
a touchdown unannounced in a cornfield.
That's got all of myth's markings. But
blue highway down through western Ohio?
Sure. A Buick tilted on the roof, drink specials
at the half-moon bar, owner's office hanging
over the stage. Yeah, I buy that. Don't you?
Just not '55, not when the "King of the Airwaves"
had already headlined *The Jell-O Program*
and jumped to the tube. More like
when he was Ben K. Benny, fresh out
of his teens, smeared in black face. "Fiddle
Funology." A man's got to start somewhere.
I played the Carousel once (you had to see

that one coming) back in the late-70s,
Duluth to Albany in a run of opening acts.
I was reaching for whatever Pryor and Martin
and Belushi were using to burn like that.
Drove myself into town, as the joke goes,
then blinked right on out of it.
This Mom-and-Pop with a meatloaf special
served up on a warm plate by a girl
mouthwatering as the pies, who
when I handed her the tab, shot me
a "take me with you" glance, I swear.
By the end of Benny's set the lot's crammed
with pick-ups, folks lured off the road
by a wild ham-radio call. It's long past last call,
and Benny comes off only to piss and refill
his tumbler, then back up in the ragged spotlight,
running through Kitzel the hot dog vendor,
the vault in the basement, "Your Money
or Your Life!" and a few squeaky bars
of "Love in Bloom." Slowing down
for an eerie imitation of Rochester, *sotto*
voice, eyes wide, elegant hands dead
at his sides. The crowd erupting when Irving
finally pulls him off; they part for him
like the Red Sea. But here's what gets me:
Benny doesn't fly out that night. No,
he sleeps it off in the hangar. Daybreak
he wakes the pilot and they take off
as the sun rides its hotrod chariot
into the sky. The plane banking over
the great lake of green. I can see him
closing his eyes (a gigantic field oak
blankets a farm house in its shade)
to rest for the first time since
who knows when. Me? I stink up the place,

a carpetbag of glib jokes not flying
with the farmer set. I lurch through
"Eggs Benedict" memorized off Woody's
Nightclub Years. This John Deere hat stands up
in the back and shouts "Go Home!" I've got
a smart-ass comeback but nurse a bottle
in my room, instead, hoping the girl
will see my light on and knock furtively.
Hey Mister, you in there? In the morning
I pay up, drive on, the road I guess
a kind of home.

Katie Smith Says, "A Woman's Body is a Battleground. I Should Know."

Arielle Greenberg

After I was killed they found the perfect nursery, all complete:
soft-backed rocker, the uneasy bones of the changing table draped in lotions,
stacks of flannel squares like milk teeth lined in gum-pink silk.

This is the room to which I would lure her, my full blossom,
my fat thing, so I could cut the baby out to be my valentine.
I called her to pick up some misdelivered things,
gifts we both would need. I took her almost name,
so we could be the twins we were meant to be.

When she came, I faked a deep chorus of rupture,
hurried her in, doubled over.
Like one who knew. I locked the door.
Set at her with my knife-arms.
Clapped my hand to her mouth.
It was to be a kiss.

But biology knows a secret it keeps from the honor roll:
intuition. Self-preservation. Survival.
Adrenaline, that makes the blood go round the clock.
Under my big shirt I had only a toy soldier's heart, melting in tin.
Under hers, the real deal, so she fought back and finished me.

Also, there's the trick of melatonin.
The sun sees better those with babies,
loves them, damages them,
little rivulets of spider blood in their fucking lucky faces.
Breaking them down, thickening their skin. I was and am pale as bird's-eye.

If I kept animals they would have known, too,
and left me be like the soft wolf cast out of the herd.
The dogs all follow the chosen ones, the swollen,
furrow into their pussies, hunting heat and colostrum.

Neighbors, though, are stupid, and believed me.
I had a victory garden registry, all the bounty
of sterile bottles and waterproof sheeting,
tiny silver scissors and nasal bulbs,
plastic nipples to keep the outlets at bay,
desires waiting to be harvested. I will need these things,
I told them all. I need them.

Oh what does it mean to be *warlike*? Like a war?
What does it mean to be *Southern*? *Articulate*?
I lived on God's little acre, in a time of God.
The good people of God. God bless you and goodnight.

My recovered memory pitches again
toward the black-winged fairies like nesting dolls, tiny things flickering
in the thickets of sexual trauma, neglect, burning, holy love.
And do you believe in fairies? Clap your hands if you do.

Leaving Saturn
Major Jackson

—*Sun Ra & His Year 2000 Myth Science Arkestra*
at Grendel's Lair Cabaret, 1986

Skyrocketed—
My eyes dilate old
Copper pennies.
Effortlessly, I play
*

Manifesto of the One
Stringed Harp. Only
This time I'm washed
Ashore, shipwrecked
*

In Birmingham.
My black porcelain
Fingers, my sole
Possession. So I
*

Hammer out
Equations for
A New Thing.
Ogommetelli,
*

Ovid & Homer
Behind me, I toss
Apple peelings in
The air & half-hear
*

Brush strokes, the up
Kick of autumn
Leaves, the Arkestra
Laying down for

*

New dimensions.
I could be at Berkeley
Teaching a course—
Fixin's: How to Dress
*

Myth or Generations:
Spaceships in Harlem.
Instead, vibes from Chi-
Town, must be Fletcher's
*

Big Band Music—oh,
My brother, the wind—
I know this life is
Only a circus. I'm
*

Brushed aside: a naïf,
A charlatan, too avant
Garde. Satellite music for
A futuristic tent, says
*

One critic. Heartbreak
In outer space, says
Another,—lunar
Dust on the brain.
*

I head to New York.
New York loves
A spectacle: wet pain
Of cement, sweet
*

Scent of gulls swirling
Between skyscrapers
So tall, looks like war.
If what I'm told is true

*

Mars is dying, it's after
The end of the world.
So, here I am,
In Philadelphia,
*

Death's headquarters,
Here to save the cosmos,
Here to dance in a bed
Of living gravestones.

Like This

Frank Giampietro

*—Monsieur Mangetout had eaten nine tons
of metal and glass by October, 1997*

The first thing I ate that I shouldn't have eaten
was a tiny moon sized shard when my brother
dropped my glass of milk on the floor.
No one saw me do it. It was a secret—glass in,
down my throat, but not a single nick,
then in my stomach. Mine. Then came:
A quarter found at the bottom of the big-kid slides,
a bet. A dull razor blade, a bet. A new razor blade—
my father's. Because the first one tasted of rust
and this one more intimate—I loved my father,
but he didn't love me. The scabbard, sword,
and head of my old broken toy Napoleon.
One of Father's spare mandolin strings.
Mother's broken locket. She cried and so I belched
it back for her—a small resurrection in my mouth.
I felt I should try to broaden my palette then.
Tried a dozen plastic guitar picks of various
shapes and thicknesses, the Q pages
of our last year's phone book, some
pieces of wooden molding from the window
by my bed, but it was no good. I began to sort
of crave King Metal, Queen Glass: sardine tins,
Grandmother's stained glass cross and the lead around it.
A fork with veal with Viola, our first date.
Then I began to make money at it: 18 bicycles,
10 used, 8 new, 15 shopping carts for charity,
7 Japanese TV sets, 6 cheap chandeliers,
2 bunk beds, a child's coffin, a pair of beginner's skis,
a computer hard drive, a Cessna light aircraft

for Brazil TV1 (it took 37 days). How do you do it?
They ask. And I don't answer.
Instead I think of Father's new razor blades,
my reflection in its reflection,
in his mirrored medicine cabinet on the back of my tongue.

Man on Extremely Small Island
Jason Koo

—*after a Mordillo cartoon*

I think I must be sitting on the kneecap
of a gigantic woman: stretched out
on the sea floor, one long leg folded in,
triangulating heavenward, her knee
just breaches the surface enough to make
my seat. How she came to be here, how
I happened to wash up on her kneecap
shore, why she never puts her leg down—
these are questions I do not pursue.
Instead, I try to picture the woman's face:
eyes lidded, mouth upturned in sleepy
pleasure, she can just bear the tickling
my body gives her; naturally, I'm afraid
that if I move too much a giant hand
will come whalebursting out of the water
to thwop me like a golf ball into the sea.
So, still as possible. Once, I did an experiment:
I got down on my belly—gingerly—
seal-wagged my upper body down
the eastern slope of the knee, and sent
my hands snorkeling—a distinct shudder.
Was that her thigh? That shudder
nearly broke my ribs, so I've never tried
the opposite slope for shin. Sometimes,
as is my way, I begin to feel ungrateful:
why couldn't it have been a breast
instead of a knee? I could lie down,
feel cared for, sleep. I could relax . . .
The irony, of course, is that from the sky
the knee probably looks like a breast,
with me as nipple, so, when you notify
the Coast Guard about my situation,

be sure to warn them of the resemblance.
Not that I expect anyone to find me.
By the time you get this message—if
you get it—I'll have been swallowed up
by a storm; the fact that I haven't been
already I <u>would</u> call a "miracle," but
when you throw yourself off a ship, lose
consciousness, and come to on a kneecap,
can anything else go by that name?

Miracle. And all those years I asked
for a smaller nose. I said to God, Just
give me a chance. This isn't a nose—
it's a melon. Just make it a <u>little</u> smaller,
something a woman can convince herself
to live with if I am a good enough man . . .

When I came to that first strange morning
I thought I'd washed up on a giant nose.
I said to God, Very funny, very very funny.
Hilarious. I'm dying here. You kill me.
Then I put my nose into my hands and wept.
But now I think kneecap—I won't give God
that satisfaction. And my sea-goddess,
she has no nose. Just a space where mine
can fit.
            I'm running out of shirt.
You might be wondering where I got
this bottle—someone must have thrown it off
the ship. There was another message inside.
I'm alone, it said. Find me, find me.
I threw it in the water.
                        Strange—
I used to hate sitting in my apartment,
night after night, hearing murmurings
in the apartments around me; now
I stare at the endless, sunshot blue
and try to imagine walls.

(Moan): Robert McFerrin, Sr.
L. Lamar Wilson

You doctors say my lips may never part again
to make *beautiful* & *sensitive* drip from mouths
that once spewed *nigger*. I did it in '55 when
I put on Amonasro's sword & shield at the Met,
the first Colored man on that stage. I wanted to sing
Radames or Wotan or Count di Luna or a romantic lead.
I guess this would have created too much controversy.
I told some *New York Post* reporters then what they
wanted to hear: *I am not attempting to carry the load
for all Negro singers.* Like I had a choice.

I knew I was lyin', but the whole damn thing
was a farce, so I learned my part. I mean,
an Ethiopian love story with the whitest gals
they could find? Letting me play Aida's daddy
but not her lover? I reckon it was easier
for white folk to ignore how their tragic heroine
would have been conceived. The heat of the grind
of pale & pitch flesh. The coil of my baritone
around her mama's lyric soprano. The ache
of my seed in her virgin womb. Guess
my powdered face got washed away
in all that white onstage, night
after night, week after week.
I was stagin' my own revolution
long before them badasses callin' themselves
Black Panthers were chillren playin' Jacks
on the corner or fishin' at the creek.
I been makin' black folk sound pretty
a long time. Hell, I even put the Mississippi
in the great black hope's throat.

(Bess, you is my woman now. You is. You is.)

Even Sidney Poitier needed me. That was my misery
boilin' over in his eyes, bubblin' out of his gut.
I taught him to roar *Amen!* years later with them German nuns,
to sound like he was smilin' & cryin' at the same time.
We *were* America the beautiful back then, blacks makin'
doors crack with our grace & quietness, then open
enough for the rest of y'all to sneak through.
Now you say I had a stroke. May never talk again,
much less sing. But you don't know it took me
years to convince my daddy it wasn't
no sin to give 'way our secrets, that just 'cause
I don't say Jesus don't mean they can't feel him
when I breathe on 'em. When my boy Bobby
come by my bedside with his jazz yodelin', I know
he needs me to show him how to put a little extra
moan in at the end of the phrase. & I aim to teach him.

The Monster's Bride Questions the Motives of Her Creator

Tiffany Midge

Those plugs jutting out from her neck:
she's curious, what are they for?

The fiery thoroughfare of crisscrossing scars
from temple to jaw, brow to ear:
should she look for something implicit there?

One eye brown, pilfered from an orange-haired
prostitute in Potter's Field; the other fixed askew
in her head, a child's like-new ornament:
is he a misogynist? Did his mother abandon him?

One arm, the muscular backhoe of a fieldworker's
connected to the jagged star of a hand:
she wonders, is she expected to work?

The vagina, intact and as pretty as postcard sunset:
should she ruin it for him?

The abdomen owns the legacy of multiple births,
a miller's wife spitting out babes like peas:
is there room to grow more?

What hair that's left is black as licorice,
sparse on her scalp like a locust-run crop:
does he secretly love his sister?

Her dresses, hung in the closet like sides of beef,
taffetas, crinolines, colors of esplanade sherbets:
should she dance for him?

At night, locked in her chambers,
she hears desire's low growl, smells iron, lust, rain:
what does it mean? Is it for her?

My Kitchen
Molly Tenenbaum

—after Julia Child's kitchen, Museum of American History, Washington, D.C.

Come to me, countertops,
up to my touch, up like loaves
to the curve of my hands.
Window, window, fly to my eye,
fly like circles I'd shape
with my fingers and swoop
like new eyes to my face.
Window, window, bring me birds,

and here are the birds, the very same birds
whose pictures and paragraphs flash
from the field guide, guide
that slides out from the shelf and flares open before me,
shelf that swings down to me, each time I need it,
the phone book of this very year,
in this, my town.

All tending toward me, converging,
handles of pans, spatula wands,
all winging forth from the pegboarded walls,

walls that sped from the sky
and fixed themselves, plop, all around me, walls
that leapt, yelping and climbing
all over their paws to be near me.

And come swimming paintbrush, finny blue fish,
refreshing the trim every year in my best
cool warm colors. When I waved, when I wished,

when I stood in my apron and asked
for an easy purée, for a quick even mincer—

how they rushed to their tables, nodding and drawing,
the blade engineers, the twirler designers, and look,
you, and you: Here's your own magic slicer.

And as for the ten thousand hours
to re-invent bread, open before me,
you panels, you photos, you story unrolling.
Here's the dough in its cradle.
Here's my husband, with the clay tiles and the water sprayer.
Here are the three diagonal cuts with a razor.
And look, one of me with the master baker.

My Life as Orson Welles

John Olivares Espinoza

Hogwash with what you know:
My father invented the automobile,
mother was a stunning cross-eyed pianist,
my brother Dickie spent most his life in the nut house
because show-biz talent evaded him.
I, deemed a prodigy at eighteen months,
played piano, violin, and learned magic tricks
from the Vaudevillians by the time I was four,
and by six, it was opera, theater, concerts in Chicago,
where my mother died of jaundice.
And after taking custody, Father died too,
of the bottle-tipping disease.
    My inheritance allowed me travel to Madrid
where the bulls and I chased Ernie Hemingway.
I was nineteen playing Tybalt in the Mercury Theater by day,
while stalking Broadway as The Shadow at night.
Bored out of my wits, I had the nation believing
Martians were invading Jersey.
Twenty-three years old and already a household name.
    Two years later, in the process of going up against
Billy the Tycoon, a man who believed a man couldn't be crushed
by the motion picture, I had directed the greatest film
America ever saw or will ever be made.
But I was crushed, too.
Nothing worse than Judas being banished from heaven
than being blacklisted from Hollywood,
losing all creative control, having all contracts terminated.
When my second wife, Rita Hayworth, got too fat
our marriage dissolved faster than an effervescent
for my heart burn. Physical appearance is a virtue.

    Despite nine hundred Golden Globe nominations,
and one Oscar, despite all the Lifetime Achievement awards
for over fifteen-thousand appearances in films,
I became Hollywood's most celebrated Has-Been
doing Farmer John TV ads where I promised to "sell no
swine before its time," performed magic tricks
on talk shows, like a child parading his charms
for the nickels he'll finagle from his aunts.
    Let me be the first to tell you I started at the top
and worked my way to the bottom: Trickle-Down Theory in action.
    I steadily grew obese, reaching five-hundred pounds.
What surprise my heart didn't give out earlier than seventy?
In L.A., I once ate eighteen hot dogs at Pinky's
in one sitting for God's sake. Call me The Boy Genius,
The Wunderkind of Kenosha, The Pariah of Burbank.
Call it destiny, but I call it prophecy for the after-life:
In my last screen appearance—*Transformers: The Movie*—
I voiced the part of Unicron: a monster who devoured planets.

Notes in the Margins of *King Kong* (1933)
III: *We'll be millionaires!*

Reginald Harris

> *He's always been a king of his world—we'll teach him fear.*
> *We'll be millionaires!*
> —Carl Denham

My skin flakes off into their waiting pockets,
the rubbed together hands of promoters,
handlers, hangers on. The frenzied Press

crushes in with flashing light bulbs, to plaster
me on the front pages, turn newsprint
into clinking dimes. I am what they can get,

for me, the going rate, my life cashed in,
the iron bands on my wrists translated
into diamond bracelets for their latest girl,

the knowledge of me breathing in their darkness,
all their fears embodied, worth its weight in gold.

Ornette Coleman's Out-of-Office Reply
Ed Pavlić

This? It's a bone crystal. New growth.

It's a full-fluted pain bristle. No

mistaking the hand-hewn Gullet of It All.
   Note the rhythm. A brand new

      dimple in bare flesh within a stun-gun's easy
range of ivory tickled

      in the shadowed side of the room.
Here, keep it. Watch it, wash
      away.

Heavy minerals remain. Let high mountain air

      drink the blue and leave salt rivers

on the sun-brown back of Dr. Fear's

unstudied understudy. Watch out. It sees in the dark.
   Ms. Curiosity Killed It.

      You can almost feel it all
happen. Can almost hear the chrome eye
   of the engine wink

your name. Me? I'm the keeper.

    Curator, really. By now you must know the routine.
The perfume and the smell of glue

   on an empty
gum-line, the stone's throw from noonday

to nowhere. You've pad-prowled
   your fair share

   of throat-garbled nights, called their dream-stolen
names. You've tasted dust from legs opened
   and tangled into treble

clefs and gauzed hands to stem the bass hum.

   You've gone back to check the slip

   knots. Herr Sleight-of-Hand, rag in mouth

and tied to the posts. Doused the bed and tossed
   the match.

   Behind barn door number three : the Deputy
Provost of Insinuation
   cuffed to the nickel catch

beneath the sink. If it's still you on the line, leave

me a message, lover. This isn't news
if you've cupped red

hands and blown our secrets into pools of rain

that freeze by morning into nerves

of steel.
You've slung vendettas back at false
ceilings and cursed the clean

shaven sky. Chin flung up

and veins chalked beneath the skin,
you were there
when I told the sun to go back down,

dared the moon to try it

with its own broke-down luck in the lost and found.
Or don't.
Sit there quiet and work

that loose flap of skin. Admit it. You can't

bring yourself to leave it alone,

that trap door in the floor and the balloon-eyed bottom
feeder hanging by its tail

in the smoke house. Let's don't mention
the broken picture
   window you carry around

in your pockets. Go ahead, hold back

   and let the easy gait wear the legs raw. Or not.
It's up to you. Dig in for chaos
   and exact change

   for the bus. Here it comes. Dig deep and make
no mention, the red
   river

of knuckles down your leg. No one will notice.
   Put your lips up

   to my absent ear and tongue-touch me

a stolen prayer. It's not music, it's the hollow howl,
   frenzy of the invisible

   stain, the blood-curse of songbirds
gone extinct and gone down

   a slope slippery as the green

stretched thin

on crooked old Mssr. Nothing From Nothing's false eye teeth.

Sarah Bernhardt Plays Hamlet

Meghan Brinson

I.
When I was 17, my father died.
I came home from Europe to a clean house
full of my relatives. My cousin
mowed the weeds and trimmed
the hedges. My grandmother
baked bread and boiled potatoes
for salad.

My mother in black,
leaning on my uncle's
arm. Her hair shorter than
I remember, hiding from me
behind my uncle's square
of blue and green silk.

II.
The dirt fell into the grave
one handful at a time. The birds
sang limericks in the willows,
K-I-S-S-I-N-G, as if my father
lying in the earth was erotic,
an embrace.

Relatives came with their green
bowls molded like cut glass: casserole,
Jello salad, fried chicken, deviled
eggs, baked and sliced ham, barbecue,
yeast rolls, as if there was a hole to fill
handful by handful. The smell of carnations.

III.
In the greenhouse, back by the pecan tree,
my high school friend Leon and I
touched. "Your mother
is worried about you," he said, unhooking
my bra. His mouth was sweet, tasted
like lime Jello. Inside me there
is a hole that cannot be filled. The smell
of lilies, touch of rue. Here my father

rode me on his back, he threw me
into this air, he is not here to catch me.

IV.
The creek smells sweet, like blueberries.
Bugs dimple its surface, skim across
light-hearted. The afternoon starts to darken,
to get cold. The lightning bugs sing
elegies to their dying race, pulse
of lights.

In between my toes, something wriggles
through the sandy bottom of the spring bed
that runs out to meet the creek
snaking through our farm.

V.
The night finds us on the sandbar,
my favorite spot, cicada song.
Leon puts his head in my lap.
By the time this story ends,
we will all be dead.

Setsuko Hara

Cynthia Arrieu-King

A bristling fir
whispered about my vanishing. The great silence.

How, fade to black,
I, the girl of your dreams, am also this tan middle-aged man
I swept into suits
and hanged. No marriage, your Eternal Virgin
in black and white. Black
and white flips a skirt, a frown until I, so famous,
fly like a buck into woods no one can see.

They knock. I don't live here, I say.
I keep the cedar door to.

*

Here in the house, a moth bats
a lantern, holding to a flame-opulent scrim.

Slatted sandals. This clatter of plums—
I'm a chime
films end with
after twenty years of poses,
striding into the fake hall as you wanted
tilting my head
to a crinoline kimono. Catapulted to billboards
glutting the seashore, I lived this thought:

No one's going to burn my bones
until smoke stops its creep from the kettle.

No smoked femur of mine will
mix in water;

a wash to paint a portrait of sad ether
a black to give the impression of bottomless eyesá
filled with whatever you
wanted.

The blunt kite
of appearing, and now I shade the hanging wash,
my hand
a visor, my hand breaks up old ash.

The sun an unexpected hand.
I say, behind the door,
She doesn't live here.

*

It's been years since I tired, tiptoeing for light meters.
The fecund night of other people's feelings
and now I hide,
a black LP played in perpetuity.

I brush the air unseen. Is life disappointing?

Yes.

*

Kurosawa. Ozu. Narusa. Inagaki.
Go on, claim with all names,
grab noise at sea, and unplanned seafoam chilling my calves
for the twenty-third time. You can't
film this yourself. Out there

withers a million me's in celluloid.
I accepted your fifty-cent tickets—

that hardly assuaged
my brother struck by a train before my eyes,
hardly your tripod
my face gone among chrysanthemums
and today,
a long still of myself:

Radishes in rain.
Oyster-dumb, not hoping for grit or a pearl.

*

I feel your undying admiration,
tiny boxes of white cream on spoons.

Snow lands on everything you knew of me
Snow beyond a dry indigo curtain
this backwards, unseen breath.
Into a kettle's voice I disappear,

a smile useless without a fence.

My heart thuds
an all-interior vista
almost big
as what you loved so much, the idea
of this steady sea—these happy eyes.

Today on Maury
LaTasha N. Nevada Diggs

I am a 19 year old shifting fabric/folds of gathered polyester/lane bryant plus
     purple lycra/cotton button down blouse stretched over more than baby fat

effort grants me mute response/bad posture/to hunch over to reduce
     appearance/to shoulder true cup size/the pubescent yeastiness

a dash of neckline/a thin gold chain quick sanded into flesh/triangular steps/soft
     my weight is not a seasonal occurrence nor is it retrograde

I don't follow the rotation of the moon/no one taught me such things

        if I could be 15 again, I would be unfat

the topic/cheating boyfriends/hidden video/and/sexy decoys/my doe eyes cloudless
     open to cool/close to dry tears/brow upraised to monitor breathing

turn/shake/left knee over right/right arm hiding my gut/pace/undone nails/chewed.
     heat blown hair turn to fuss.

a seat away is my first love/cherry popper/finger blower/scamps near laughter
     the lisp/enamored by the close caption:

        "So what you doing tonight? How much do you charge?"
        "Can I get a sample now?"

        if I could be 16 again, I would be unfingered.

words of blow job offer/hidden black-white projection/english dub to catch
the whispers/appointments after 11/replayed/appointments after 11

tongue in her/ her/the mouth of maury's hired help/hired milk maid
      brought out to the stage to confirm what I've done seen.

her dress size/five times smaller/her hair/feathered and done/her nails/manicured
      unbitten/I was that cup size when he first said I love you

      if I could be 16½, I would be unpregnant/unchildbearing.

      unlied to.

Track 4: Reflections

Jericho Brown

—as performed by Diana Ross

I wanted to reflect the sun.

I wore what glitters, smiled,
Left my eyes open, and,

On the ceiling of my mouth,

Balanced a note as long as God allowed,
My head tilted backwards, my arms stretched

Out and up, I kept praying,

If the red sun rising makes a sound,
Let my voice be that sound.

I could hear the sun sing in 1968.

I learned the word assassin
And watched cities burn.

Got another #1 and somebody

Set Detroit on fire. That was power—
White folks looking at me

Directly and going blind

So they wouldn't have to see
What in the world was burning black.

Violin (Larry Fine)
Sean Singer

Away from the air which is its only
resource, and apart and away

from the Stradivarius door, we know
window means eye of wind.

Here is pale marble, like a flat alabaster ship,
barely there, hearing only its echo, of its inside water.

The dark music by which a violin tunes its pear
reversals, again lights like a square in stone choirs.

The pain goes away
on payday.

Sequence of violins and their dark pegs, rolling
like a victor civilly putting a rubber mouth over his mouth.

There is a silence that will turn: a hammered vitula
actually sparking with upper and lower bouts.

Maybe we're at the junction
where we will not need this anymore.

Yellow spigots and leafy mirrors–
abandoned grain buttresses and pillows of mud.

Devouring our orange holding since the afternoon
everyone's milkweed & mezzotint.

Beetroot powder, ivory territory...
volcanoes may have peaks but a peak is not a volcano.

Some of us aren't even here, some
have happiness mixed in their lilac eyes.

the vodka to Miss USA Tara Conner
Marty McConnell

lies don't sit well on dry lips, pretty pretty—
admit it. I made you. rocked you to sleep
after each man left. when the hotel paintings

crawled out of their frames to shame you, I
took you mirror to barstool to blackout just
like you asked when we stared, deadeye

down, shot glass to bar. it was mutual.
we had a deal. I gave you everything
I've got and now you cry therapy. maybe

you didn't read the fine print, sweet thang.
this here's a lifetime agreement, a pact
backed with blood and sworn on the flag,

nothing you can give up so easy.
when you were waiting tables
in Tahoe, who brought you home

every night, laid you down dreamless,
took the Kentucky out of your sleep?
it was me gave your tongue its wink

and vaseline charm, got you through
the Mint Jubilee and the Showboat
Float, out of Russell Springs

and into pure Manhattan. you owe me.
what are you going to do dry, my queen?
the stammer will come back, and the drawl

thicker than a mix of shit and molasses.
you'll be back. give your daddy my love
when you see him.

It Kept on Burning

The Fires of Social and Political Consciousness

Ajal
Brian Turner

*—The appointed time of death which Muslims believe God has
determined for every individual; it cannot be delayed or hastened.*

There are ninety-nine special names for God,
my son, and not so long ago I held you
newly born under a crescent moon,
and gave you the name which means *servant
of God*, and I did not speak of tanks,
the thunder of iron, missiles flying
over the rooftops of our city—I whispered
the call to prayer once in each ear.

It should not be like this. Abd Allah,
many years from now, your own children
should wash your body three times
after your death. They should seal your mouth
with cotton, reciting prayers in a wash
of light and grieving, a perfume of lemons
and jasmine on your skin.

It should not be like this, Abd Allah.
I wanted you to see the Ctesiphon Arch,
the Tower of Samarra, the Ziggurat of Ur.
I wanted to show you the Arabic language
written on the spines of the sawtooth mountains.
I wanted to teach you our family history,
and see where you might take it.

I cannot undo what the shrapnel has done.
I climb down into the crumbling earth
to turn your face toward Mecca, as it must be.
Remember the old words I have taught you,
Abd Allah. And go with your mother,
buried here beside you—she will know the way.

All the Trees of the Field Shall Clap Their Hands
Eduardo C. Corral

Are the knees & elbows
 the first knots
 the dead untie?
 I swing from a rope
 lashed
 to a beam. Some men
along the Yuba river
 toss coins
 into the doubling water.
 Visible skin.
 Memorable hair.
 Imagine: coal, plow,
 rust, century.
 All layers
 of the same palabra.
 Once
 I mistook a peach pit
 on a white dish
 for a thumbprint.
 Wolf counselor.
 Reaper.
 Small rock.
 The knot just under
 my right ear
whispers *God is gracious,*
 God will
 increase. The soul,
 like semen,
 escapes
 the body
 swiftly.

Ballad of Greg Withrow
Alison Luterman

1)
Love blindsided me.
Crept up in those dumb white
sneakers they make waitresses wear. This girl said,
"You seem like such a nice guy."
And she put eggs in front of me. I ate them,
though by then I was such a mess of mud inside
I couldn't hardly speak human.
Dirt with a pile of eggs in front of it.
Except she smiled or something.
So I went back. Went back for her smile
and her number. Love crept up
on dirt.

2)
She was new in town and didn't know.
She never seen the likes of what I was up to.
My job: big man on the hate rodeo.
Ride into town, get the white kids fired up
telling them how the niggers and spics
and jews had all the money, all the jobs.
Why they weren't getting any.
Under my direction a few black heads might get smashed
like pumpkins the day after Hallowe'en,
or the body of some gook
show up in the tall weeds outside of town
with no one but his family to count him missing,
and them not even able to tell the cops in proper English.
I wanted to be like Hitler, or better, Genghis Khan.

3)
She didn't have family
neither. And my old man
used to like to
kick me downstairs from when I could walk,
until one night he kicked me out entirely.
On the streets the Nazis was family, they took me in.
Because I was Aryan, white like them.
And we was someday going to rule again.

4)
What happened before doesn't matter.
What happened after I take as payment
on debts past due.
But I'll tell you something:
Love opens you up worse than a knife.
I've been stomped on with steel boots,
punched in the stomach, had my head swung into a wall,
into a toilet. Love is worse.
There's nothing to hold onto.

5)
See, we was family to each other.
She had no idea, she didn't know.
Little by little love was ruining me.
How could I eat her eggs and go out afterward
and preach kill the nigger? Kill?
I'd lift my head and it was another man,
a black man, eating his eggs
with maybe someone who loved him waiting at home
in their bed for him to make her warm.
And I couldn't do it. Love was ruining me.

6)
I tried to get away quiet.
Out by the back door. But hate—
Hate really does not want to let you go.
It thinks it owns you. And I owed
something, now. Would have to pay.
Still, when they came for me I was not ready.
Came with their baseball bats and smashed my jaw
so I couldn't talk to no more reporters,
and say that Hate thing was a mistake.
After, I wouldn't tell police who done it.
Hell, it was me who done it.
I trained me to come after me
in the middle of the night and leave me
in a pool of my own blood.
That's who done it.

7)
When I turned on her she left
and I don't blame her. I'd have drove her to the station
myself, if I knew what come next.
After the news that night when I kept on telling
the wrong I done and that I was sorry. They got me good—
nailed me to a six-foot piece of wood
like the savior of hell, and I come stumbling down the streets of Sacramento,
the nails in my hands, and blood
running down my side. And the white folks passed me by.
Like this I know God has a plan.
And nothing happens that He don't see.

8)
Cause my own Aryan nation had warned me:
I was as good as dead already.
And the others, they were afraid I think. My own people.
And then the black couple come.

And the man says, "Is this who I think—?"
And the woman says, "We got to take him down"
And the man says, "Hell we got to, *do you know who this is?*"
And she says, "'Course I know, everyone in this town that's got a radio
or a television knows. Jesus, lord have mercy, help me
with these nails."

9)
And like this I come to speak before you.
Except I cannot talk right
on account of the jaw still being wired
and because I don't know hardly
what to say anymore. When I hated I knew.
Now I don't know
nothing, except the things I told you.
Love opens you up,
worse than a knife.

Bring the Rain
Khadijah Queen

—*Uruzgan, Afghanistan, July 1, 2002*

there is a B-52 in my bed.
scimitars dance a careful dance
on my sand-loaded tongue.

this is the world where letters writhe against my teeth—

tear at my face like *nan*—
and I eat it, the black bread—

black my blackened ankles, black the sand of my feet—let

the precious bombs fall

I submit
I submit
I submit

my olive legs pale open to the rubble of caves,

a ruined wedding, loved bones muscle skin turned ash

the dance is a dark one
(where are my children   where is the rain)
when blood pools on the floor
I scream over the music

and I sing it, the black bread
broken in half by steel

the prayers in black fields of sandstorms
and I fold them—the black hundred
bleeding limbs into one
thousand tons of fire

        dropped over
        and over
        and over
        and over
        and over
        and over
        and over

        on screaming blackbird days

                        and the blasted rock of night

            and I untie the cord of panic

        bruising my throat
        take these weapons from my mouth

          and speak

Bronze Age
Shane Book

Their revolution painted on a wall. Revolution
scent in the rust-colored dirt, and the rat-heavy
palms, and the blue diesel smaze over the former
capital. We waited. On the corner, insistent laughter.
On the corner, a turned over bus—flame bathed

to the metal. Our tape measures cocked,
as per our orders. We were given
a belt each and a night. Mine was short-haired,
with jagged white gear teeth and a dirt-sniffing
mechanism for quicker dirt sifting

and much data to desist. Lots: "Encada barrio..."
and "our ideas are our weapons." Among other things.
Revolution, revolution. Faint image of the revolution's
big man on the plaza clock. Drawn in wrought iron.
Splashed on a smock. The sounds we watched for:

night wind cracking canvas sails; wood stick
rhythmically striking wood stick; hastily made
motorcades' ragged sirens. The revolution?
Through our high powered geigers: twin-stroke
underbuzz of revolution's engine; the puttering

three-wheeled revolution; the landless campesinos
beaten by pots and pans into land and nothing
we could do. They resented our husks.
"Of two eyes one always lies," this we knew. We planned
removing the other, replacing it with Jefferson dirt:

dirt of the sea, empire dirt, wind down from the north
dirt, father dirt, dirt of scallions and ghost
galleons. The elephant god Jefferson. Trident
in one hand, another with axe, snake in another
and in another his reigns, steering his eight rat team,

as through the green clouds they steam.
On Jefferson's neck a lush green alligator hung
from a bone chain like a hymn. As always. Family
bones, yet distant; somewhat empirical and fencing
the hill, long shards of oxidized metal. There went
tradition, bronze titan. The balcony scene:
swarms of wetblack hair surrounding
wetblack rocks on the tree-less frozen
sand expanse. Once the show trials were over
we would get to work, but quietly. Such were our orders.

Swimming style analysis, certain constellations
notated from the tattered revolutionary cupolas'
ceilings, hands to secure a detainee's head (placement
and number). In their revolutionary stories the sound
of dirt on animal skin drums was like the sound

of a blinking eye roving wild in its socket was like...
Their revolution had its big man and its new man tales
of the monolith sky. We had our love.

Chin's Monologue in the Bucket
Ching-In Chen

—*after Thylias Moss*

here i make   here i jump   skillet to skillet   i'm stirring
i'm shit up an egg   a chick   a runnel of oil   a boy in line
a boy in time

                                       here i make what i want   i make what i
            can
i'm a fan of the fork   i'm not corked   i make
what i want   i make what i can   i make what i make
here i make   here i make the dirt   wash away the plug
the side the cop out the door the pig   in the griddle here come to my door
on the side i can't leave but i can make i can joy i can pass
thru the window the steam i make i make your heart   jump and on oil i make
what i make and you can eat and you can stamp   you got the craving I got
the make i got the follow i got the eye i make what i make   and you take what you take

and then stampede

                                    i can't hear in this box
                                    i just make what i make
my heart is souped up i zipped up i'm making
until you walk
                      walk away with your smug
                                  and your fake

Chorus of X, the Rescuers' Mark
Iain Haley Pollock

X say search party,
say month,
say day,
X say live wire, gas leak,
say floodwater
say dead dog, dead cat,
X say no dead bodies,
say one dead body,
say two,
say three dead bodies,
say four,
X say kitchen,
say bedroom,
say attic,
say the family Bible floated next to me
three days before the waters carried it off,
X say that dog was a loud-ass, mean-ass bitch anyway,
say rain & wind on the roof was like every song I heard,
the slow ones & angry, Sunday ones & off-tunes ones,
pretty ones & ones that growled, played all together on tuba,
on trumpet, on banjo, on every instrument man saw fit to make,
X say God you been flooding us too much,
say we here and you never be rid of us,
say most of the family moved north & west, got tired
of humidity & high water, called when they could,
X say it got easier to die in water than live on land,
say if you loot this you only stealin from nature
and that bitch always take back what hers,
say you missed me buried under plaster & paint shreds
& wood & door & shingle & pictures of my grandbabies,

say my worst sins were pride & white lies recited
every morning like momma's daily prayers,
X say lungs full of flood in the end
took me higher than liquor ever did,
say blackwater love me more than my daddy ever did,
say pestilence, say quarantine, say lamb's blood,
say slave ship, say witch trials, say Wounded Knee,
say the monk doused himself in gasoline,
say God, say man, say
                    not all of us are saved.

Dear Laramie, Dear Liar, Dear Once Upon a Time

Jeremy Halinen

Matt and I were walking hand
in hand down University Avenue,
sipping sweet tea in bright light
sent about eight minutes before
by the sun, sweet nothings
slipping
now and again
from our lips,
which couldn't have been more
calm,
when two frat boys
approached us with lazy
grins on the faces
below the brims of their hats.

We nodded at them
as we passed.

That night, we drove out of town,
parked at the edge of a field
and made love awhile
by a split-rail fence
in light sent long before we were born
by some stars.

Elizabeth at Seabrook

Kevin Clark

—Nuclear power protests, 1977

Even today, brushing blush on my cheeks,
I can re-imagine the turning face
Of that young guardsman irradiated
By dawn sun—or the fissured power plant.
He said, Ma'am, you know my orders: It's time
To separate the men from the women.
One afternoon walk I'd seen a flower
Arranged in a Fibonacci sequence
Of new helical rays. What was its name?
The artist says beauty walks math spirals
Out past numbers, out past all reason.
That's a moment to live for, isn't it?
On the damp armory floor, the men sat
In circles, then the women around them.
At the center were piled our tied shoes.
We were surrounded by a tight square
Of masked soldiers holding shields, Billy clubs.
I stood to tell the lieutenant of our
Consensus pact: The instant a guardsman
Touches any one of our group, every
Man and woman will strip naked. Like that,
Rouge shadows blossomed on his cheeks the way
A thumb touch might shame any fresh petal
Into darkness. Their retreat took seconds.
Then we sat alone in the new silence.
I had always believed that peace was won
Unarmed in the face of odds.—Who could know
Naked skin would send them into shadow.
They gave up and let us out. For two days

I slept and dreamed. At first the nuke sent up
A mushroom cloud. Then night, distant voices,
My mother, a ring of linked friends, moonlight.
I'm strolling through the wetlands, alone,
Wearing only my hiking boots. The sucking
Muck holds steps like kisses. Fibonacci
Florets billow in the sky. When I wake,
That flower's lost name burns me alive.

Emmett Till's Glass-Top Casket
Cornelius Eady

By the time they cracked me open again, topside, abandoned in a toolshed, I had become another kind of nest. Not many people connect possums with Chicago,

but this is where the city ends, after all, and I float still, after the footfalls fade and the roots bloom around us. The fact was, everything that worked for my young man

worked for my new tenants. The fact was, he had been gone for years. They lifted him from my embrace, and I was empty, ready. That's how the possums found me, friend,

dry-docked, a tattered mercy hull. Once I held a boy who didn't look like a boy. When they finally remembered, they peeked through my clear top. Then their wild surprise.

fodderhouse
Quraysh Ali Lansana

—harriet tubman

dis mornin milk of sun
seep through de lookhole

devils crouchin
on de walls udda side

night is busy worrisome
day a tirin idle

lord hide de outcast
betray him not dat wander

six chirren   five women
seven grown menfolk

saints grievin today
dey trampled yesterday

run chirren run wid yo grief til it heal
cry out til you ride above tears

Forget
Tamiko Beyer

I forget to eat. Sometimes I even forget to breathe.

—DJ Keshav Jiwani, San Francisco, 2003, waiting for
 his asylum application to override his deportation order.

1. Karachi 1978–1985

When stones smash against the apartment walls I gather
    Mummy's scarves—brilliant red flecked with gold I set
the needle carefully down Asha Bhosle's voice high and delicate drowns
    the curses I dance like the film stars dance
like the myths Swirl scarves around my body blood
    red and glistening Tabla thrums and strings
sing like kites in the wind I dance night
    into dawn forget myself small boy with secrets
become Sharmila Tagore with her diamond
    smile My mother and sister laugh until
tears run down their cheeks Papa looks through me through
    the wall where the mob shouts and I dance harder for forgetting
forgetting who we are and where we have always
    been Only this heartstring Only these heartbeats

*

Inside Ahmed's room I press my hands against the cool stone floor Boys jumbled
    on the bed Porn stolen from Ahmed's American Uncle on the TV
The man's hands tangle in her golden hair His face the map of pleasure
    Close room heavy with the funk of boys I escape and
Ahmed corners me in the vestibule Takes out his glistening
    Cock—*Take it you want it*—And I do
It fills my mouth sweetly Drunk
    on his smell and smooth brown thighs I ride until he explodes
bitter milk in my mouth He sneers Buttons his pants *Tell anyone and you*

173

die Out on the street his rough voice follows me home My throat raw
and powerful I exhale the scent of boy

*

After Mummy caught me pinned under the taxi driver's dank
      hulk she hit me harder and longer than any man
who had sunk his hot flesh into me My sister found her with a tava
      in her hands my curled body just light and space and blood on the kitchen floor

2. San Francisco 1997–2003

Here there are boys who kiss me gently on the thin skin
      behind my ear Who cup me close in movie theaters and on Dolores
Park's bright slopes When afternoon sun pulls
      away the fog's sibilance I add
muscle and flesh to each of my battered bones

*

The records spin like dervishes I mix
      coy flutes and the high voice of my childhood
drowning in electronic pulse the blond boys and girls
      with flowing skirts dance their limbs have never needed
to forget their feet firmly planted
      in concrete America they dance night into dawn and I the alchemist
blend sound into light I heartbeat I glisten

*

The towers are burning
      Penciled drawings of men who smashed their bodies into flames
flash on TV screens across America I do not look like them

*

In long lines we touch our pockets heavy with Pakistani
        passports and visa papers long expired creased one hundred times
The immigration man's teeth are so white I am blinded My body buzzes
        florescent My mouth forms words I can hardly understand
              —Gay   Hindu   Asylum   Please—
The immigration man's hands are pink and perfect They stamp
            a piece of paper and slide it across the plastic desk
into my own bitter brown hands I deportee I refuge I stumble
        into misty streets Lose my way home

*

I forget to eat   sometimes I even forget
      to breathe   let the phone ring   let me stand here   bones
disguised by fog   unremember
      myself   wait to lift into darkness   disappear
into night's thin membrane   heartbeat to still

Forneus
Jeffrey Thomson

—*Forneus, the fifth satan, teaches Rhetoric and languages, gives men a good name, and makes them beloved by their friends and foes.*

This is historic times. I think we can agree
the past is over. It is a time of sorrow and
sadness when we lose a loss of life. There's
no question that the minute I got elected
the storm clouds on the horizon were getting
nearly directly overhead. Make no mistake
about it, I understand how tough it is, sir.
I talk to families who die. Families is where
our nation finds hope, where wings take dream.
I tell people, let's don't fear the future, let's shape it.
One year ago today, the time for excuse making
has come to an end. We cannot let terrorists
and rogue nations hold this nation hostile.
Security is the essential roadblock to
achieving the roadmap to peace. We are
making steadfast progress and I'm determined
to keep the process on the road to peace.
And free societies will be allies against
these hateful few who have no conscience,
who kill at the drop of a hat. The only way
we can win is to leave before the job is done.
I promise you I will listen to what has been
said here, even though I wasn't here.
I am a person who recognizes the fallacy
of humans. They have miscalculated me
as a leader—when I am talking about myself
and when he's talking about myself, all of us
are talking about me. See, in my line of work

you've got to repeat things over and over
and over again for the truth to sink in, to kind
of catapult the propaganda. Anybody
who is in a position to serve this country
ought to understand the consequences of words.

George Wallace at the Crossroads
Jake Adam York

No guitar. Just the one, quivering string.
Abnegated gut begun to hate itself.
The throat's weary chords, his hands.

I enter by whiskey, set to
work, retune the flesh.
My favorite music rises.

Everything I touch holds the song
already. The fallen star's
swallowed question. Hot night wind.

This body's never quiet.

As he walks off, into the east,
they fall again, and the whole state
burns in the light.

Gila

Rigoberto González

It's no curse
　　　dragging my belly all day
　　　　　　across the steaming sand.
　　　I'm as thick as a callus
　　　　　　that has shorn off the leg.

If you find me I can explain
　　　the trail made by a single limb.

　　　　　　I'm not a ghost.
Don't be afraid.

Though there are ghosts here—
　　　they strip down to wind
　　　　　　or slump against rock to evaporate.

　　　Sometimes I crawl beneath the shedding,
backing up into the flesh pit for shade.
　　　Praise the final moisture of the mouth, its crown
　　　　　　of teeth that sparkles with silver or gold.

I make a throne of the body
　　　until it begins to decay.

　　　　　　And then I'll toss the frock—
death by hunger, death by heat—
　　　off the pimples of my skin.

　　　Don't you dare come into my kingdom,
peasant, without paying respect on your knees!

179

What generous act did I commit
in my previous life, that I should be
                rewarded with this paradise:

a garden in which every tree that takes root here
                drops its fruit eye-level to me.

Installation / Occupation
Philip Metres

—after Vera Tamari

1.

there was a time you couldn't paint   red white
green or black   could be a flag   imagine

you couldn't paint poppies or watermelon
now you can paint all you want   & yet this state

of uncertainty   will the doors hold out
can you leave your house can you walk around

this occupation   when the tanks come
crack down   drive the sidewalks for fun   for weeks

all these smashed cars lining the city streets
my friend's red Beetle   flipped over   its legs in the air

so in a field   we paved a road to nowhere   & placed
the crushed   in a column   as if in a rush hour

line of traffic   we had an opening   at our piece
a huge party on our road   & then walked home

2.

before dawn a column of Merkavas
came back   my house was opposite the field

& I could see the tanks pull up   & yield
two heads emerged from turrets   trying to read

the scene   then went back inside the hatch
& ran over the exhibit   over & over

again backwards and forwards   then shelled it
& for good measure christened it with piss

I caught it all on video   this metamorphosis
of the piece   there's the story of Duchamp

once the workmen installing his exhibit
dropped a crate of paintings   the floor

shattering the glass   Duchamp ran over
thrilled   now he said   now it is complete

Listen

Seth Michelson

—for Nâzim Hikmet

I write this from exile,
in an attic, in jail:
I twice have died, in 1915 and '22.
But also I've lived:
I climbed Ararat, swam
the Bosporus, studied algebra,
chess, the world's seas, how to sing!
Yet my suffering was enormous:
broken bones, broken country—
so much of me crushed
I now must crawl to my meals....
But still my heart pants
like an old sheep dog for his flock,
so I write this to you
from exile, in an attic, in jail:
The importance of man
is a lie of the will,
only lightning or love
can shatter a blackened sky.

Liu Minghe Speaks

Francisco Aragón

A hyena upon an animal still breathing, he questioned me
I was told it would last for days
His voice clutched my frozen heart
My lungs burned my temples throbbed—night revolving my eyes
A silent tribe of spiders began spinning a web in my brain
Bells occasionally howled—homeless spirits endlessly moaning
I was handcuffed to a window, so I stood, or hung from my wrists
Several of my lower teeth left me during my visit
To open, with a withered hand, the lid of a coffin, and climb inside

At first, I didn't butter my hair
I breakfasted on air, on rock, on coal, on iron
My clothes were rotting rags, my bread soggy with rain
I ate by lowering my head into a bowl
I ate fever with my watery vegetables
For sixteen months my hands and feet were shackled
I slept on boards, or on the ground—a book
Les Poètes Maudis my pillow, my only companion
My skin was ravaged with mud, my armpits full of worms

Enormous province whose sky is flecked with fire and mud
Weighing on me like a lid
Pouring down days as dark as nights
Sometimes the rain mimicked the bars
Funeral processions—no drums, no music—filed slowly inside me
Hope wept, stabbing its stalk in my skull
Sometimes I saw in the sky endless beaches
I tried to invent new flowers, new tongues, new stars

Fear and suffering evaporating in the air
The hallucination of words

On my hospital bed that smell comes back to me still
I have dyed my hair black to erase those years

Memory
Allison Adelle Hedge Coke

When disease rode trade blankets
wove way across oceans, rivers,
my People reeled. So many crossed
into the next world, my fullness ruptured,
poured as sores upon then-tainted blistered skin.

It was too much for Memory, to bear.

Since time ago, slowly erased all
eye could see, truth held
within my reaches for falcons'
sure vision. It is in these vaults
time, place, I exist even today.
In the end, all will dissipate, join me.

My Brother Jay, A Trilogy
Nagueyalti Warren

I. In the Eighties, My Brother Jay

Mamma says the worst has happened. It's morning and daddy is fixing
his eggs in the little black skillet. Mamma's eyes are red and swollen.

She has not combed her hair. She looks like she doesn't care.
Frying eggs spit grease on the chrome stove. Daddy's jaw is set.

His ears go back. *Deserved it*, daddy says. *Damned son-of-a-bitch!*
Mamma drops her juice glass, crashing, blue splinters on the floor.

*That's my child you talking 'bout. My son, and I ain't no bitch you
son-of-a-bastard.* They don't see me standing near the toaster in my

flannel teddy bear jammies granny sent. I'm shaking and start to cry.
Boy made his bed hard, now he got to lie in it, daddy turns from the sink,

pops pepper on his eggs. *Jimmy that's your son you talking 'bout.
He ain't in the damn bed by himself. We in it too. We all affected.*

Mamma's crying, her nose dripping. *The hell you say.* Daddy's temple
veins thump on his head. Mamma sobs, *It's a death sentence. It shouldn't be*

a death sentence. Daddy slams down his fork, *He sinned.* Mamma shouts,
We sinned too, but we didn't die. We just got pregnant and got married.

Is Jay dying? My voice shakes and they both jump and turn around to me.
James died a long time ago, daddy mumbles, but mamma sighs and she

pulls me to her coffee breath, *He's sick baby.* I'm seven, my big brother
is nineteen and daddy says he cannot come home and mamma says we

are going to get him and bring him home and daddy can take his ratty ass
and go straight to hell. We take the Greyhound to San Francisco through

that gate that isn't even golden but red, red as blood Jay spits when he tries
to eat, like red snot running from his nose when I give him pepper pot soup.

Daddy stays in the house but will not talk to Jay. Mamma says pay him no mind.
Jay's tears slide from his long black lashes. They look like jewels on his face.

His cracked lips do not smile and he can't sing songs off the radio, not even
Rapper's Delight. At night he sweats. I wipe his face with my Cyndi Lauper

cloth until mamma makes me go to bed. I pray that Jay won't die because he is gay.
Daddy says all gay men die and go to hell. I think heaven is the happy place.

Maybe I'm confused like when I thought the wafer was the white skin
of Jesus and refused to eat it.

The last day of school I come home to see Jay loaded into an orange and white
ambulance, red top rolling round, doors slam, and it screeches away down Imperial

Highway. Mamma crying, daddy holding her up but she sees me and grabs my hand.
Get my keys. I'm going with my baby. Come on, mamma says.

Daddy won't come. *You old stubborn fool! May your soul rot in your pious shit.*
Mamma backs out the truck and we follow the siren's whine to the emergency room
         door.

Mamma running almost falls but I catch her arm and we have to wait for Jay
to get a room and daddy comes and we are waiting and Jay's friend Jerome comes.

Daddy jumps up and socks him in the mouth knocking out his front teeth and
         blood and
the police take daddy away and Jerome is crying and mamma is crying and I am crying

and Jay slips away at eight fifty two p.m. when it just starts to rain and lightning
streaks the hospital windows, thunder rumbles, drowning out my mamma's screams.

II. In the Eighties, My Son Jay

He looks me dead in my face, my man face and tell me he don't like girls
except to be his good friends, hang out in the mall and all. I'm not seeing

what he means, not knowing what the hell he is saying to me, his daddy.
Him smiling, looking like a cat what swallowed the mouse, licking his lips.

He say dad I'm homosexual. I hit the wall with me fist. Bust hole, a man hole.
I taught you to be a man. He steps back saying, it's just me dad. I am just what

I am. Out my house. No nasty shit in here. Okay he says quiet. Hurt catch
on the turn of his thick lips. He looks past me, liquid brown eyes full of regret.

My throat dry. My hands sweat. I feel tears freeze in the top of my throat.
Why my son? What I do? What I don't do? What I can do? Heavenly Father!

He goes down the back steps, his mamma staring at me, telling me to stop him,
but I'm the one sending him away from here—away from everyone who knows

me. I'm done with it two years when my wife come waking me up with that
phone call saying he sick to death. He can't bring that sickness up in here.

She curse me. Brings him anyway. What a man can do? Woman/mamma crazy
wild about her child. She spoil him up, she the one make him weak, she the one.

So I bear the shame. Disease without a name I tell my friends and they don't pry.
My son, six-foot one, ninety-nine pounds. I pray. I cry. Then I wait for him to die.

III. My Son Jay, In The Eighties

He was a gorgeous baby, so lovely I had to always dress him in blue
or people would take him for a girl, thick hair curled around his oval
face, almond eyes with lashes thick and black, his cupid lips smiling
whenever he saw me. He walked early, talked before he could walk.

Named him James Harrison Walker, after his daddy, but Jimmy wouldn't
let me call him Little Jimmy. We agreed on Jay who grew so big and tall.
He was a perfect boy, so easy to love, so talented, artistic, and perceptive.
His father was angry when Jay came out the closet, but I wasn't caught
off guard. I didn't want him to be any kind of macho man. He was love.
A man who would not even kill a fly or stomp an ant. He just wanted
to be free, was so much like me, flesh of my flesh, bone of my bone.
Now he is gone. Just wanted to express himself like anybody else.
His own daddy made him feel like his life and love were wrong, like a
man can be only be one thing, but my Jay was so fly—my mariposa.

A Note Found in the Tomb of Tutankhamen
Matthew Shenoda

—for the British Museum

Possessor / ignorant of the converse

One geology / cancel another
One past / haunt another

You who does not understand that our speech is prayer

When every arrow of my body
Shoots towards heaven
The hieroglyph of my spine
Made run through my front

Shattered in the folds of my hand
A young boy I was
Rested to this place to be one with Ra

They took me to the valley at Thebes
peace my soul from tomb robbers

Hidden / eternity
Sealed with the doctrine of eternal existence

Now you have unsettled the cataract of the Nile
and disturbed the very sun that shields you

Hard-headed Brit
Did five attempts to steal me not warn you
White man / always to himself a hero
Howard Carter / tomb robber

Take the sterling from your Lord Carnarvon
You cannot buy yourself eternity
This life was never material

Who believes / believes
Impotent in your knowledge   beast
Grave robber / blinded by primitive massacre
Unable to not know how

Why was never enough.

Unbeliever!

Alive in my death mask
Eternally a cobra
I am become my own protector
What am I to do in these strange times
3000 years I lay whole
shrouded in my new name
lay distant from the heresy
and you who unwrap me
make my bones degenerate
for a glimpse / think yourself worthy of my touch

unable to embrace mystery.
I sing the song chorused by palm fronds in wind
You have missed the message

You have not seen everlasting.

Rosemary Talking Belfast, 1975

Laurel Rust

That barbed wire, it was set up in '69.
The Peace Line, they call it.
Soon there weren't any houses on either side.
Blown up, they were, molotov cocktails
in milk bottles. It's the Protestants
over there, the Catholics here.
As though we needed a fence.
You can tell by looking at it, you can.

Patrick, my youngest, he's not here now.
It's his birthday, and every year he goes
to his twin brother's grave, and I'm glad
it's on the coast, I am, and not
in Belfast. It's many years now.
I don't like to remember, it's true.
He's bent on revenge, that boy is.

First you must know
it was one of the soldier lads
brought Patrick home. My husband
was interred then, in Long Kesh. As good
as dead, he was. Some men picked up Patrick
and his brother coming home from school.
They told his brother
to sit on a stone and cross his legs,
and he did. They shot him
through both knees. That was what they did
then, and then they shot him
through the head. They gave Patrick
bus fare home, a couple quid.

But this soldier lad took pity, saw him
walking like a ghost, left his place
on the tank, just like that. A Welsh lad. I could
tell by the red carnation in his cap. Barely
sixteen, I'd say, the age of my own now.
The Brits send the Welsh and the Scots
because their own crack too often. This boy
came carrying my own over the fence,
a terrible day, a shooting day
on the Falls Road. And he comes
into my house, you see, crawling across
the garden with my wee boy beneath him,
breaks the window with his gun
and sets him down, here, in a Catholic
house. And then he goes out. They're shooting
outside, and they're shooting
on the telly. My own boy is trembling.
Where is your brother? I yell,
where is he? And the soldier lad gets caught
by the trousers on the fence. My own boy
sitting at this table, white as the tea cup
you're holding. The soldier can't get over,
there are bullets everywhere, and not
the rubber ones now. I went out
and I got him free, that was what I did,
there was nothing else to be done.
He brought me back my one son
and not the other, Patrick
has not forgiven me.

Listen to that racket, will you: the Brits
must be making the rounds again. The tanks
roll down the Road and we all stay inside
and let the dogs out to bark.

Skinhead

Patricia Smith

They call me skinhead,
and I got my own beauty.

It is knife-scrawled across my back in sore, jagged letters,
it's in the way my eyes snap away from the obvious.
I sit in my dim matchbox,
on the edge of a bed tousled with my ragged smell,
slide razors across my hair,
count how many ways
I can bring blood closer to the surface of my skin.
These are the duties of the righteous,
the ways of the anointed.

The face that moves in my mirror is huge and pockmarked,
apple-cheeked, scraped pink and brilliant,
I am filled with my own spit.
Two years ago, a machine that slices leather
sucked in my hand and held it,
whacking off three fingers at the root.
I didn't feel nothing till I looked down
and saw one of them on the floor
next to my boot heel,
and I ain't worked since then.

I sit here and watch niggers take over my TV set,
walking like kings up and down the sidewalks in my head,
walking like their fat black mamas *named* them freedom.
Well, my shoulders tell me that ain't right.
So I move out into the sun
where my beauty makes them lower their heads,

or into the night
with a lead pipe up my sleeve,
a razor in my boot.
I was born to make things right.

It's easy now to move my big body into shadows,
to move from a place where there was nothing
into the stark circle of a streetlight,
the pipe raised up high over my head.
It's a kick to watch their eyes get big,
round and gleaming like cartoon jungle boys,
right in that second when they know
the pipe's gonna come down, and I got this thing
I like to say, hey, listen to this, I like to say
"Hey, nigger, Abe Lincoln's been dead a long time."

I get hard listening to their skin burst.
I was born to make things right.

Then this reporter comes around,
seems I was a little sloppy kicking some fag's ass
and he opens up and screams about it.
This reporter finds me at home in my bed,
TV flashes licking my face clean.
Same ol' shit.
Ain't got no job, the coloreds and spics got 'em.
Why ain't I working? Look at my *hand,* asshole.
No, I ain't part of no organized group,
I'm just a white boy who loves his race,
fighting for a pure country.

Sometimes it's just me.

Sometimes three.

Sometimes 30.

AIDS will take care of the faggots,
then it's gon' be white on black in the streets.
Then there'll be three million.
I tell him that.

So he writes it up,
and I come off looking like some kind of goddamned freak,
like I'm Hitler himself.

I ain't that lucky,
but I got my own beauty.
It is in my steel-toed boots,
in the hard corners of my shaved head.

I look in the mirror and hold up my mangled hand,
only the baby finger left,
I know it's the wrong goddamned finger,
but *fuck you all anyway.*
I'm riding the top rung of the perfect race,
my face scraped pink and brilliant.
I'm your baby, America, your boy,
drunk on my own spit, I am goddamned fuckin' beautiful.

And I was born

and raised

right here.

Spring Reply to Internment Camp, Location Unknown
Brian Komei Dempster

—*March 19, 1942*

Dear Nitten,

I look deep, see the stroke of your brush, waves growing
into canvas. With each horsehair sweep, you shape
a shore of starfish and urchin, a luminous ocean.
I write you into haiku, gulls gliding home
through fog, fluttering against our church windows.
You rattle the mailbox and approach our door,

wind clicking the brass knocker. Slamming doors,
the children pause in the hall, wait for your glassed face to grow
beyond the photograph. Behind a train window
they frame you, imagine your trip from prison, back to us. The beacon shapes
an eyelet in the fog. I link lines, straight as rails, to bring you home.
Miles away you paint whitecaps soft, and I hold Renko by the ocean.

Today, the girls molded sand while Renko cooed *bird . . . mama . . . ocean . . .*
pointed at gulls swooping through clouds like doors,
landing on castles, white plumes giving her *papa . . . home . . .*
A soft giggle when she touched a feather. *Don't cry, you won't grow
up without papa.* The boys shape
your absence into games with bats, the crack of our altar window

followed by the tinkle of glass, the window
I pick up, piece by piece. Maybe they mock the ocean,
shards of Pearl Harbor hissing into the tide. How do we shape
such fire? We haven't forgotten prayer. Like doors,
the covers parting open, your sutras growing
like lotuses from our throats. For now, our kids savor home

in their teeth, wrappers peeled from chocolates you send home.
How long will we be here safe, the children crouching behind windows,
stringing their wrists with beads, praying for your envelopes. Renko grows
warm inside the bear-clawed tub, its ocean
of lavender bubbles where she floats on a door
of water and I memorize her shape

for you, unwrap your paintings we hid in rafters. With syllables I shape
the locked gates into openings you could walk through, homeward
to Renko and us, your arms lifting her from me and through the door,
lowering her into her crib. At every window
I wonder if you find rain, miss the ocean
of winged figures inside my poems where you grow.

Shapes dissolve, and words become our windows.
We go home in envelopes, the ocean rolling us into each other.
These letters widen doorways, let us grow.

The Venerable Fisherman Speaks Again of His Days
Vievee Francis

—for the Venerable Bogwang (Lee Sang-chul)

To fish   to know
their mouths
the shimmering flesh
the thrash within   the net
flick of knife   fleck of scales

Who can smile looking back?

Once I was a fisherman
a man
of the water   blood-soaked deck and slicker
of the mud   and its secret pockets
of the water and what catches the light
          below
          water that cools the skin
a man
of the rivulet and the rived
belly pouring out its quick life

*I look over the hills
as if forgiveness might be found just
                    over them—*

I was a fisherman
I had a wife   I had children I could feed
          whose palms were plump as fish bellies
          always dancing   jumping

There was a storm   no other sign

A boat is indifferent

North or South I was still a fisherman
                     a fisherman
I had a wife who was not yet cleaved
I had children eager at play as carp

                  Some I threw back   it's true

I was a fisherman   not a spy
so when the prong slid electric between my legs
I thought it was an eel   perhaps it recognized me
perhaps   I had chopped off its head

                 Torture?

My hands danced in front of my face then   up
toward a light   A song played in my right ear
The perfect song for
         a day I could not hold
Outside my wife swam away   undulant as a strand
of hair swirling beneath the surface
phlegm   spit   blood   piss   the outpourings
of the body   I will spy

        I was never a spy

                 I have been thrown back into the world
                 with a hook in my mouth

My hands jump at unexpected times
mocking   flapping
With my feet in the iced tub I saw
        a fish at my ankles   It was my child
come to save me   I reached for—
but the fish slid from my grip   a shimmer
        under the surface like a thrashing carp
        convulsively
        mouthing   goodbye   goodbye   goodbye   goodbye

Are you listening?

I said I am no spy Ask the fish
I said Only release me and I—

Torture?

I was a fisherman I said
I only want to go home   *to be thrown back* *believe me*

    Come let's walk to the river
    Let's hear what the fish have to say

As It Was Written

· ·

Saints, Sinners, and Holy Figures from Sacred Texts

The Apostle's Wife

Adam Tavel

Tongues of flame, the secreted tents, slinking
mute-dune deserts like coyotes we wept
to know again the taste of cony stew.
My fingers sought a daughter's locks to braid
as mine thinned to silver beneath my veil.
Bishop of a rowboat, he oared an ocean
to smite Myra's doubt with a gunnysack
of splints & cloudberry. It was a land
weary from gumming a Roman bridle.

Beside his moonlit cot he chapped his knees.
The jailor learned my scars. So freed, my love
repaid my love with stones. I wait upon
his name among the news of martyrs here,
an orphanage, balming the blind girl's sores.

Black Jesus Speaks to the Cosmetic Counter Salesgirl at the Mall of Asia

Barbara Jane Reyes

Skin whitening soap make me laugh.
You know Papa Dios did not intend
for the papaya to be abused like that.
You know Mama Mary was indigena,
she taga ilog like you, sister. You see,
Papa Dios got an older name,
a forgotten name, Amang Araw,
and he love his own kind fierce.
Why you think my skin so dark.
You see, Papa Dios love native women
like he love my Mama Mary,
like he love you, indigena sister,
like he love old Manila Bay salt
dissolving on his tongue, so pure.

Daniel Addresses the Soothsayer Society
Jennifer Gresham

> *He reveals deep and hidden things;*
> *he knows what lies in darkness, and light dwells with him.*
>
> —Daniel 2:22

Let me assure you: before he dreamt
of the tree that touched Heaven,
the stump, the iron band, the dew
at his cloven feet, the king was mad,
obsessed in a way most unhealthy.
Anyone could have seen it coming.
Such a future is no more than a thin,
white shift, the next oar stroke,
the night that blankets flower from bud.

What of my own dreams? He never asked.
I dreamt of red, but was it the furniture
from a brothel or the lining of a lion's mouth?
The blood of my brothers or the back wall
of a fiery furnace, if one were inclined
to step so far? Or maybe it was the heart
of a rhizome, deep within the soil's
clutch. Add enough red and the landscape
turns black, if I may be so bold to say so.

Just as the astrologer will let loose
the hem while simultaneously
cinching in the waist of his prediction,
just as the palm reader hides a poor eye
for distance, so must you be unapologetic
on the platform of obscurity. Reject the need
to be unnecessarily articulate, ramble, tell

the same stories with different protagonists:
one day the chipped rock, the next
the crushed chest of a bird.

Every dream comes true if you wring
them like rags. Why not let them totter off
to the river blanketed by fog, faces
already unfamiliar, two coins
in their pocket, braced for the inevitable?
Trust me, you'll forget them.

From the Book of Ten Instructions
Carolina Ebeid

—Abel

In the catchweed & nettle country, my brother's region,
where there are nephews of nephews now older than I,
where the hour is an heirloom dusted off & little rusts,
I watch my melancholy brother at every cutthroat,
harvest morning. Over there, Love is the sinew, the gullet.
Father is the drinking-well & Mother, the banked embers
       in early light.

Brother is always the scarecrow he fastens to posts.
When I was young, I understood that nature spoke
in many tongues & only to me. This was the chronicle
of life: Prairie blossoms just beginning, a late frost
entering them violently. The first of us to go
into the ground from which my father came;
       this is my vocation.

And this netherlife has its own heaven & its own seas.
Like pilot birds steering the lost & weather-burnt
to land, I am useful here.

His Cassandra

Maria Terrone

> *Pilate's wife sent a message:*
> *Do not interfere in the case of that holy man.*
> *I had a dream about him today which has greatly upset me.*
>
> —The Gospel of St. Matthew

He ruled, but I had his ear—
mine attuned to stirrings and murmur,
betrayal that could rise like a swarm of wasps.
And my eyes saw what his could not.
He called me his Cassandra and half-believed.
Each morning as he left, smiled and kissed
my brow still beating
from visions that shook me
sole to skull:
sun plunging through sky, water climbing
up our doorway, a legion of horses rearing.

I did not ask to awaken that day to howling,
to see that strange one stand
before my husband, who washed
his own hands in a blood-steeped bowl.

That vision never left me.
Soon after, Pilate did—
said he needed a woman
who had no dreams.

It Didn't Happen That Way

Elizabeth Austen

It wasn't a lure, dangled
by some fallen angel.
She found it, mid-path
no tree nearby. Unbruised
red-yellow round

sprung from the gravel.
She entered the sweet
fruit, wet flesh
breaking on her tongue. She didn't
ask for it. Wasn't
looking for it. No one

tempted her. Unless
the apple itself, longing
to be known, can be blamed
for the light bent
across its skin
for the mid-day heat
transforming sugar to scent.

And him? She didn't say
a word to him. He found
her, slack-jawed
skin flushed and damp
as if he had lain on her
pressed into her—

he found her, swallow by swallow
savoring the taste of knowledge
her eyes fixed, focused

somewhere beyond him
as if he no longer existed.
And one more thing—
she didn't tempt him. In fact
she never offered it.

He pried the fruit
from her hand, desperate
to follow, and bit.

Jezebel Remembering

Valerie Wallace

It was like the first time
your hand touches a married
man's thigh; or when you lean
over the velvet rope, right
before you touch the painting;
or the moment you slip
the lipstick from the shelf
to your purse; when you cover
your crying child's mouth
and say Shut up; it was the moment
you join your husband's enemy
on the ledge while he smokes,
and you place your hand
at his back, then push.

Lord's Own Anointed

Kevin Cutrer

If Henry Hébert seems a little off
it's due to the fact he was whopped upside
the head by Harley Swearinger's 2 x 4
one afternoon ten years ago outside
the mower shop when he had made a joke
about the woman Harley lived in sin with.
They say his eyes went bugged and bright before
his knees collapsed and he fell on his face.
Never the same, they say. Not ever the same.

Lost his job, lost his stitches, got the Spirit.
You see him in his short necktie, suspenders
holding them awful pinstriped pants up high,
his belly like a baby's poking out,
out by the hardware store, by the old highway,
holding his imitation-leather bible,
grinning his one-gold-toothed, immaculate grin.
He stands out there to greet the customers,
not hired nor shooed away by management.

He talks a funny way I can't describe,
not that he ever talks that much at all
but mostly stands around and grins at you.
They warn of idle hands, but idle tongues
are just as bad, ask Henry Hébert why.
He's the most thoughtful-speaking man you'll meet
in this or any town, if he will say
a word or two about the holy scriptures.
The preacher calls on him to pray each Sunday,

and every time he has a different prayer
more blessed than any message that young pastor
with all his years at college could invent.
It's never rambling, or too rushed on through,
but sentence after sentence simply sings.
He prays with all the energy a workingman
puts to his pillow every night to sleep,
that hard-won peace that only comes from struggle.
He seems a little off but, child, he's on.

Na'amah
Davi Walders

So loud this din,
thick this dung,
the heave of never
ceasing hungers.

So tiny the beak,
fragile the branch,
her wing serene, a
gardenia against grey.

    Noah, look.

Punishment

Shelley Renée-Ruiz

And Jephthah made a vow to the Lord, and said
"If thou wilt give me the Ammonites into my hand,
then whoever comes forth from the doors of my house
to meet me when I return victorious from the Ammonites
shall be the Lord's and I will offer him up for a burnt offering."
—Judges 11

I leaned against the splintered fence post,
obedient, waiting, tugging the dog back by its ruff
so I could be the greeter, only girl of his to welcome him
into the cool loose circle of my arms.
Home from war, I wanted to wash the blood
from his stiff clothes in the creek; from his face
with my palms coated in salve and olive oil.
The sky yawned wide over the open field
as trees inched their leaves closer to their trunks.

I have lain beneath them on the mountain,
eyes closed to the roll of wind over my body as I called
for a mother to run her hands across my forehead
push me into the pulse and undulation of sleep
rather than wander back to a churlish home
father gulping from a dirty cup
he slings against the wall behind me.
But I welcomed him with fanfare.

He wrapped thick fingers round my arm
and pushed me toward the mountaintop to mourn
my virginity. I called memories of a woman
to calm me, enfold me in robes heavy
with the scent of field grass and slip
a silver coin bitter on my tongue
to pay passage to another world.

Father ties sticks in bundles with twine
for a small pyre, girl-sized, that struggles to ignite.
Sounds of crackling fire weave into his groans
as he grapples with flint to spread the flames
and calls me to become a smudge in history,
name lost in sacrificial ashes; charred skull; a curled fist;
vertebrae scattered like seeds of stone.

Put Me Back, Jesus (from Lazarus)
Kelly Scarff

There were doves in me,
their throats were the calm
lilies of Spring. They grew

inside, cooing and preening
each new vein until I
was beautiful again.

Their beaks were horns
beating through my ribs.
Each tender sound echoed,

spread warmth through my chest.
There were doves in me.
Their clipped wings

hushed me into a stillness
as the music took over.
I could hear their notes

bending my organs,
caressing this silent heart
that no longer waits for you.

Rebecca to Isaac
William Robert Flowers

I saw you, walking like someone who is lost
in a foreign city. I saw you walking like a child,
with your empty hands hanging, and wondering
at your shadow, which seemed to fear the weight
of your steps. I veiled my face before you, Isaac.
How long since your throat lay
against that rough altar, and you asked him
to bind you tightly, so that your trembling
would not detract from the sacrifice?
And when he leaned on you with his terrible
hands, his hard stone weight like a cataract
pouring from his forehead, his ravaged mouth,
how his breath fell in that moment and hung
there, as a dead limb hangs from low branches.
Then a darkness so complete came over your
soul that the angel's voice never reached
you; the bright hands that gripped your father's wrists
couldn't draw your eyes from the shadows
dancing on stone. Some said later
that your eyes grew weak from the tears of
the angels falling into them, as you lay helpless
on the mountain. Isaac,
                                        how could you bear it?
Bound on that altar of stone and broken wood,
feeling celestial tears falling into your eyes,
like birds in the windows of abandoned buildings.
You must have stared, every day of your life,
into the sun, blinking to clear their light away—
and though you tried to burn it out, you could not,
you saw as the dead see: everything both near

and far at once, a panoply of instants borne by
every moment, dancing in the light of sacrificial
fire, the shadow of your own ashes.
                                        Now you see
this woman coming toward you, a delivery arranged by
your father—him, whose weight you always
feel pressing into your neck—now. I've nearly reached you.

Salome Gives Seven Explanations for a Kiss
Nina Corwin

> *On Herod's birthday, the daughter of Herodias danced in front*
> *of the whole group. Herod was so pleased that he promised her*
> *"I swear that I will give you anything you ask for"... she asked him*
> *"give me here and now the head of John the Baptist upon a plate"*
>
> —Matthew 14

I kiss you, John the Baptist, entranced by your blank stare
Because your glassy glances follow admonishing
　　　　　　　everywhere the dance takes me.

And I kiss you, John the Prophet, for a taste of the apocalypse
Because from your lips flows the milk of millennia
　　　　　　　sweeter than the seeds of pomegranates.

I kiss you, John *Au Jus* upon a plate,
Because blood is the only baptism I have to offer.

Because marrying martyrs is an exercise in futility
So a kiss is as close as I care to come,
Leaning close as breath because I *need* to know
Dear John of the Populace, does God *see*
through the eyes of martyrs or does He only give you talk?

Oh John, my Recalcitrant Conquest, your coyness of flesh
gets under my skin, so I kiss you: that sin be no stranger
from my lips to yours tonguing the honey of redemption
as I sacrifice my soul for the gospel of promises.

> *Last night, I dreamed I carried your child*
> *and a will not my own moved my hips.*
> *Birthing history is strange labor, my love.*

I've played every veil of this village comedy
because lust is the singular trump card
I was dealt from this love-lousy deck.

So I kiss you, John the Modest, because
in every undulation, every sweaty pirouette or two
It was secretly for you that I danced.

Oh John Who Must Be Jaded
by this latest turn of circumstance
I tell you, dance may be my commerce
but my covenant is in my kiss.

Sarah's Story
Susan Rich

I watched their figures moving light as
embroidery stitches back-lit against fine cloth;

mid-summer, late afternoon baked in a lapis
blue inhalation—a day fit for any God—even Him

and those good looking angels He brought in,
their bold hips swaying as they scrambled the sea-

colored hills, bright dust lifting small circles above
their ankles. My husband napped, undisturbed, snoring

louder than our camel consorting at its bit. And so
I left Abe's arms and came to see, examining

each figure closely. It was then I sensed a stirring up,
a scouring all around my limbs, then deeper, in the interior

faultlines of my body—wide awake, at ninety—
it made me laugh and the unfamiliar sound rimmed the tent

and woke my husband, who recognized them immediately.
With nothing on but a thread-bare sheet he bowed

and brayed while I left to prepare the food—
remaining close enough to listen. People ask

if I knew burning light, but I will not reply. What I know
I'll not state in scripted sounds, just imagined speech

as if in conversation, passing time with women on the street.
What meal to fix for the Lord and his company?

Brown bread, some soup, mustard sauce and lamb's meat?
Nothing fancy but they would not leave hungry. Steaming plates I set

and served and brought back again three times. The appetite of God!
Enough to make a mother wring her hands—bottomless

yet full of compliment—always a word of thanks.
Raised right I thought, the kind of son I used to want myself—

or daughter, or any child at all—I had prayed
and raged and cried for. But now at ninety, I knew

my womb was useless as a leaking chamber pot,
that a child would not bless us. Abraham no longer touched me,

though he often bragged that other women looked like monkeys
compared to Sarah's beauty. But this was habit speaking,

a slight memory of an oasis misplaced long ago. I suppose
I loved him now and again, but our bodies had forgotten how

to coax and stroke and howl, decades since I knew his hips
against my back, his thighs filling each Friday with desire

incomprehensible. And then I returned from reverie to hear Him
say *Next year when I return your wife will be with child.*

How could I *not* laugh at such a declaration?
Of course I held it deep inside my body, the laughter

that builds and fills itself, soon bridging joy
to tears in rocking rhythmic shudders.

The Sin-Eater
Rita Mae Reese

> *one hired to take upon himself the sins of a deceased person*
> *by means of food eaten above the dead body*
> —from *The Oxford English Dictionary*

That first girl's name has long been forgotten
by everyone save me. She was young, fourteen or so,
and the daughter of a laborer. Then a carriage accident.
How shall I describe it? Her sins smacked of turnips and leeks.

How would innocence taste, I wonder. Pride is like
molded bread, abandoned cake, crumbs in a wood
that all the animals—even the birds—have fled. Save one.
Idolatry mushrooms in the mouth, adultery is a raw onion,

and hatred cooked cabbage—it is what I eat most often.
How do the living not gag on the smell? Will there be another
after me? I am old and full of ghosts. No one speaks to me
save there's been a death. But who needs words?

Most are lies anyway, tasting of pottage. People die,
you can count on them for it, God bless them.
Then over their bodies it's bread and porridge
that I eat with clean fingers. I used to follow him,

the old sin-eater, asking him questions:
Was it always the same meal? Did it ever spill?
How much did he eat? Then one day he didn't answer my knock;
inside I found a fresh loaf of bread—three slices cut off—

and a bowl of gruel and him more silent than
ever, under a meal that was venial, mortal, and rotten.

Sister Lost

Lois Holub

I. Eve Tracking Lilith

There are times I need to go down the path alone.
Without him.
Without the words of naming falling from his lips
like seeds filling my ears
so that is all I hear.

This is the way:
To wake before his dreams release him,
start down the path in the wet of new morning.
Like a ring of water I widen my circle
each time I wander.

I am certain now there is someone else.
Someone whose footprints fit mine
but are not mine.
I know where I have and have not been
and I find the signs of her—
        the smell,
        the sounds of her—
that linger just inside
each place I did not go before.

Today I shall pass through the stillness,
let the shadow of her steps become my own.
My hands are full with the need
to reach across the truth for her.
I want to see her, and I am afraid
of nothing but the silence
where her name belongs.

II. Lilith to Eve

Oh yes my sister, I have watched your wanderings
through this place called Garden.
I am here, unseen but sensed,
unbounded by shall nots,
and certainly, my dear one, unnamed by him.

I feel your life as you cannot,
the life taken from you with promises of sweet beginnings
and savage threats of suffering.
You are tracking the mirror that knows your own name,
that knows your own body,
a landscape that rolls
rich and fertile down to the sea.

I have seen you, sister,
and have ached for the caution of your heart's pulse
strong enough for life but not for passion.
A heart afraid to bite its fruit of fullness,
afraid his sword will spring forth to destroy.
You have yet to learn that what shall be destroyed
is not your self but his lies.

I know I must approach you
and I know the way it will be told:
The serpent, the tree, and the fruit,
the curses and exile,
as if snake is not sacred
as if tree is not friend
as if apple is not gift
and as if you, my sister,
are not power of birth, death and life everturning
at home anywhere you squat to bleed,
with eyes to see through death's slave dressed as Angel,

with body to ignite his soul in grief for what he has lost,
with voice to name yourself
and hands to fling wide the gate
on your way out.

After *Happily Ever After*

Fairy Tales, Creatures, and Other Imaginings

Dido to the Little Match Girl

Anne Shaw

Barefoot in the snow, you're a specialist
in pathos, I can see. Even at six you have a knack for it.
But take my word for it, honey: You can't just sit there freezing
by the wall. I know how it is to want things,
to tie yourself to the bed because it burns. I can see you're *that* kind of girl
dreaming of a lavish room and cake. But let me tell you something: you can be queen
of the airwaves and still the signal's weak. Don't like
yourself too much. I used to believe two bodies
could cross out each other's grief, that a girl
could take some comfort for herself. But once it starts, a heart will not stop
breaking, that's the thing. I'll tell you how it's going to be:
go with the man in the car. When he asks if you're a pervert
nod and tell him yes. You don't have to know what the word means. Just
do what he asks. Because the more you practice giving up
the readier you'll be. You won't be twirling in a dress
singing, *make me a match*. Build yourself a bedroom in a house
of straw and thatch. Just strike one, then another. You dirty
little bitch. Because the place for a girl like you
is not on the common street. The place
for a woman who burns is in the fire.

Gretel in the Tunnel

Henrietta Goodman

Brother, why must we enter?
The mountain opens—in the night,
a blacker hole. My shoes twist
on gravel. This is the mouth
of the monster in every dream:
black teeth, the smell of rotten leaves.

No light at the end. Without touching the walls,
how will we know where the path bends?
Is this a lesson—your gentle taunts,
not-quite-hidden exasperation? Nothing to be afraid of,
unless you're afraid of *nothing*—this hole
could devour us, press us flat, eyeless,
like the fish that live deep in caves.
At whose mercy are we?

When we reach the threshold
I want to be carried out into the lighter dark,
because, truly, I have given myself to you.
Without you I would run, panicked, headlong.
Without you I wouldn't be here at all.

And when you sit on a rock under
the blurry moon to rub the marks
of my nails from your arm—
don't you know the only way home
is to go back through? What will I make
of the gift you offered, that I could not accept
and could not refuse?

Mermaid

Erica Wright

I

I used to think the devil
lived in Fayetteville, Tennessee,
though there's a sort of godliness

in the abandoned music shop
where a Romanian teen once
bellowed at me over a violin,

To play, this hand must be stronger.
This after getting glass in my shoes
from the parking lot,

after wanting to be the source—
smashing bottles to watch
the greens and browns make oceans

to lose your sons in.
At bottom, you get infrared glasses,
see God in scales.

Here I must be watered—
every morning a spectacle—
and there's a woman for that.

II

I prefer the quarantine
where we banked on makeshift
weapons—anything that could

file to a point over the toilet.
We put our faith in herbs.
Shirts were swung out the window,

and even this was faith somehow.
For those of us who fell to scarlet fever,
panic had to be swallowed whole.
Bats tucked into our chimneys
before the final hush of light
silenced over the ridge.

Maybe we didn't think of them at all,
not so much nestled as crammed
one on another in the square foot

of brick, but one summer,
I'm telling you,
there were bats every night.

III

Stag, you say, as if you meant wildlife,
not a polite word for driving oneself
to a party and chatting up

other old ladies who'd rather—
and would there were a polite word for this—
be elbow-deep in the goldfish pond

it took outliving one husband
and shooing three children out to earn.
I like fireworks as much as the next.

That is not the question.
Now is the hour of miracles,
when no one's watching.

Throw me back.

Pinocchio's Elegy for the Unreal

Ariana-Sophia Kartsonis

Here's the rub: you're on your own.
What breaks isn't replaceable anymore.

Gepetto's hand on your unhinged knee
won't set it right again. A torn

finger can't be carved anew.
You prayed for this: Real Boy,

then, at last, a skin of your own
to hide within. Real boy arms

are limp arms against a sea
of troubles. Now the stuff

you're carved from rots,
touches all it can then forgets

the touch. Not to mention pain
broken skin and bones the heavy

human heart and the way you get the part
where Hamlet says: *and by a sleep we end*

the heart-ache and the thousand natural
shocks that flesh is heir to.

This is for you, Geppetto,
deep in the sleep of death.

Listen up, Old Man (who once pulled my strings,
knit the motion to my dance, tied to me

somewhere inside even now,
only I can't see the cables, can only feel their tug,

like loss's magnetic field between memory and gut),
I miss the certainty of my ligneous hands.

Everything's either too far away or not enough.
I can still hear the toys talk, still hear the whispers

of the inanimate world, the soul of objects.
I wish you'd told me about the way it feels

to be watching life from a dying body.
Your workshop's veiled with cobwebs,

every old tool dreams of your hands,
your smoothing grip. In the corner,

a spider unlaces a luna moth, a dinner
too huge, too gossamer to be real.

The Tale of the Dead Princess
Donna Prinzmetal

—*after Pushkin's poem*

This time when I died
I was daughter to a Tsar,
baby daughter, motherless
and the new wife, the inevitable, as always, slave
to loquacious mirror,—this time
stunning dark eyebrows, mine, and
complexion *beyond compare*,
got me deserted in *the dark wood*, left
for wolves.
               I felt my way through
oak trees, found a barking friend,
loyal companion in the lonely
days of the hunt, gleaming orange heads of dahlias,
and *seven hearty knights* in this old country
house. My only visitor,
stepmother's chambermaid disguised,
of course, and bearing the usual
shiny red fruit, something banal, innocuous.

This time, my canine howled a warning, but what harm could be
one small bite—succulent, delicious sleep.

They found me that way, lifeless, even after the dog
ate the rest of the apple knowing sacrifice.

They carried me in crystal to a *small deserted cave.*
"Sleep in this coffin," the elder knight said.
I would like to add that my dear father, the Tsar,
did not lose a wine's sip of sleep wondering
where I had gone.

Lucky, lucky me, he was not the only man
in my life: Prince Elisey on *mighty steed* asked
the sun, fallen in a pool of splintered light,
and the ransacked moon but no one
knows everything. He
asked the wind, always a good second choice, till
he found the crystal coffin, sobbed his eyes
red as my two red lips and he slammed his fists
into the glass and I awoke.
        "My, how long I've slept!"
The mirror, miscreant, remained intact,
while *the vain queen* could not be content with second best.
Father, I presume, remained alone after that.
One of the knights gave me away
at my nuptials. Now,

where I can't breathe,

I inhale only when it is safe.

Thaw

Thorpe Moeckel

1

Worrying the snow that goes
sun-struck from pine, bright
while squirrel claws oak's gray
edge, I scratch my carrot-nose,
cinch my coat against the warmth. What
I need is what I fear: to learn
not to melt, not to freeze too hard.

2

Crow lands on my head and bellows
in that awful voice of his—such fright!—
"if you bleed water, say,
and my blood is the blood of shadows,
then what do you weep, what—
winter's purple?" "No," I squeak, seeing farmer
aim. "Crow blood, of being so forward."

3

Warmth makes me and warmth undoes.
So while it's possible, I court
the shadows—what other way?—
all that's flat: the sun's lows,
inversions of smoke. Still, to sit
shrinking, my inside feels reborn,
as if body was breath and centered.

4

Who shivers touches me, who grows
plants that blossom at night,
licks metal, and on a frigid day
runs naked, inhaling to whistle. Whose
favorite color is ice and favorite
shape is round, yes, who rides the Northern,
prefers the drowned over the charred.

5

The land doesn't speak to me; it knows
I'm what it says. Dusklight,
water's ways—it could be May;
I'm going, going fast. Such prose
warmth is. Earlier the child gave me fat
strands of ivy for locks. Then wonder,
that whiteness, tied them in a braid.

6

Warm sun again; I'm slick with flows.
Always, in such thaws, I grow polite
remembering rivers. Odor of clay,
cedar, root—this branching, towards rose,
stone, where motion—elegant bat—
is stillness, and elsewhere
worry's wind: will, surrendered.

7

Three parts, none the same—potatoes,
that easy. Child packed me tight,
knew stains made me pure: hay,
muck, leaf, coal for eyes, a nose.
No winter brain, not that:
she began with a flake, added one more
then another, and so on, outward.

To the Stockyard Bulls
Paul Nemser

The bull-gargoyle
addresses the bronze
bulls who once stood
by the gates of
the old stockyard
in St. Petersburg.

My bronze brothers, they cut exactly where our hearts were.
They knew us in the chutes and bellowing on blocks,

in wrapped paper parcels tinged with blood—
handed to women in chicken-print kerchiefs—

chewed in grand style by brush-bearded men in crimson vests
and long coats, who crumpled into chairs after dancing.

And here you are—tilt-headed, nostrils huge,
tensed to leap when there is no need to run,

having outlived the slaughterers and their house,
their long-tongued hounds lapping offal.

Trailered to the peeled pink gates of a former meat plant,
your bronze is more solid than the stage-set columns,

your legs more stout than the truck tires
heaped in squat, white-pink garages. Don't despair, brothers,

the gods ignite any and all. Some who leave streaks
like window water, others pent up in monumental pause.

They enjoy sitting inside us, ribbed bronze for a chassis.
In cool belly hollows, you'll feel a stirring

just as grass begins to push through gravel,
though your ears cradle gray-feather snow.

The Watchtower
Traci Brimhall & Brynn Saito

You could guard the city if you could bear
your own loneliness. The night
could offer you wildflowers and moonlight

and your bright face reflected in the waters
below. But how will you rise above me
if I continue to seduce you with the illusion

that violence is honest? Look at the sea,
the bereft immensity. No ships approach.
But do not confuse that with safety; absence

is the heaviest tide. Watch for the sea wind,
and watch for the wildest enemy
within you. Once sunrise shows

its unmerciful love, you will know this:
you must save yourself more than once.
Look at the sea again, count the sails of

continuing departure. Count the cut tongues
in the blood coral. I see a bright ring
around you. Come with your torn heart

to the bottom of the reef. The shipwreck
you find there hides in its hull a rusted rapier
and whalebones and a compass. Beware

the gleam of forgotten gold. Beware
the dark bite of sought pleasures.
Cut your hair and climb through the swaying.

Then open your body to the windless night.
The light inside you
will guide the burning ships to shore.

The Werewolf of Green Knolls

Tony Barnstone

1. Pooch

> The frat boys playing pool yell "Hose her! Hose her!"
> when Dan and I walk in the bar, and Daniel
> just grins and takes a bow while I, brownnoser
> that I am, toady, doormat, flunkey, spaniel,
> duck my head low. "What yours, sweetheart?" the bar-
> man asks, but Danny cuts me off, "Get her
> a Miller Lite." The bar-man smiles a far-
> off, sad, I've-seen-this-one-before smile. Cur,
> tail-wagger, mongrel, pooch, I tremble out
> a "Thanks," and take the beer. Here in Green Knoll
> you take what man you find, or masturbate
> at home. Tonight he comes then leaves without
> a kiss. I hate what I've become: his hole,
> a pussy, jellyfish, invertebrate.

2. Snarl

> Across the windshield, rain was diamond-strung
> in streetlit strands as Danny's hands invest-
> igated how the cup held to the breast.
> Out in the wet, a wolf-like stray with hung-
> er on her narrow features howled. I clung
> to Dan, who laughed. But I saw her possessed
> red eyes and whined, "Oh, Dan." "Give it a rest,"
> he growled and ripped my skirt. He had begun
> and wouldn't stop until he had me spread.
> He held me down and from his teeth a thread
> of drool spun down and clung to me like dew.
> Danny was tugging wildly at his fly
> but I was done. "Get off!" I snarled, "I'm dry,"
> and glared until he sullenly withdrew.

3. Little Piggy

> I told Detective Abernathy-Todd
> about the wolf, then couldn't help but weep
> for Danny with his ripped-out throat. The creep
> *was* my boyfriend, after all. The odd
> thing was the way they found us: Danny, his
> eyeballs wide and throat a gash, and me,
> covered with blood, out cold, my clothes torn free,
> but both doors locked. So try to answer this:
> how did the wolf get in? And how'd she close
> the door behind? The wolf got in, somehow,
> big bad she-wolf. It makes me want to howl
> in lunacy, to change my life like clothes,
> strange towns, new man. *Come in, by my chin-chin.*
> Am I deranged to welcome the wolf in?

4. That Time of Month

> The problem is I find it hard to switch
> back to a woman after the full moon
> chips off a piece, blood hunger a typhoon
> of whirling teeth inside my narrow bitch
> skull as I skulk the narrow alleyways
> and spread my dangerous loins for happy boy-
> dogs. While they snap and nip, I burn like Troy,
> like Alexandria, my red eyes blaze
> like Tokyo, Nagasaki, burn like silver
> moonlight, white fire, burn like their hot red cocks,
> their hot wet blood on my wild tongue. Who stalks
> me now? Another dog. His haunches shiver.
> He smells the blood, the sex. His nostrils flare.
> He walks toward death in her sleek coat of hair.

5. Wolf's Best Friend

My new boyfriend dislikes the long dark hair
stuck to my sweaty rump. "What a buzz-kill,"
he grumbles, flopping out. He sulks, but still
he drops his eyes when I give him the stare.
He says at night my eyes are red and feral
and that I grind my teeth and snap the air
as nightmares thrash my human limbs. I care
for him in my own way. "You hear that serial
killer attacked a night watchman last night?"
he says at breakfast as I make the Quaker
Oats. I just grunt. "We have a giver-taker
relationship," he tells me later, "Right?
You always take. When are you going to give?"
I answer nothing. But I let him live.

6. Whine

"I'm wearing antiperspirant," he says
peevishly when I snuffle and sniff
at his armpit. I don't answer, but gaze
at his pale limbs, blood-animated. "If
you want, I'll take a shower," Nathan blurts
when I push my nose into his crotch and snort.
I give his rump a nip. "Hey! Don't, that hurts,"
he whines, but it was just a taste. I sport
with him a while, lick him until I find
he's hard enough. He moans and moons at me
until I let him take me from behind.
After I come, I growl and then push free.
I bite his lip when Nathan tries to kiss.
He sighs, "Oh, well." I go to take a piss.

7. Rabbit's Revenge

Animalistic sex, just like that song,
I want to fuck you like an animal,
I want to feel you from the inside—call
it what you may (perverted, twisted, wrong),
but it's addictive. Sex became a feast
and I her meat that she would sit and eat.
Her tongue, my god! And just that hint of teeth.
And how she looked at me, a famished beast.
But things got wild. Lunatic. She'd prowl bars
for other men. My friends would edge away
from my strange hickeys, bandages, bright scars.
She'll get help now. It's not like she's been jailed,
no cattle prods, steel bars, slop on a tray.
Really, I feel like I'm the one who failed.

8. Feeding Time

It's feeding time here at the loony bin.
The guard tries to slide food through the door slot
but it won't go since I have jammed the hinge.
He scans the cell through the door's window slit,
sees just some skinny girl, scraped fingernails,
frenetic hair, no threat and comes on in.
He makes me think of Danny with that grin,
but with my teeth around his throat he wails,
or tries to wail. They tried electroshock
and I attacked the lab technician, so,
therefore, the padded cell. How could they know
there are some things you can't keep in with locks?
I prowl the parks and people run from me:
haunted harlot, demon, woman, free.

The Werewolves
T. M. De Vos

We darkened,
flickered with hair and chitin,
eyeteeth dropping yellow
from their buds.

We forgot speech,
the decoy howls of the prey
you considered before me.
Whatever you force
has a dim urge, under its skin.

Bitten, I roll with you,
paws on your chest,
shearing, your face, neck,
the braid down your back.
You throw me off like a fox,
red coat snapping.

Day spills, a cap of bluing.
A soft, kind animal
is chewing through you,
cleaning the bulk from your ribs.

When Red Becomes the Wolf

Jeannine Hall Gailey

In my dream you brought me fried bologna sandwiches.
"But wait," you said. "You don't even like bologna."
I wolfed them down without answering.

I have never owned a red cape, that's asking
for trouble, I knew. I dyed auburn hair brown.
In the forest by your house,

I met someone gathering wood. "Nice axe,"
I said before wandering further.
I was obtaining samples for my botany class.

How many daisies make a statistic?
I thought of Persephone, her dark gash
that allowed Hades passage. Which flower?

I was hungry, and tired. I entered someone's
cottage, it was dark, and there was an old woman.
I volunteered to take her to get her hair done.

I mentioned I was born under the sign
of Lupus. "No," she corrected, "Lupae."
Later, eating sandwiches, we discussed you

and also whether I could wear her fur coat.
"It makes you look feral, with your green eyes,"
she said. Oh grandmother, what a big mouth you have.

From the Page to the Pen

Authors, Their Characters, and Everything in Between

Case History: Frankenstein's Lesions
Laurie Clements Lambeth

When the great doctor's assistant—Fritz
or Igor, some hunchbacked henchman—beheld
the row of preserved brains afloat in glass,
did he pause to consider the irony

of such delicacy housed by potential harm
before he let drop the jar marked "GENIUS"?
First the shatter, then the spill, then the plop

rather like a peeled orange dropped and opening
a little, swirl of corpus callosum stretched
between tilted hemispheres. Panic,
then he picked another: not the abnormal

brain of a murderer, frontal lobe dented
with insufficient fissures (as Whale filmed),
but what he read as "Abby Normal,"

a brain atrophied, mottled with grey lesions
visible only when sliced in the autopsy theatre.
Mine was the one jar that did not break,
and I sloshed against its walls with each lurch

of the hunchback's pitching, tilting ramble.
Nobody sliced me; I was too precious
whole, tight bundle of tissue disembodied,

"just resting, waiting for a new life to come,"
said Dr. F. He didn't know how much I'd like
to rest, stay out of bodies for a while.
Alas, now I work this body

as best I can. The monster (how I hate
what they call us, but I suppose it's true)
presented no symptoms at first, capable

of strength to match his proportions,
performing feats of violence when provoked
in his chamber. It was all going so *well*,
I nearly forgot about our illness. Then

he began dribbling his trouser fronts (too
humiliating for me to acknowledge
personally) and we took a while

to recall the simplest words: "fire" fell
to nothing, then, "f . . . , f . . . , f . . . , fancy? fast?"
Which made Fritz think we liked the torch's dance.
Torture. We did away with him, yes, but

perhaps I just didn't know our own strength.
It took some getting used to, as I had
formerly inhabited the cranium

of a cripple who willed her corpse to science.
Just when things began working smoothly, brain
and body as one, the body began
to cave to the ills I had brought it.

The legs moved less freely. Our feet felt heavy,
as though they wore sixty-pound boots. I hear
that was Karloff's trick to imitate our gait.

That man got it right, a very good likeness,
probably because he more than anyone
comprehended the absolute effort
needed to heave one foot forward, and the next.

Laughing villagers toddled along roadsides,
saying we walked like a duck. Echoes
of the cripple's life. Quacks, taunts. No duck,

but a monster too weak to chase them down.
Torso before feet, we shook only the earth,
tipping into the woods. Left Arm, pale hand
stitched to deep brown wrist, tried to pull a limb

from a tree to use as a walking stick,
but the fingers would not tighten as I
intended. Right Arm assisted, but could not

force it from the trunk. We plucked a flower, limp
hand round the bloom, not the stem. Petals and phlox
sifted through our weakened fingers
to the ground. What else to do but plod on?

We learned to lean into trees for support,
the way a drunk would lean against walls
following a night's consolation. The creatures

in the eaves fled our advance, left us alone
with our sensations, or lack of them.
All along I thought this might happen.
With grief more than horror I've greeted

each fresh apathy in our limbs. I dare
not share this with Dr. F., or my toes.
They'd be so numbly . . . disappointed.

Within me, though, I feel something changing:
not the spread of lesions, more a tremble
in my cortex, as though this broad skull
sutured shut is not enough to contain me.

When we look down to our trailing feet below,
it happens, that theremin playing
our abdomen down to trill in our legs,

and I'm close to bursting. Curse the skies that watch
us buckle, the shock of our birth night's storm
now played out from within, as L'hermitte
discovered and named. I want to say

there is no discovery, only repetition
and return. And the rage that pulses down
this monster body, frail and more fierce than fire.

Confessions of an Invisible Man

Steven Cordova

The stars have their starry-eyed astronomers,
the soon-to-be-possessed their demons; birds
have their binocular-eyed watchers and those
about to become extinct have sworn defenders.
Even the most common citizen has an enumerator:
a bean counter, a census taker to say *this
is where you live, this is how, with whom*

(no one). I am the one sitting next to you—
to you—but you will never see me.

Copyright

Gregory Pardlo

—Paul Green

Of course I know the story of the scorpion
and the frog. I've known Biggers all my life.
I've cast down my buckets where I've
stood with them, shoulder to shoulder, our bodies
bent like double helices in the fields. And
when the mob came for Dick didn't I sit anyways
outside his quarters all night like a jailhouse lawyer,
him ignorant of the nature of his custody?
It was me who kept the townsmen at bay after he
provoked them. My cousin among them
had watched him grin and wheedle,
consort with white people carelessly, our naïve
and guileless women, at the civil gathering where
he was my ward. And later, because of me,
his offense went unanswered, un-atoned.
I know the hearts of men are governed
by the endowments of nature. And some children
are faithful. Some are made to obey.

Elizabeth Barrett Browning Speaks of Spirits

Liz Dolan

I can hear them thumping
the accordion under the pleated folds

of the muslin-draped table, the shrill syllables
of the dead boy. White as snow
a hand rises and sinks, rises and sinks,

creeps over the edge and crowns me
with laurels. Is it Dante? Robert never

believes they speak to me
and my dearest Sophie,
who gifts me with Damascus

slippers, a Holy Sepulchre rosary,
a portrait of me he scorns,

memento mori from the thorny white rose.
She is my medium. Say it is
my morphine. Say I do not fly

on pinions of my own. On the road to Rome
gardenia-soaked spirits rattled in our carriage.

I tell you after Robert cast the desiccated wreath
from our portico onto the cobblestones below
an icy mulberry vest buttoned my soul.

A Foot, A Poem
John Poch

—from Diary of a Seducer *by Søren Kierkegaard*

Unknown, take care your carriage-high descent
in the dark. How this anxiety augments
your loveliness, your step to the rough street.
I could show you a story in a book by Tieck:
a lady dismounting from her horse became
so horribly entangled—this step remained
her most definitive.
                                    Poorly built, the ladder
on carriages can cause a scattered
approach, a dire departure, or a fall
into a servant's arms. Therefore, of all
professions, servants have it best: these slips
reveal the secrets of such a young miss.
But don't jump, think of the slow, lax attendants
(enamored of their own velvet resplendence)
who might not catch your fall. Watch your silk dress,
and make concessions for this foot's finesse.
For my regard, let that same foot, with care,
fall forth into the broken world and dare
to find a steady walk. Though should you not,
then follow quickly with the other foot
your graceful hurry, just as God intends.
Like Cuvier we can observe an end
of such detail, that a lovely foot can divine
a loveliness. I'm thinking of your spine.

Hamlet Beside the Stream

Adam Vines

Cruel Fortune, cattail braids, hydrilla tail,
I see you stalk the swan, her lotus neck,
her downcast eyes. The stones below are washed
of fissures, scars, their place of birth. From the womb,
my heir would start to pock and leak.
Beneath the stream's insinuating ripples,
where eddies hold the dead, where leeches wait
and lampreys nibble scales and flesh from hosts,

the sowbugs scuttle, feeding on hyacinth's
decaying leaves and bloated roots detached
from the banks. As April gnaws on winter's sick
and courtiers wring out your amber hair
then close your eyes, I press my palms in clay,
cursing the god who made our hungers weeds.

House of Galicia
Jonathan B. Rice

> As in the past the future is maturing
> So the past is rotting in the future...
> —Anna Akhmatova

I don't mind the talk of younger men
who lead their women out beside the shore

at night, and bring them to the coming point,
a shudder for a bastard child. They speak

to me in pity-looks, saying as they pass—I sit
near the blind saint's park—Wretched husk,

watching father, palsied to that oak-slat bench,
you're untouchable, a widower refusing death.

I miss caresses of all kinds. And dream the body
bared from calf and thigh to wetted gash of sex,

abdomen and navel, birth-home and above,
the cooling flesh of mid-moan breath and echo

of that rising heat. Tonight I mourn the girl
who, rising from the imprint of her lying down

in sand, chills beneath the young man's shadow,
moon or no, when he buckles back his denim

slacks to take her home and leave her there.
I watched her unsupported shadow weaving

towards me through the slipping dunes
and down-coast breeze, which mourns her too,

though, knowing more than me of breath
and time, will lament, I want to say, for latitudes

of days, and leave the outline of her form
whisper-thin and falling, shape of arm of wind

and shape of breast of wind and shapeless
voice scattering across the flat meridian.

*

Once there was a girl for me. In awe of her
I kneaded all myself across her taking form

and stayed each time to rest. That was no
wasted prowess. No slacking loss. Those

drifting hours in and out of sleep we named
each child we could not have, and I imagined

them, the spirits that they were, wise and cold,
refusing us and passing on toward other cries

of coupling. And years of this, it closes fast,
a fist across my thoughts: What were we then?

I never asked. In the silence of our little rooms,
in the barking of our arguments and stirring pots

and searing pans, the kettles screaming for their
instants and then lifted, I am lifted, bodiless,

to hover in my past, a watching presence.
That haunt I always felt I fear I have become.

*

Rachel of lifted skirt, of leaning down to wake me—
for years of standing at a lathe—Rachel wringing

blouse and linen, nylons like shed snake skins
and every working shirt I wore, ringed with sweat

and stinking before their drowning and their wringing,
your name and voice are ringing in my thoughts

so often now I ask, Can you be gone? and see
the little yard I left you in, two Septembers' worth

of indifferent weather ago. And see myself
in the bath-steamed mirror, lifting brush and razor,

your untranslatable songs lapping every year,
your blue blue blue Ukrainian eyes dimming to

the weighted grays of cloud fields steeping snow,
of stone, wet slate, granite. You are gone.

And I am thinned to breaking if I fall, a seated
statue, still a little warm, noting the going out

and the returning, the usury of a youthful
woman I do not know. I watch you walk inside

instead of her and want to follow, want for any
slap or curse or swear of love within our old,

animal embrace. Some night, when no couple
struggles in the sand because a pitiless gale

mangles every dune, let me rise from the nodding
stupor of my body to remember the word

or thing you said would be your signal,
what you'd murmur or shout or make stir

after you'd gone. The photograph of your mother
with her thinned family fell from the wall,

bursting frame and pitted glass across the floor.
That was it, and no, a woman shouting to her son

in the street beneath our bedroom window,
Bohdan, your father's name, the boy's as well.

We did not know then. The woman or the name.
Neither. The kitchen filled with whispers in late

August waking me from sleep which comes in
crushing bursts. I fold my arms. I bow my head.

No prayer verse nor dream will follow. Once
I thought this noise was yours but is the girl

beneath the man who walks her out, saying
against the wall whatever she must say for him.

This morning pilots flew low over the tenements,
a demonstration of strength beyond the open water

and back, their formation perfect. The echo lasted
hours, only minutes, twenty seconds if I counted

as your mother counted the workers Stalin's
digging left in the Dusse-Alin Tunnel. I see her

with her only story at the kitchen table, telling us,
speaking past us, after others' moaning grief not

passion through the walls of her rationed youth.
I see her near the open maw, ticking numerals

without names. More are carried out. A single
jet engine fixed to the front of a giant truck, cools.

Then restarted, it's angled to the tunnel mouth
to melt the solid ice. The offcast light is too brilliant

to watch. At her feet is uncle, is brother, is brother,
is father, unrecognizable, hers, no one's, hers.

She must stand back. The cold settles in like hunger.

If Robinson Came from the Heartland
Kathleen Rooney

then this must be the brainland.
Do not disappoint, he demands

of the city. *Do not be fooled*,
he commands himself.

Does he want a master, or
does he want a companion?

Unmusses the bed. Hungover,
he feels the promise of the place;

as well, that the place may break
him like a promise. Pulls back

the lace curtain: the sun burning.
The blank faces. All right—

he's here. But to be near is not
the same as to be close. Ann,

his wife, must arrive behind him.
I'm in trouble. Where are you? he

jokes into the phone. *Another time
zone*, she answers. *How do I*

know if I'm any good? he asks,
but the connection's gone bad

& there's only a comfort tone.
He's got to make a plan—

to make a drawing of a hand
without looking at a hand.

In the fever-world, my dearest

Jehanne Dubrow

In the fever-world, my dearest,
our hands aren't clean
for very long, the brambles
biting in our palms,
deep thorns across our life lines—
      here, even the shrub
surrendering fruit to the picker
resents the sacrifice and wants
its juices given back in blood.
      If you are hungry, starve yourself.
Make a desert of your thirst.
Don't fall asleep
           Here, my dearest,
there's only wilderness where fields
should be, only the blackberries
concealing knives,
        cherries pitted with buckshot
to choke the unsuspecting throat,
and peaches whose centers hold
dark stones of cyanide.

The *Kama Sutra*'s Banished Illustrator
Chad Davidson

I only drew the woman. Raised cheekbones
curving impossibly in my hand, the slender
neck, hair pulled back like rope: all

female after brushing the vagina's conch
in agni. I shaded with my stained finger
around the breasts, gave her arms, karma.

Her pupils swelled, anticipating the loss.
How I coveted the way she seemed
to stare at my palm while I labored—my subject.

Any artist will tell you they're not easy,
the eyes; I grinded them into reflection.
She never saw past the image I gave her,

just as I could not stop scorching her skin
with reds and ochres saved for Brahma's eyes.
A flame of curry stained her mouth's rim.

Here, a hand rose for wine a lover brings.
His name would well up in her parched throat.
Before the night, she would accept him again,

whom I refused to draw. It was a trick
to make ecstasy—the floating legs,
head tossed back, the half-eaten plum—

contrary to her leisure. In fact I stole
my sketches long before I finished,
before she bled back into my hands.

Letter from Zelda

Marjorie Manwaring

My darling Scott, I feel so exploded
I can barely write, like a gourd
not knowing the hand that shakes me,

my mind a million seeds.
But weren't we once grand—a Ferris
wheel in Paris, spinning ourselves silly.

I never loved you more than when you bent
over your desk, pen gouging paper,
never hated you more—

your pen always blackening,
always my paper white as dogwood.
And though you cried,

your relief heavied the air when you left me
in this room—where everything is cream-colored
rest—no silver shoes, dance floors, gin, or us.

I've planted a sunflower seed—I give it water
from the pitcher on my bed stand.
One day its yellow head will be as full as mine.

Li Po Of Course Drinking

Kenneth Pobo

I lug wine to a mountain—
sit, and poems visit like ants
tickling my feet. Maybe

Tu Fu will return. When I
saw him last, we discussed
dust. Even the Emperor's

pleasure is a snapped twig—
Tu Fu agreed, but though
I called to his back

I knew I couldn't join
or stop him. Another sip.
The wine tastes like crushed

wood, bitter, yet I drink more.
Look, a violet. Perfectly shaped,
slightly brown at the edges.

Love Letter to Hans Christian Andersen

Jennifer Fandel

Hans Christian Andersen never married.
On the day he died, he was found in bed
with an old love letter in his hand.

I have skated deep circles around the pond
waiting, but you never come.
The snow piles up, the ice grows thick,
and when I call through the boundaries of trees,
your name hovers in the frozen air.
My breath is smoke in the cold
and my hands turn stiff in my mittens.
We can have quiet happiness, Hans,
should you walk from the forest
to this pond where I wait.

Spring near, my breath soon
will disperse with my loneliness.
The snow will melt, the ice thin
until one can see the water beneath.
Forever, I feel I've stood here,
looking through the trees.
The ice will break with the warmth,
but even if your footsteps come,
I am not foolish enough to believe
that you can save me from time passing.

Should I receive no word from you,
I will know the truth and will believe it.
Until then, I listen to the vowels of the wind,
the consonant ice breaking, traveling downstream.
I know from these sounds comes your voice
and truth and this daring action,
opening like seed from spring-thawed ground.

Love Song of Fergus

Israel Wasserstein

> *And who will drive with Fergus now?*
> —W. B. Yeats

Pass me and know me not:
I, who once was king, now sleep
in clearings wrapped

in restless stars.
For years I kept my kingdom
with sword-arm, but man

grows weary of battle,
and each night my tower
closed around me.

If I grew old and discontent,
and each morning I woke
from restless sleep,

if the forest whispered
my name, if the evening
grew heavy with the ache

of open spaces, and the oldest
song called me west,
west toward the sea,

who was I to resist?
Listen: the night is wide,
and everywhere the echo

of countryside and thicket
calls to us, brothers, sisters,
urges us to seek ourselves

in shrouded corners of the world.

Marcel at the Station House
Natasha Sajé

> If you find yourself being questioned about a crime you did not commit,
> resist at all costs the impulse to be helpful.
> —Social psychologist Richard Ofshe, UC-Berkeley

Where were you the night of July 10?

I am unable to say from what place, from which dream, anything comes.

If you were to commit a crime...

I would prepare the hundred masks that must fit a single face.

You would plan it?

How many persons, cities, or roads does jealousy make us eager to know? I'd think about details.

Like hair and fibers?

Like *boeuf à la mode,* like water lilies, like Vermeer's *View of Delft.*

You went out to dinner that night?

I observe, I speak with servants, I remember.

But sometimes you do the things you think about?

Nothing is so satisfying as the imagination's rendering of it.

Because you have a bad memory?

Hours go by and I remember the tremors in my thighs.

So how do you…

I like to watch famished rats clawing and biting each other.

Are you kidding?

The day my mother died she took her little Marcel with her.

And how did it feel when you first put your hands around her neck?

A slight ripple, like sipping linden tea or feeling a fingernail trail against a taut stomach.

What was she wearing?

A Fortuny gown, pleated red silk, and diamonds. Red shoes, of course. Everything of those days has perished, but everything was born again.

Did you love her?

I prefer to remain closeted with the little person inside me, hymning the rising sun. He would make me happier than she.

There's a lot of evidence. We have a lot of evidence. We have your hair.

I'd curl it to face the photographer. I'd wear my velvet jacket, and the apple trees would expose their broad petals of white.

You were nervous? You stuffed the body in the trunk?

No, I would have laid it on an old satin coverlet, after which I would have consoled myself, if I felt well enough, by walking along the avenues. I would have taken my walking stick, I would have sung at the top of my voice. I would have taken a few grams of Veronal.

Are you sorry?

Ars longa, vita brevis.

Which means?

I am acquainted with sin, in one form or another. Dostoevsky writes about murder, but did he commit it? Laclos was the best of husbands.

But you?

I don't invent things. I've become braver, thinking of my journey into the self like climbing down a well without a rope.

You used a rope?

O! The trinity of braided strands, the coarse erotic fibers.

I'd like to try a polygraph, if that's all right with you.

Maudie Defends Her Spinsterhood

Donna Vorreyer

When I first turn the dirt for the garden
each spring, I am stumble-drunk with
the smell—old and new rolled into one.

It's the same with cakes—flour and sugar
and simple lumps of butter, all lifeless on
their own, full of breath when combined.

But not everyone can see both sides. Some
can't understand that a woman without
a man is not the same as a woman alone.

It hasn't been easy—neighborhood wags
watch every move. We meet in brief trysts,
midnights and mornings before the moon

winks and disappears. She is like talcum,
like molasses, sweet and rich, a cool sip
in the evening's drought. I speak my mind

about most things, but keep this secret
close lest it spread, like seeds of nut grass,
giving them something new to hate.

Excerpt from "Musica Humana"

Ilya Kaminsky

—an elegy for Osip Mandelstam

[In summer 1924 Osip Mandelstam brought his young wife to St. Petersburg.
Nadezhda was what the French call *laide mais charmante*. An eccentric? Of
course he was. He threw a student down the staircase for complaining he
wasn't published, Osip shouting: *Was Sappho? Was Jesus Christ]*

> Poet is a voice, I say, like Icarus,
> whispering to himself as he falls.
>
> Yes, my life as a broken branch in the wind
> hits the Northern ground.
> I am writing now a history of snow,
> the lamplight bathing the ships
> that sail across the page.
>
> But on certain afternoons
> the Republic of Psalms opens up
> and I grow frightened that I haven't lived, died, not enough
> to scratch this ecstasy into vowels, hear
> splashes of clear, biblical speech.
>
> I read Plato, Augustine, the loneliness of their syllables
> while Icarus keeps falling.
> And I read Akhmatova, her rich weight binds me to the earth,
> the nut trees on a terrace breathing
> the dry air, the daylight.
>
> Yes, I lived. The State hung me up by the feet, I saw
> St. Petersburg's daughters, swans,
> I learned the grammar of gulls' array
> and found myself for good

down Pushkin Street, while memory
sat in the corner, erasing me with a sponge.

I've made mistakes, yes: in bed
I compared government
to my girlfriend.
Government! An arrogant barber's hand
shaving off the skin.
All of us dancing happily around him.

[He sat on the edge of his chair and dreamt aloud of good dinners.
He composed his poems not at his desk but in the streets of St.
Petersburg; he adored the image of the rooster tearing apart the
night under the walls of Acropolis with his song. Locked up in the
cell, he was banging on the door: "You have got to let me out, I
wasn't made for prison."]

Once or twice in his life, a man
is peeled like apples.

What's left is a voice
that splits his being

down to the center.
We see: obscenity, fright, mud

but there is joy of shape, there is
always
more than one silence.

—between here and Nevski Prospect,
the years, birdlike, stretch,—

Pray for this man
who lived on bread and tomatoes

while dogs recited his poetry
in each street.

Yes, count "march," "july"
weave them together with a thread—

it's time, Lord,
press these words against your silence.

*

—the story is told of a man who escapes
and is captured

into the prose of evenings:
after making love, he sits up

on a kitchen floor, eyes wide open,
speaks of the Lord's emptiness

in whose image we are made.
—*he is out of work*—among silverware

and dirt he is kissing
his wife's neck so the skin of her belly tightens.

One would think of a boy laying
syllables with his tongue

onto a woman's skin: those are lines
sewn entirely of silence.

Nabokov, Naming the Animals
Billy Merrell

I was speechless. Still he came to me,
Sat among these saffron rooms, called me Father.

I showed him the earth and he took it
In his mouth—I had him name things:

The first was simple: he lisped an angel.
But when he caught her between his palms

And she crumbled, Nabokov wouldn't stop crying.
Even as I turned the leaves to fire,

Let the first of the flowers unpetal, trying dumbly
To explain how things are meant to die.

More came, and he named each,
Though he let them live—

Orange Albatross; Paris Peacock;
Wood Nymph; American Lady.

He gave the world its first
Question Mark, first Small Postman,

First Harvester. Nabokov's butterflies unfurled,
And he never grew tired of them,

Though Paradise did. All he had to do was speak,
And another wrought angel flitted out of hiding,

Hungry for color, lighting our sensitive skins.
A breath would send them off; a stillness would call them.

If I had had a tongue, I would have stopped him,
Finished the job myself. But I woke Adam, the lonely one,

Who saw their millions and believed
He was in Heaven.

Ophelia Drowning
Carol Berg

I had no idea he would be
so warm the water this other Hamlet

greenly stitching me into my twilight
blanket   my deepening blanket

How his wriggling words grip me
with their hooked thumbs and glittery fingers

His ropey tongues tugging my spinning flesh
My hair blurs out   my dress he muddies

Me in my watery yesterdays   He is my
foaming lullaby   He tastes of red

feathers fluttering in snares   He shudders into me
like a buzzing star   Tucks me into incandescent sheets

He murmuring is blue promises
He is my   is my   is my

I am spreading into
I am almost home

Paul D's Haiku for Sethe

Derrick Weston Brown

I always loved trees
Long thick limbs swaying brown boughs
Sethe   be my Oak.

Poisonous Persona

T. R. Hummer

I, Fernando Pessoa, am not myself, and never was. Pour me another absinthe,
  de Campos, and I will pour one for you. Pour me another soul.
You might say that when I was born they left my bedroom door open, if by "open
  bedroom door" is understood a metaphor for metempsychosis.
Or you might say that my birth was the fanfare for the end of the personal ownership
  of selfhood, that I was born a metaphysical communist
And stand ready to die a dedicated drunk. Is absinthe drunk in Portugal? Do persons
  live there, distinct from one another, freestanding?
The problem with Portugal is that it is a flat character in the drama of Europe.
  Look at England, look at France: they stand before us whole—
But here we are a beehive of probabilities. One of my heteronyms, for instance,
  has invented the Absinthe Clock that measures half-lives,
The shorter the better. It works only on Portuguese soil, and sometimes in Brazil,
  but in Spain it grinds and wheezes and pukes out Quixotes
Like pater nosters. Quixote was Quixote, and he is ubiquitous always as himself,
  just as the Pope tends to be the Pope, or absinthe absinthe.
But I, Fernando Pessoa, am not myself, alone am not myself and am never alone,
  with so many indistinguishable others inhabiting the mental avenue
Where I walk from the office after a day of translating myself into the terrible prose
  of salesmen, to the bar and the shadow of my absinthe.

Robert Frost, The Derry Farm, New Hampshire, 1906
Andrew Mulvania

> *I am sure that anyone standing in my place tonight, charged with*
> *the happy office of greeting Mr. Frost on his birthday, on his massive,*
> *his Sophoclean birthday, would be bound to feel, as I do indeed feel,*
> *a considerable measure of diffidence.*
>
> —Lionel Trilling, March 26th, 1959, Waldorf-Astoria,
>   in celebration of Robert Frost's eighty-fifth birthday

He sat reflecting in his cane back chair
on the bitter wisdom of old Sophocles
in the Oedipus at Colonus: *Never to have been born*
is best, / But if we must see the light,
the next best is quickly returning whence we came.
That would surely have been true for poor Elliot
and he had—hadn't he?—taken the poet's advice,
returning from the arms of Frost and Elinor
to wherever "*whence we came*" from was—if anywhere.
The other children—the four left—were at play
out in the pasture down by Hyla Brook.
He'd written about that once in a little poem
he'd called "The Trial By Existence"—the thought that all of us
come "trailing clouds of glory," as Wordsworth had it,
from some prior life of which we have no memory
and that whatever pain or joy befalls us
is ours by rights as what we somehow chose.
But had the children chosen this country life
of isolation?—for lately he'd noticed they'd grown strange
from having only one another for playfellows.
It was fine for him, misanthrope that he was,
but the strain had been too much for Elinor
and, after Elliot died, something within her
died with him and a wall went up between them.
It couldn't be true that Elliot had *chosen* to die,

to be ensouled for only four short years
and then go back. No, Sophocles was right—
this whole business of living was for the birds,
those goddamn chickens squawking to be fed
even now in the chicken coops behind the house.
Still, there were days like this one: children at play
in the near pasture, April sun warming the fields
and the back of his neck where he sat in the chair.
Yes, maybe it wasn't so terrible after all.
White wings burst briefly upward in the air.

Sebastian's Arrows:
Lorca's Last Letter to Dalí, August 20, 1936
Kara Candito

> *You do well when you post warning flags*
> *Along the dark limit that shines in the night.*
>
> —Lorca, "Ode to Salvador Dalí"

What part of your dream logic will tell you
    I was not looking for science or your cock?
I stumbled into the orchard with my hands bound

and my pockets stuffed with bitter oranges. The Law
    is an affectation. Its roots are bare wires.
The mind reaches only as far as the fingers. Today

I am *map, grove, moan;* a boy in cold bathwater crying,
    father! I play pallet to the frozen aqueduct
of your wrist, which is a firing squad, the shallow

grave where I bleed beside a matador and an old
    schoolteacher, his beard full of famished doves.
Tonight in Cadiz, the fortuneteller wears a collar

of bees and horse thieves turn bacchanals into lullabies
    outside the walls of the city. Every gypsy boy
clutches my death mask to his chest. If forgiveness

is a smile of bullets, then my name means *antiseptic*
    and it will sting each time you touch a paintbrush.
There is no one who can sing without hearing

the cries of pinned olive trees. There is no one
    who can say we did not lie side by side, tucked
into the twin coffins of our lives while Spain

emptied its ashtrays into our mouths.

Speaking as the Male Poet
Keetje Kuipers

I would like to write the fistfight poem, which I have never had
the pleasure of (I hit him once but he wouldn't hit me back)

or I might visit a prostitute (girl, woman, professional or not)
and then confess to you my shame (oh, to be the doer of the deed!)—

the death of a pet, a reference to Greek tragedy, a snowy drive in the dark,
a hospital room I wouldn't have to describe because just knowing

I am perhaps very bad and very broken and certainly very, very,
very smart would be enough. you might then want me to cook you

scrambled eggs in my boy-kitchen or simply ignore you from
behind the black rims of my not-really-necessary reading glasses

and I could say things to make you swoon, things like Codeine,
Oldsmobile, shortstop—words that were ordinary but now, coming

from my pen, my born in the suburbs of Boston pen, my son of trains
leaving every hour pen, my jeans tangled around my pale white calves pen,

might have a new meaning that would make you think twice, as in,
why didn't I think of that? and they would be clever and sad

all at once, and wouldn't you want me, would want to wonder at me,
how I came to be transformed, and maybe who my mother is (lost child,

peter pan) and how she feels about the lies I'm telling you.

Walt Whitman Sings Happy Birthday to Himself
Matthew Nienow

Down the uneven plank stairs, down to the cellar-world
of thick smoke and high ceilings, the busy clanking
of heavy glass,
the low rumble of a hundred men, the drumming
of feet, the whine of wooden chairs scraping
along the wooden floor, whispering
with grains of sand, the world above carried
to the gritty floor by the feet of men

who have come here, as I have come here, to celebrate
or curse the fact of our being here and I,

I have come back to Bleecker Street to name myself
among those who have lived longest,
to bathe in the lingering smoke and drink to myself,
which is also to drink to you,

for we are of the same flesh and must sing to say so,

until we lean into the creaking steps
and sway into the first astonishing moments of light,
blinded, raising a hand to block the sun, to fall quiet
at the city still asleep, and we are filled by this quiet, rising
from the underbelly of this swine filled city, which we love,

and I, warm from the long night among other men, smelling
still of smoke and earth, run my fingers through my beard,
one arm slung over the shoulder of an old friend,

and sing myself another year in this lingering body
which has served me so very well.

The Wind Over Pasternak's Square
Todd Fredson

Aren't the leaves like women, women
knotting lace in the marketplace
chattering at passers-by? The passers-by reaching overhead
to weigh the heft of the pears
with their bared fingertips.
The girl opens my nightshirt
to listen
but my heart is two beds down, an idea
of Spring, as if
I have been the wind.

And if I have been the wind
then there is no question.
So let's pretend that the bird has not ruptured its breast
pressing the first
briar of the year into its nest.

Or, if I have fallen asleep against the wind, always
in the act of forgiveness, then please

determine this,
this very particular thing
that hovers over itself like a scorpion's tail
then drives itself in.
Dryness concedes rain.
The day nods over us—and now February begins.

The Muse Talks Back

Artists and Their Subjects

Agitation: *frida says (a translation)*
Alessandra Lynch

i will cut off all my hair & use each strand
as another bar of music   each bird an unbridled note

i want the dark birds   they're more easily read
they can use my hair as nesting threads

you have said you won't love me without
my woman-power—what protects—my veil

i say: my burden—what strangles—dead tendrils
of pleasing   pleasing   appeasing

follicles which have no sheen or motion
i sit on my hellish yellow chair without my hair-shirt

in my man's suit & small man's shoes   my legs wide
like a man's   smoke issuing from fingers

immaterial   green bird in my lap

Baedeker for a Life Cut with Danger
Rodney Gomez

—*John Valadez*, Car Show, *2001*

I don't have night's number. Wouldn't know it
if I went through a phonebook
with a highlighter and a bloodhound.

Where's it hidden in her halter top,
the Aztec tats he plays loud as tom-toms
every time he takes his t-shirt off?

I worry about the sun in this backyard
barbecue. What if they added wrong
and it's heavy enough to go black hole?

There go my tax returns. There goes the bread
I baked in the shape of a rosary.

Better to sing a war ballad. When I was a kid
all I wanted was to nurse a bloody rifle
between my thighs. I could've galloped
with Villa, a flask of pulque slung across my waist.

But don't mistake me for a sympathizer.
I hoard rejection in my cheeks
and porcupine needles for your outreach.
During the day, I'm a strain on group
identity. Rolling twenties in a street

lined with palms, samuraied by Hurricane Dolly.
Pouring myself into a junked Impala
with the winos from the VFW.

I know a little Spanish, the bristly kind
you speak when you want a Granny Smith
at the grocer. The tongue throws off

its crutches. You've got to think in a deeper
hunger so a round brown stomach can carry
your swollen arguments. So what are you?
And there is silence.

Notice how nothing that matters has a mouth.

Beethoven's Maid Writes a Letter to Her Mother
Angela Narciso Torres

His doctors have ordered fresh air and quiet,
far from Vienna's crowded streets.
Barely a week since he arrived
and already the Master has broken
three plates. Yesterday he hurled a saucer
because the coffee was thin. *Thirty-two beans!*
he boomed as blue Delft flew. Picking violets
for his tray, I saw him at the window, head cocked
as one listening, ear pressed to a wall.

                       The pianoforte
roused me before dawn, crashing like the herd
of Lipizzaners at the fair, then soft and pleading
as Papi's face the day I left. When I brought
his breakfast, he wore a dressing gown, quill
in his hair. Music papered the floor. Mama,
at half-a-gulden a week, who knows when
I'll see you again? But this morning he paid me
twice my due. When I refused, he raised both hands,
saying, *I have no time to think of sums.*

Mornings he walks by the creek, papers
tucked in his arm. He notices neither heat
nor cold—wears linen in any weather.
Today at noon, beneath the cracked
elm I found him, blue fingers drumming
his knees, pages scattered like doves.
Nothing stirred. That's when he gripped
my arm, demanding, *Do you hear?*
Tell me, Anna—is that quail? Mama, I lied.

Coy Mistress
Annie Finch

Sir, I am not a bird of prey:
a Lady does not seize the day.
I trust that brief Time will unfold
our youth, before he makes us old.
How could we two write lines of rhyme
were we not fond of numbered Time
and grateful to the vast and sweet
trials his days will make us meet?
The Grave's not just the body's curse;
no skeleton can pen a verse!
So while this numbered World we see,
let's sweeten Time with poetry,
and Time, in turn, may sweeten Love
and give us time our love to prove.
You've praised my eyes, forehead, breast:
you've all our lives to praise the rest.

Diego is Painted by D. H. Lawrence in the Desert

Rane Arroyo

We laugh at the whiteness of
his back and ass, that he doesn't
know that the sun will paint him
red soon, that the yellow of
his nudes is nothing compared
to a cactus pear eaten at noon
after Chihuahua tequila shots.
Such innocence has to be saved
from itself. We take off our clothes
so he can paint us and learn about
the brown of a perfectly baked bread,
the brown of stones older than gods.
Diego, my amigos laugh, he looks
at you and sees something and cuidado,
beware, never take off your gold cross.

*

Frida makes sure David and I
are never alone for too long.
I pretend not to speak English
because she is angry at me
and at everyone but her painter.
He's just a model. I grab the shovel
for the impossible garden they
want by the back door. *Soon,*
David says as I leave, *you, mountain,*
me, soon. His Spanish is broken,
but honest. Frida follows me
so I take off my shirt to show off

my chest and the fierce heart
she will never know. David waves
to us and I wave back just so
Frida's jealousy eats a feast.

*

We sun naked on the mountain
after his mining of the rainbow in
his palette. *Hombre,* David says,
*do you think the sun is an unthinking
tantalizer?* I can't answer in English
so I nod. He throws his voice
into the staid canyons: *the nexus
is worthy the thorns that protect it!*
His sex is relaxed, a serpent not
from my world. I break words too:
*you, me, us, mountain, mystery, fire
inside the heart, corazón, God's furnace.*
Now he is ready to paint me as I am.

*

Artists and obviously future lovers
show up for Frida's party to show off
Davíd's paintings (*He's earned the accent mark*).
I'm pulled from the ranch because
I keep my fingernails clean. Frida eyes me,
but I know how to pour wine and stand
invisible until beckoned. Davíd refuses
to attend the mock-Paris mockery of
a salon event. He's painting in the desert,
and I risk being fired by seeking him out.
Juan the Beloved, he says, pulling me to his
chest. He and I know my name's not Juan.

*

His death far from me is astonishing:
so other old worlds are real. No one
says anything directly, but la taverna
gives me free drinks on hearing the news.
A spurned widow or widower (no one
asks me) is bad luck for business.
I drive to our mountain and undress.
Gestures must never burden the dead.
I throw the gold cross into the cosmos.
It sprouts wings. Again, I'm left behind.

*

Frida burns all the paintings of me
as the alchemist, vaquero, the sun's
chosen one, worker with optimism,
and the erection that casts no shadows.
And she has demanded I see the burning.
And she knows of my knowledge.
And she spends David's money on matches.
And she has a young lover already.
But I've not disappeared, Fraülein, I say in
perfected English. I've read all his books
aloud in my obscure house. On cue, she
needs to hurt me, *there were many others.*
She doesn't know that David gave me
paintings that are now my windows, and
that I look out of them into the desert
where we learned not to be enigmas.

Fernande Olivier: Woman Sleeping, 1904

Diane K. Martin

I detest Sundays. I tell you, they smell bad.
If that Sunday I lay in bed with a book, I'm sure I didn't read it
but thought only of that first night with Pablo—how the wind took
the trees in Place Ravignon, how the rain soaked my blouse
to the skin. At Bateau-Lavoir, Pablo blocked the way in.
I'd seen him around of course, that Andalusian the artists and poets
all followed. (One night,they marched drunk shouting:
Up with Verlaine! Down with Laforgue!
Or was it the other way round? No matter.)
Well, there he stood in the doorway, in his arms
the smallest wet kitten. *Voici Minou,* he said, laughing,
she is as wet as you. Then he made me see (vraiment) his
new etching. You know the one I mean—two
blue people, blue wine, the piece of blue bread?
He scratched it in zinc with a hatpin found
on the floor of a brothel. Pablo, Pablo, his face so old,
his black eyes coal hardened to diamond. His hands,
delicate as a girl's, held me, removed my wet hat,
then my shoes, my stockings, slowly, and my lace…

On that muggy Sunday I lay in bed with my book,
remembering this—the air so close, it didn't seem possible
I could stir by my own volition, more like the Fates
pushed me—to leave Laurent for good. I packed
my things into Pablo's trunk, got him to drag it
across the hall to his place. *Mon Dieu,* it stank!
It seems his pal, Appollinaire, had the bright idea
to clean the floor with paraffin. Then they used bleach
to rid the place of paraffin; then eau de cologne
—that made it smell even worse.

But there I stayed seven years, as much
a part of his studio as the mattress propped
on tin cans, the iron stove, the yellow bowl.
We lived for Beauty and Experience—
we smoked the lovely opium with *les autres*,
staring into the flame of dreams. We had
nothing to do with those *petits bourgeois* farts
who lived in the classy parts of town. Weekends
we might buy Pablo a shirt for a couple centimes
at the open-air market. In winter,
tea left in a cup would be ice by morning.
Summer found Pablo painting shirtless
in the heat, red scarf around his waist.
Some days we ate only macaroni or dined
in cafés on credit, running up bills so high
they let us in so they had some hope of payment.
Once we were so hungry we cooked and ate
a sausage Minou dragged in. But sometimes
a dealer came and left quite enough for wine,
and Pablo would buy me lavender perfume
in cut glass *bouteilles*.

       Oui, certainment, he loved me,
or the idea of me, or the idea of love. You can see:
he watches as I sleep. Day after day, I lay
behind a curtain while he painted and held court.
He said he would starve for me. (But what I had to do
to get him to wash!) He enshrined my hat
as if it were a holy relic. He forbade me
model for the other painters, or even shop or clean.
So I slept and read, got used to being
la femme decoratif, as Gertrude called me.
With me in his life he left behind brothels
and blue canvasses. Rose hues bloomed,
saltimbanques began their strolls. Still and always

he was a man who gnawed his own bones,
who only ever thought about his painting. That was all
he ever wanted to do, though doing it did not
make him happy. And there was no asking him,
Pablo, what is the matter?

        As for me, I get bored.
If I'd been a man, I could have lived by my skills.
I hated being locked in (like the white mouse he
kept in a drawer), while one girl or another
at the Lapin Agile sat laughing in his lap.
And so, I never meant to leave but did
and then could not find my way back.

Frida Kahlo Speaks:

Barbara Crooker

> *Fidelity is a bourgeois virtue.*
> —Diego Rivera

There are two Fridas, the one you want,
and the one you don't want. You might
have thought I wore this white dress
for you, Diego, piled this hibiscus in my hair,
threaded azul chunks of sky around my throat.
But I did it for myself. *I paint myself.* Look
at me. I wear a necklace of thorns;
a hummingbird hangs between my breasts.
My heart is a bloody shrine trapped
in a corset of pain. But I will rise,
a Bird of Paradise. I will enter your body
like a jolt of caffeine. *At last I have learned
that life is this way, and the rest is window-
dressing.* I will carve *Viva la Vida*
on this watermelon, like a tombstone. *I hope
the ending is joyful, and I hope I never return.*

Josie Bliss, October 1971
Carolyne L. Wright

Nombre definitivo que cae en las semanas
con un golpe de acero que las mata.

—Pablo Neruda, *Residencia en la tierra*

When they brought me the newspaper
headlines with your name translated
to the round dark petals of our script,
I knew you'd finally found your love.
I'm happy for you, Pablo.
After all these years, silence
between us like seabottom jewels,
the Bay of Bengal with jellyfish *armadas*
patrolling the beachheads from which
I could wage no campaign against loss,
your face in the photo
grown heavier—faithful, at last,
to the body's vows with earth.
Our season of mangoes and brainfire,
the paraffin lamp guttering out
on the other side of the curtain,
white jasmines in my hair
and naked feet you said you loved.
Forget those foolish nights
I circled the bed with a knife,
a dance the old women showed me—
panther's ritual, incense I burned
to weaken your instinct for betrayal.
I was your first love,
wasn't I? No spell
bound with camphor and inflections
missing for thousands of years

in our mouths can change that.
Remember how I said my fears
would end with your death?
When you gave death the slip,
boarding the westbound freighter,
leaving your freshly-ironed shirts
to fend for themselves, and books
like a row of hostile witnesses,
in languages you returned to
every morning, every night you cried out
in your sleep—it was I
who died: into the betel leaf
and fringed anxiety of palm,
sarongs and Malay silks stacked
like jute bales in the courtyard.
Airless nights and the ache of salt
between my thighs, my body closed up
like a village in wartime.
No steamer passage across an ocean
littered with telegrams and the summons
of fair-skinned women, no hampers
of saffron rice and clear plum wine
to remind you, no conjures of sweet oil
and scimitars could break the spell of flesh
to which I lost you.
You wouldn't recognize me now,
Pablo. I've blurred with age
and sons and the long war in the East.
And the one daughter they took from me,
whose secret name meant *Heartbreak*
in our tongue, and in your language,
Song. Veiled in blue silk for the voyage,
she vanished from the docks at Singapore
into abject air, water the color
of a beating. Now I'm alone,

refugee of the blood's terrain,
memory's backhanded apologists.
No husband to uproot the strangle-vine,
no one to put a stop
to these voices—my share of messages
you could never bring yourself
to send. What else remains
of what we called our lives?
The house with the jagged bamboo fence
went back to the tribe of liana
and baobab and climbing fern.
My brothers in their blood-colored pagodas
came for me, snake bracelets on their arms,
their tongues heavy as bronze
bell clappers. In Mandalay market
they sold my true name—a powder
against suspicion and English ways.
Since then I am married to quarry stone
and razor-palm green air,
desire that honeycombs the brain
like limewater, fool's-gold gleam
in passageways of no return.
Gone the parrot's emerald laugh,
the incantations of monkey flower
you used against the shadows. Gone
the history of broken clay you told,
gone the hard fruit wrapped in *tilak* skin
that began our countries' sad,
metallic generations. Gone your tongue
in my mouth, sweet anarchy of the hands.
Don't look for me, Pablo,
if you come. I am the first wife
and widow of my own refusals.
In this neighborhood of narrow doors
and shadow longings, the retreating steps

of my blue daughter, machine-gun
voices of my sons, I have forgotten
how to open dawn's orange fan.
No more do I search through books
full of dreams' high-water marks,
no more glide from room to room
listening to your pale breath,
my own lost pulse along the heartwire.
No more do I throw myself down
and kiss the chalk feet of the bearded god.
Stay in your land of stone's tremor
and women like the avalanche's blessing.
I couldn't bear the hidden fault lines
in your beauty, and I no longer answer
to the empty net, the long-knived
moon—warnings between the hand
and its caressing, names you gave
me for my fury and my joy.

Marc Chagall: *Blue Violinist,* 1946

Claire McQuerry

We have come home from the cold, even children—
they float up the street in bluing
light, smoke from dinner fires.
All the chickens cooped and roosted.
The pigeon seller in his ramshackle rooms,
the baker's cottage with lantern
windows, a whiff of warm bread.

In my painting the sky is winter descending,
the clouds an open field for snow rills, a moon's
bald intrusion, fiddle's keen and glister over our roofs.
I stipple in a little heat: red
the hue of still smoldering coals.

Whole villages abandoned, or swallowed
by surprise of flame, violent and complete.
First, airplane engine no louder
than the mosquito's whine.

After, stone wall, lone chimney, smoke.
I don't think of this every day.
Newspaper clippings, a survivor's story, or the earthy
fumes of woodstoves lifting on a cold morning
double me over in sudden grief.

Somewhere under this sky I paint, I'm a child.
Father bathes first, and the water
glitters with mackerel scales
that swirl like galaxies or oil
sliding over the surface of soup.

His beard steams as he dries himself,
while I undress, shivering in my skin.

I lower into the basin and listen—
the rustle of cigarette papers, father
just through the curtain.
He dusts tobacco down the center of the paper,
curling each slip: a tube, no wider

than a woman's little finger. The oil lamp
casts a tent of light for his hands, as if
the raft of cigarettes, the knotty wood,
his articulate fingers, comprise the world.
Overhead, frozen bed sheets soften,
uncontorting. Scent of lye and wind.

On Sketching *Pippa Passing the Loose Women* (1855)

Anna Leahy

I drew people well. I drew
people out of themselves.
These are unrelated talents,
but I was happy to embody both.

I portrayed good Pippa and the prostitutes
equally ably, virgin and harlot alike.
I captured their expressions:
mutual curiosity, earnest interest.

Even the geese stretch to see.
I rendered the human form well, too.
Render: to create a version,
to give something in return

like the women exchanging glances.
Rend: to slit, to split apart.

Picasso's Heart

Molly Gaudry

Part One

His destructive mornings, ours.
We mimicked his maneuvers,

every quirk: sidearmed steaming
croissants from the roof; used

cricket bats to smash his thrift-
store teacups, our still-boiling

Darjeeling exploding high,
splattering on sidewalks below.

We cared nothing for the peasants
who sidestepped our shards, who

had learned and carried umbrellas,
had ceased their vulgar gestures:

raised fists, bitter complaints. We
had been them, once. Were, still.

Those mornings we forgot that.
We wanted to be like him. It was

our sanguine period. Who knew
what that meant, but he called it,

not us. Why did we care? Art?
Back then, it seemed so magical.

Art was everything, everywhere.
It was in clouds (smudged), rain

(dripped), puddles (pooled), rivers
(streaked on our canvases), the sun,

the sharp edges of buildings, shadows
long leaning lines (our photographs),

in the color of our breakfast fruits,
our meats at meals, in the shine

of our lipstick, hues of our blusher.
We saw it in the tiny hairs on our toes

and upper lips, plucked (our selves
as models for the hairless bodies

we molded from chicken wire,
paper pulp, potter's clay, marble).

Truth is, we were godawful-terrible
and knew as much. Hobbyists, at best.

We were a machine: predictable,
idealistic, full of noble ideas. Art

pushed at us, but we were strangers.
Until oysters. Before, in his presence,

we silenced. He kept his back to us,
hunched, unrelenting. We were bare

before him. We played subtle. He
wore earrings, ruby. He fucked

a few of us, sure. Rumors, words.
Who would believe? False, words.

Besides, most of us were lesbians.
Which brings me to oysters, flesh-

plumps that turned the surface
of our skin into ochre longing.

Picasso fell, sunk. We wanted
to be like him, not with him,

not like that. But he had a saying.
It was, "Joy waits." Was it his

joy or ours? They wanted to know
but I didn't care. There was a girl

and I was unmindful. I wanted her
in my bed. I wanted her alone,

but there were so many people
in the world, infinite options

of others for her to choose. I went
want-mad. She was nothing. Wistful

thinking. She was a sword. She cut.
She wasn't a lesbian. She said,

"You'd like to lie beside me,
but who's to blame?" It was a slip.

It wasn't meant for me but him. I fed
her oysters, made a crown of the shells,

and we pretended we were artists,
famous, as we unbuttoned her top,

my top, while Picasso watched—
the only way she'd have me. All right.

I wanted to stay forever in his studio,
I was so happy. But so quick, that day

that ended, as they began, with tea.
Impressive. Always, with the Darjeeling.

Unfailing. Did he need it? What means?
What fuel? It took me away. I drank

too much to prolong the event, make it
last. From the roof I watched her fall.

"Who's to blame?" she asked. "Joy
waits," he had said. What a night.

Under those stars, an empty corridor
in which I squatted, aching, trembling,

thinking how one male in the bunch
steals souls and sends them arcing,

racing to the street below. I had fears,
but they were no longer for my wallet

but my heart. I might have left but
nowhere else to go, I stayed. And paid.

⎯⎯en Studies for a Self-Portrait

Jee Leong Koh

Study #1: After Albrecht Dürer

Double eye. Double bind. Double blind.
The dark paints the dark in the dark.
I am the Christ. I am not the Christ.
I am not making claims, or so I claim.
So watch my eyes, my eyes work so
black and thin. They ensure, they endure.
When the doormaker throws the sun in
my face, and shows my eyes are brown,
you shan't take my word for it any more.
Word can stand down, leave by the door.

Study #2: After Rembrandt van Rijn

The guarantee is your willingness to pull faces
at yourself, and to let the weather do likewise.
No plastic surgery. No wrinkle cream. No hair dye.
Laugh lines, you mock the errors in the text.
The creases supertitle a slow crash, you explain.
This face is, you claim, with a golden flourish, *me.*
Well, in that case, who am I? Who is this writing
about you, making you up as I paint and repaint,
giving you the best lines, begging a few laughs?
Who is this dour worrier, but your dear guarantor?

Study #3: After Vincent van Gogh

God sank a mineshaft into me for a reason
I could not see in the coalmining district.
Coal dust ate the potatoes and the beer.
When a man slammed into a woman, dust
climbed in their heads and formed a cloud.
I carried away what was mine, and burned
black to blue, red to rose, yellow to gold.
I burn the stars and each becomes a galaxy.
I burn the fuse of flesh and my face bursts,
a wheel of fireworks, a vase of sunflowers.

Study #4: After Egon Schiele

Look at me, cock in my claws,
combcrimson from scratching.
Skinny arms kink round my back,
but can't kill the screeching itch.
The hand can't scratch its bone.
I snapped off the black arrows
but their featherless beaks stab
the katydids, their broken feet
scratch in the scattered flesh.
I stretch the canvas on the rack.

Study #5: After Frida Kahlo

I dream I am a wreck of a woman.

I am not grand like ruins, I am not a broken column.

I am the traffic accident on morning radio.

A bus handrail is sticking in my uterus like a huge thumbtack.

My collarbone hangs round my throat like a necklace.

I dream a monkey is picking up bits of my spine with his pale hands.

The monkey is carefully arranging me back together.

I hear the Professor say the monkey is the traditional symbol for lust.

My monkey is very gentle.

When he is finished, I will take him to my breast, and offer him my nipple.

Study #6: After Andy Warhol

Why be a man when you can be a brand?
Be copies the machine clicks to the market
to compete against other copies for a niche.
Not Nietzsche, but Benjamin. My fancy
education. My immigrant genes. My coming
out or not coming out, and other agony stories.
What are they but printings on silkscreens,
recognizable by the cock or the shock of hair?
I'm waiting, like a dupe, in a photo booth,
wondering if I should pay for duplicates.

Study #7: After Yasumasa Morimura

After strapping the tits to my cricket chest
and pulling the famous hair over my scalp,

I talk to Marilyn about loving Art, playing
dumb blonde, being closeted as one thing.

She answers, with a toss of her head,
her nipples erect as the stalk of a fruit,

Grab me. I demur. Soft from politeness
or fear or disbelief. She takes my hands

by the wrists, presses them between her
thighs. *Now we can talk about anything.*

now we can talk
about anything

Steady, My Gaze

Marie-Elizabeth Mali

—after Frida Kahlo's "The Little Deer"

This female body, bound
by want and hunt, rotting
flophouse, movable casket.

Bleeding, I run. A storm gathers.
Lightning antlers to the sea, trees
shudder leaves to the ground.

I will lock racks with God.
Find yourself another
woman to wound.

What man doesn't wreck
fights for each breath
until God finishes the job.

Not the Poet, Not Me

The Other Faces That You Meet

All My Wives
Cate Marvin

When I say my wives are cages, I don't mean I'm a bird.
Collapsible shelves, they hide their usefulness when not
in use. All my wives contain terrariums: terrible and fetid
atmospheres in which their salamander selves linger atop
damp rocks. Their hands are damp as the tissues they ball
in their hands, though none of my wives could make a fist,
not even if I asked, no, not even if I commanded them to,

an amusing idea I must someday revisit. My wives are like
the Small Mammal House at the zoo, their rooms kept dark
so visitors may view their nocturnal truths, that anonymous
wakefulness we sleepers do not care to know. None of my
wives are like lanterns, nor do their ribs sing with canaries.
It does my wives good to run my errands, for it keeps them
purposeful. I do not allow pockets on their shirts or skirts.

Theirs are unforgiving interiors. A woman's hands should
always be in plain sight, preferably chafed from dishwater
and cold. A woman's hands should be kept raw from wind
and sewing. When I want my wives to come out, I turn off
the lights and crouch to listen as they compare me: *Who do
I smack more often? Whom shall I take for my queen?* They think
I take pleasure in belaboring this decision, yet to think of it

is to imagine I might some day purchase a book I've never
desired to read. When I snap the lights on, they scatter like
roaches. Why read when there are so many worried brows
upon which to set the delicate glass of my gaze down? One
of my wives petitioned, once. One of them dared to cry.
They've tried to make me sad with their eyes. Let them try.
I would rather buy a hat, a walking stick, move alone within

my chamber, pose before my mirror. I do not need a queen,
I do not like tantrums. At times, I shudder, alone in my bed,
when I consider how their desires must churn like the onset
of inclement weather. They could be one, she could be one-
hundred. I just saw her shadow skulking down the walk. She's
drunk, as usual. Her shakes, her heart-murmurs, her general
unease. Pity the creature. She has a disease. If it gets worse,

I'll be forced to consider treatment. All my wives have four
legs each. What we call arms may as well be legs, so it seems
to me as I kneel behind each, not knowing one from the other,
only their asses' moon-curves aglow in lamplight. With such
anonymity, we are pleasured. It would not do for them to undo
the tiny latches, the wire doors to their cages. It would not do
to lift the lids of their terrariums. Something untoward might

escape, roam the grounds. For then I should be afraid to walk
alone at night, my new hat atop my clean head, walking-stick
in hand, as I move onward, staking out crevices, damp places
that lock my eyes: the fragrant earth I move atop my inheritance,
the herd of them breathing behind me in the dark. At the thrill
of their whispers, I stick my stick into the ground, turn on my
boot's heel. My wife, on her four legs, waits quietly in the hay.

Anthropologist Dreams
Rachelle Cruz

I want to curtain
her voice and body,
reveal her
cage of sin.
Screech-owl,
harpy of want,
she calls me in dreams
sweaty and disturbed.
Population of ghosts.
I always run after her.

Half-clad Lilith.
Her genealogies of lust
house my pleasure
in measuring
deformity.
Monsters unfold
on my sterile table.
Thief of seed.

In her thatched
dwelling,
above the trees,
she lifts a finger
from a woven plate
frayed at the sound
of stolen cries.

For every good woman,
gasp and teach

your children.
For every good man,
heed this warning.
I want to trap
her body of ruin.

Emboss her name
in every encyclopedia
of maladies,
symptoms
destructive to mankind.
Tame her,
name her mine

Aunt Rose Baptizes the Greens
Derrick Harriell

Your uncle Pete done been gone for couple days now,
sister May say brother Jenkins seen him shooting pool
down where them fast women suck bankruptcy
out weak men. Brother Jenkins was down that way
preaching the word, but swear Pete was preaching
a black dream to a red bone. This morning I made catfish,
expecting him to bust the door down,
complaining how Evelyn can't cook an egg
how her coffee stale as her morning loving.
I even left the back door unlocked.

But I spoke to sister Mitchell on the prayer line
and she say sometimes you got to help a man
find his way home. Cook his favorite thing, crack
a few windows. Put on his favorite dress, play
some Otis Redding. Go head and line the table
with pecan pie and Black Label. And if his ass still gone
drop some salt pork in them greens, unlock the front door.

Autumn Somewhere

Leigh Phillips

Dear Eleanor,

There are pianos in you.
They are threatening to shatter together.
They are threatening to shatter into God.

This is the letter I should have written in June of 1974. I know what you're holding.
I can hear the song of you slipping into an overcoat, letting your chignon spill
its curls to your neck. Rivers and rivers: I can hear great things. A novel of flesh
called "You, Appearing." On the threshold. In a door frame. The Arrivant, again
and again. Enter, to me. Trembling on the stoop of flesh. "Who is there, yes and
come in."

No.

This letter I will burn before I ever let it touch you. Nothing should ever hurt. I
want you to tend to the roses, sift bags of potting soil and sunlight, taste John's
lips, arrive over and over. The letter I will writes sounds like this:

Dear Eleanor, how are you? I am fine. The weather here has been a delight and
my days are filled with years. My years are full of shimmering and my body is a
lake of lost things. Over years, I have written books and taken nightly riverwalks.
I have collected maps, postcards, and a drawer of antique thimbles. I have a
collection of clocks, they all ring differently.

Dear Eleanor, bells and birds. Time? It is time to turn to you in a dream of 1976
and say. This letter will not survive. My other words will live, but these will not.
I love you. Some words just have to be destroyed. Angel, I am leaving Flagstaff.
Soon I'll be an Angel, too.

You're my certain slant of sunlight. To be older is to shiver. My hair pours a silver faucet, running with a faster I. I'm coming. Do you ever wonder who remembers? This summer, winter. So many sweaters. I still smell you sometimes when no one's looking. In the dark, the moon glances the bridge of your nose on the floorboards.

John, please kiss Eleanor's bridge so I can sleep and be beautiful tomorrow. Tomorrow I thought I'd do some writing. My hands shake so holding is often very difficult. These are the winters in me. I am so warm.

Sunlight, my—

Daisy

billy they don't like you to be so free
Mary Hammerbeck

threading years bright fabric in the grand market place
billy watches him counting his fingers, thinking cry

when they're falling down honey all around you

tips her head back to see nothing's clear squinting
memory catching, slipping all her bones remember

there was a time she slept through whistles, roosters

on the border radio Warren Zevon pleads *carmelita*
hold me tighter, I think I'm sinking down

on the outskirts of town, strung-out, lost on some

billy feels right alone like a cowgirl on a fence
trying to decide one of many lives she'd loved best

straw in her teeth, feeling mean, playing solitaire

again seeing him like an overdose little to no
control over the sink-sink from heart to fingertips

her kicking dust around foot forward, away, up in a cloud

what've you got to lose, billy americana, one-eye-open
sleeper, writing your poems on trains, dreaming restless

just cuz you don't like his words *in any way, shape or form*

he can give you diez reasons or less why you should
spend the north winters in his rooms deep sleeping

número uno, pointing, billy love is need and need is love

número dos, thumb out, you can't catch this feeling easy
& billy can't shake the thought of all the footprints it took

número tres, three splayed out, laid down like money

you remember the size of his eyes when you wake up wide
keeps telling billy things she's tried to forget sundowns & sunups

like rose gardens rushing in all petals and thorns opening

& closing his lids there's tears snaking down dry country cheeks
billy sees it like Angel y Diablo him having come after her like this

Clairvoyant
Gillian Devereux

I know this is all fake, and yet I believe.
Even the most intelligent among us wants
to know the future. Some obvious trick
works the act—a stage trap, a gypsy switch,
an audience plant. No one this pretty sees
the unknown. A tired, listless audience

crowds around me, caked in dust and misery.
They're desperate for rain, for work, for magic.
They're desperate for a charm to halt the dark.
I'm desperate too, for this girl who pretends
she has all the answers, who poses on stage,
her gown molded to the curve of her body.

The fabric skims skin and bone, frames the slope
between her breasts, and then, suddenly, falls open
to reveal a naked thigh. I can't remember
how I got here or where I'm headed. I can't move
beyond the shape of her face, smooth and cold
like a crystal ball. I want to help her con

these farmers and railroad men, help her read
their minds, their fears. It's done with mirrors
in some shows, but in others the girl takes
a partner who speaks to her in a private code,
all his words chosen and deliberate, all his
syllables heavy with some hidden meaning.

—Clean—

Matthew Guenette

There was an octopus in the fish
tank nicknamed Vishnu. There were managers
like lifeguards in their lifeguard chairs watching over
busboys in their busboy wilderness.
There were shadows of customers still
sticking to the tables that had
to be unstuck with lemon juice. When a customer
dropped her lobster, time seizured so
I turned to my daydream where
the restaurant wasn't
a superfund site. There was a simple code: you could ignore
the schedule & not punch out for breaks
& take two hour breaks & steal beer from the coolers
& get stoned on the dock

AS LONG AS YOU COVERED
FOR EACH OTHER AND KEPT THE DINING ROOM UNDER
CONTROL.

        & when a busboy was cleaning a table
his hands should resemble a hummingbird's
wings. & when the condiments were being organized
a skilled busboy should spin the ketchup & shakers
like pistols before holstering them in the tray. Only then in the customer's
mind would a table really be clean.

Corpus
Leslie McGrath

> *If you can bear it so, be dead*
> *among the dead. The dead are occupied.*
> —Rainer Maria Rilke

After they washed my body
and threaded my arms through the sleeves
of a dress I'd bought in the thirties
in a Cuernavaca market, they looped a rosary
around my folded hands. A bloom
from the bougainvillea is tucked behind my ear.
I am dressed for church; I am beautiful
in death. Oh, the perfume of my hands
rises from me like prayer. I am gone, yet here
I lie waiting for the man
to come for me, to wrap and box me,
to burn what's left. Unusable,
this brittle spine, these still feet.
Unusable, these folded hands,
hands that tended, arranged,
wiped clean floors cleaner still,
hands that chose the melon,
sliced and served it, threw out the rind—
the unusable rind.

Doomsayer

Luke Johnson

It's doom and gloom, same doom and gloom
down decades. You see these buzzards coming
to roost on streets where pricks like me tell you
the truth? Take your picture, go on and smile.
I'll flip the bird and walk. And soon, too soon,
it'll all go blank. You think I'm the one who's crazy?
Revelations. The time is now and when
the cock crows, when God's almighty balls drop,
find me in the gutter with light. You're gone.
We're nothing, just flies buzzing dumb over
a universal pile of trash, big ol' black rats
on sewer-pipes scuttling to Armageddon, sniffing
the napalm air and twitching the end of our tails.
You know it's only God can love a rat.

Dwarf with Bottle

Curtis Bauer

Can you blame me, really, for sitting
where they tell me to, and alone
at the table in the middle of all attentions,
like mine all on the bottle I want, the one
they won't give me, its neck a lonely mouth
never closing, but stopped, silenced
by lips, like mine wanting a kiss, not
of the wine but the love wine gives
back in the mouth's embrace? Big
thoughts get caught in the blur
of its round mouth. I am disgusted
by the artificial flowers. This coffee,
this hard donut I'm given disgraces me.
I've been beaten by men like those
in the diner booth smoking, for asking
for a smoke and not laughing
when they laughed. Their good
women stay quiet, smile, sing hymns
in the choir on Sundays. I want to drink
big, but I won't drink with them.
I don't love them. Just their height.

Etude

Sandy Longhorn

After my daughter learned to dance, I called
her *Stepping Water*. She walked with that much grace.
Some days I watched her test the law of gravity—
the wind her patient lover. With a threat
like that, I only did what any mother
would do. I weighted her with gems and coins
sewn in the hems of her long scarves and skirts.
Earthbound, my wounded kite, she would not be consoled.
When I stroked her hair, warm from gathering
the sunlight falling thick as rain through her window,
she no longer pressed her head into my palm—
once her sign of sure forgiveness. Now she pulls away.
I watch her stretch her liquid limbs.
I check the seams of silk for evidence of wear,
numbering my days in the time it takes
a thread to fray. In my nightmares, she gifts
the hills with her bounty-weight as she twirls
and twirls, until all that's left is silk.

The Facial Reconstructionist has Cocktails with the Girls
Jacqueline Jones LaMon

I've always had this thing for clay, to cup
my hands around a sphere, allow my fingers'

strength to grope toward definition. I know
there is an art to this, despite the grayness

of my walls. When the cranial remains lie
in state before me, I play *The Lark Ascending*,

let my mind know dawn and flight. Vaughan
Williams and I mold the timing of rise, the hover

preceding the soar. After work, my girlfriends ask
no questions of me. They stare at my hands,

inspect my cuticles for hangnails and fingernails
unkempt, survey the end of the bread that I touch.

They don't ask how I can wade my way through gore,
question unclaimed bones, mold parentheses around

a flesh I'll never know. This victim was a man-child.
I contemplate tissue thickness near his nasal spine,

the skin shade I will choose, the social construction
of race. I have another Cosmo. I think about his eyes.

The Gospel According to Lucas

Paula Bohince

The day's meanest pleasure:
threading worm after worm, entire
length and breadth,
onto our hooks—
souls hardened, visible at last
beneath translucent flesh.

This, and the praise my boss offers
as payment, calling me son,
goddamning my gifts,

while the fish, experts
in the discipline of water, the element
we borrow, fell for our tricks,
landing pathetic,
heavy in the basket between us:

the bluegill we should have sent back,
easy between our hands,
bluegill we will not eat
or admire.

Our lines cast out softly
from the furred edge of sedge, algae,
my intent to be a good man
filled with mercy

erasing as evening overwhelms,
as the argument within myself increases
in sense and volume.

Graciela and the Song of One Hundred Names
Matthew Thorburn

The sun fell into the harbor and the fishermen
caught the last light in their nets. Now the sky darkens
for rain, the salt breeze blows in from the sea.
We sit knees to knees, Graciela and I, high in the hills
in her house with its open windows. *Who could be*
happier, she asks, *than the man with two feet*
snugged tight in his stirrups? She thinks it unwise
for a man to die on the same hill where he was born,
but I will always have the dust of this place
on my boots. Now the yellow boats knock
against the dock, and soon the colored lights of Havana
will blink on below us. I wish I had remembered
my guitar, something to calm my hands, and find myself
singing. *How I long to be that swaying boat,*
the shadow following that woman's body. I sang this
for Graciela once at the Casa de la Trova,
with Roberto my brother and his second-hand guitar.
He never had a pick so he let his nails grow long.
Portabales, what do you know, she says. *Anyone can sing*
of love. And you are an old man who still wears
his hat in the house. For this I have no answer
but to take off my hat, wait for the silence to slip down
on us, blue as the scarf Graciela carries to church
to cover her shoulders. She laughs, lets down
her dark hair with its two rivers of silver. Seeing Graciela
in moonlight, in starlight, I must remember
to keep breathing. She smoothes her dress, gives me
the look that says I know what you are thinking.
You are wrong, but that is alright. At the end
of each day I walk the cobbled streets of Havana,

past the beach littered with the bicycles of swimming boys,
to climb these hills. I cannot tell Graciela
I wish to grow old with her. She would only say
we are already old. Now she asks me to sing her
the song of one hundred names. *My name is Morning,*
my name is Two Blackbirds in Moonlight, I sing.
My name is Graciela of the Red Hills. And now she sings
to me, *My name is Portabales of the Dusty Boots.*
My name is Pockets Full of Centavos. If you wish
to dance, she sighs, still singing, *you better find someone else*
to finish this song. My heart fights with my blood.
It's late. We should turn on a light or light a candle.
But why? Now we are only our voices. Then her hands
find mine, and my lips. We dance. Now we are only our bodies.
We upset a chair, rattle the dishes on the table. *My name*
is Lemons Yellowing on the Lemon Tree. My name is Clouds
Tickled Pink by the Moon. Graciela, my name
is The Blue Sheet of Morning Hung Out to Dry.

Granola Jones Cooks for the Potluck
Gabriel Welsch

The neighborhood is made of mailboxes
built to mimic the houses they front.
No trees rise over twenty feet. Not one
life exults in a front yard.

Parking won't happen easily. Quiet
in the concentration, wheel rock
on a curb, men with longnecks
rubberneck and chew

in the backyard of blue smoke
and music rising like smog. Meet,
mingle, judge. Meet, mingle,
drift, drink. Mingle, judge. Judge,

drink. Eat a little. Drink more.
Ms. Jones recognizes a woman, Kara,
from the shelter. Her two kids often
watch her husband kick her legs

as she curls and screams on the linoleum.
Jones eats a deviled egg, one she made,
the bite sharp with too much tarragon.
At the smell of a man, her breath

is angel fire, a holy sword at her throat.
She knows at once the shout in her muscles
will pull and ache through her arms later,
the strain of lifting the earth to hold

it against her gaze, torrents of fire
at her bruised back. Kara's husband
puts an egg whole into his mouth,
Ms. Jones knows it will nourish his feet,

and she hears the crack of his jaw
working the egg, as if he can chew
forever, adept at grinding, a master
of breakage, and his kids she now sees

ghosting the swingset hemmed in weeds,
the only children here, their slender legs
a shadow blur when they run or arc
in the swings tethered still to earth,

and Jones wishes Kara her angel
in leather and rage to open her sky
and give her some hope of violence
to burn her square of earth clean.

Her Head Bowed
Diana Park

Let me show you a familiar scene of snow:
a small house alone in a land of covered hills
except one slope's the roof. It's early, the sky a certain blue.
The only light is a naked bulb in the kitchen
hanging over a table set with a bowl of soup
for a dying mother we can't see but feel—
the way the home's shadow reaches a woman standing still.
Her head bowed, her breath a cold globe
directed at the ground. She's praying for her mother
to get well or die soon. We can't be sure
but we know two simple things.

One, she is still breathing.
Two, no amount of saying or sighing can open the earth.

How many times have we looked at the ground and wanted to speak up?
This is how we age. This is snow.

Holes

Ivy Alvarez

I pressed the button. No one came. The police could not find me in the dark. They were also afraid of death...it might come for them instead. They waited behind a screen of trees, for the moon to uncover itself and silver the edges of their sirens, their dark cars. The pale pebbles in the driveway are left to imagine the river that used to wet them—they must tire of always staring up, sightless and at the mercy of everything. The police step on them. They creep only so close, but no closer. My son is dead on the ground. Someone close his eyes. But I am ignored in this as I have been with so many other things. His blood is cold now, blackening, drying up, stiffening the fabric of his jacket, soaking into the soil. There are holes in him I know nothing about, nothing to do with the boy I delivered to the world, my gift, small and pure. The dark is blue and cold. The trees conceal susurrations in their high skirts, branches uplifted like arms, wailing whispers...Black cars, dark scars, my son's open mouth, empty shotgun shells whistling smoke white dancing up and out

Homewrecker

Alison Pelegrin

You'll never see a diaper from me,
whether I'm the baby's daddy or not.
Just like your sister Janelle—on the pill
and suddenly knocked up. Giving it away,
seducing me with sobs to cover for
the river trash you're shacking with. Go on.
Go by your mama's and grow the little brat
on dumplings and venison gumbo.
Oh, to be a flea on the wall of your life!
I'd pay to pass through Killian again
and count the jokers you collect with three
in diapers and a job sweeping hair
at The Gossip Shop. You'll catch the breeze
of a thousand big rigs, I bet, dragging
those potluck kids across the tracks
to meet their relatives—no better than
a salesman with a suitcase full of junk.
This time the truth is better than my fantasy—
you sneaking home after a weekend spent
pussyfooting on Trey's pontoon boat
to find your clothes in garbage bags
and a vacant lot where our trailer used to be.
Around you, crew cut kids circle on their bikes,
all the while bolder as they pedal up the drive.
It would have been easier to throw you out,
but the prize for holding the harlot's card
is more than being oops-a-daisy pregnant.
It's stares that smack like sucker punches
everywhere you go. It's standstill time
and backstab talk sweating you through

errand trips to town. I hope you pass seasons
peering through fingerprints on glass
for the storm you know is coming and the man
you know ain't. Nothing but worries walking
in your mind. Well, worries and the thought
of me at the wheel steering our trailer
down the red clay drive and across Tickfaw River,
ringmaster leading the biggest elephant in the parade.
People thought it was a tornado—sirens,
and a double-wide speeding through the sky
to land a new life in Ascension Parish.
And really, where else could destiny deliver us?
Come Friday, I'll be sniffing out fresh meat
at the Bingo Palace while you hook up
with the first redneck to listen to your barstool lies.
I'll be swallowing the beekeeper's smoke,
feeding dogs off your grandmother's dishes,
bachelor again, and king of all,
until I find me a new queen, keep her
inside draping scarves over mismatched lamps.

Ice Jesus
John Hoppenthaler

And then there was Bernie Anderson,
who was my lab partner in high school bio.
He hung out with the heavy metal clique,
so when he etched a Manson-inspired cross
into his forehead we didn't think too much about it.
We kept dissecting worms and frogs and fetal pigs.
He passed me a note once asking if huffing
formaldehyde would get us buzzed. That winter,
because he wanted a stigmata bad but
couldn't will himself one, he broke an icicle
from the eave outside his bedroom window,
pounded it clean through his palm with a rubber
hubcap mallet, and sat at his desk while it melted.
Blood and water ran together everywhere.
When they released him from psychiatric care
he was more elusive than ever, hard
to figure but, sure as shit, his right hand showed
the mark and everyone allowed Bernie a certain
eerie credibility. Later that year he killed himself.
Somewhere—maybe it was an urban legend,
or one of those stories he loved by Poe or De Maupassant,
but he bought a trunk full of frozen blocks
from the Nyack Ice Company when his parents
left for three weeks in Spain, tied a rope
to the back rim of his basketball hoop, placed
the noose around his neck as he stood barefoot
on the stack, handcuffed himself behind his back,
then strangled as ice dissolved beneath his toes.
Had it rained or if, as he must have planned it,
he wasn't found until the dark stain dried

on blacktop, it might be mysterious still
how he died with no chair or ladder there,

and I'm sure he wanted that to be a secret.
He'd think his dying a failure. I wouldn't bring
this up now except for the fact that last week
I went to a friend's wedding. The reception
was at a Holiday Inn in Jersey, and I ditched
into the staging area to bum a choke
from a waiter. We smoked out on the loading
dock and there, on a sheet of plastic behind
the dumpster, a chef was hacking out an ice
sculpture of Jesus for the First Christian Church
of the Second World Dinner/Prayer Meeting
with a chain saw, a chisel, and a rubber mallet.
It was warm for late October. Jesus was sweating—
the chef, too, who was cursing and had just
decided to do the fine cosmetic work
in the walk-in freezer or else, he said, "Christ,
Jesus will end up in the storm drain.
It's a mystery to me," he muttered as he lit
a Lucky Strike, put out the wooden match
with a sizzle on the side of his creation,
"why anyone would want a melting Jesus
in the middle of their savory quiche tarts
and meatballs, but they're paying a freakin' fortune."
Funny how ice dilutes good bourbon just
enough if you drink it with a little urgency.
Let me buy you another;
could I have a cigarette? It's scary
when so much wells up at once.
Got a match? A lighter? Drink up already;
I think our next round is on the tender.

The Jerk

Jeffrey McDaniel

Hey you, dragging the halo—
how about a holiday in the islands of grief?

Tongue is the word I wish to have with you.
Your eyes are so blue they leak.

Your legs are longer than a prisoner's
last night on death row.

You're a dirty little windshield.

I'm standing behind you on the subway,
hard as calculus. My breath
sticks to your neck like graffiti.

I'm sitting opposite you in the bar, waiting
for you to uncross your boundaries.

I want to rip off your logic
and make passionate sense to you.

I want to ride in the swing of your hips.

My fingers will dig in you like quotation marks,
blazing your limbs into parts of speech.

But with me for a lover, you won't need
catastrophes. What attracted me in the first place
will ultimately make me resent you.

I'll start telling you lies, and my lies will sparkle,
become the bad stars you chart your life by.

I'll stare at other women so blatantly
you'll hear my eyes peeling,

because sex with you is like Great Britain:
cold, groggy, and a little uptight.

Your bed is a big, soft calculator
where my problems multiply.

Your brain is a garage
I park my bullshit in, for free.

You're not really my new girlfriend,
just another flop sequel of the first one,
who was based on the true story of my mother.

You're so ugly I forgot how to spell!

I'll cheat on you like a ninth grade math test.
Break your heart just for the sound it makes.

You're the *this* we need to put an end to.
The more you apologize, the less I forgive you.

So how about it?

Letter after Dismemberment
Alison Stine

Lover, I left you because you would not slip me
      into the squares of an ice tray,

           though I asked. I was considering a jar

of preserved lemons and watching television,
      though not really, and you wondered, aloud,

           if anyone had died on camera, by accident,

if that had been captured. Want flickered in me
      and fell as though from a great height.

           But it must have been earlier when it came

to me: seeing the neighbor man, perhaps.
      Our tenement windows cut into him like grids,

           exposing an arm, a finger. Such mystery,

the divided flesh, like a photograph spreading
      onto a page—the body so piecemeal. Or the closet,

           being punished in the dark of overcoats

and shoes. I drew my knees to my body.
      I became a smaller box, and when your arms

           first wrapped around me, later, in love,

what could I want to give you—to give any man—
        but the tightest hold? To keep you secret

                as a stone? Then I wanted to be the stone.

I found a man to kill me, and cut me up,
        one who wanted the body in inches, who

                dreamed in pixel. I became divisible.

Have you hoped for anything? Honestly,

                I do not remember. Not even that first

gutter of warmth when I saw the knife,
        not even the last, now that I am everywhere,

                in earth and in ash, in the stomach

of the one who swallowed me and then,
        when they killed him, sent him into the air

                in a chambered cloud, the flies that erupted

from his belly, spun with blood, the grass,
        the goats, the milk they gave. And somewhere,

                I am in a girl, lightly fingering her wrists, how

her hands fit around them, thumb to index,
        the pressure on the vein, the world encircled,

                trapped there, the pleasure rising,

and wanting to ask for it. Then asking.

Lexicons
Ash Bowen

On the steamer Mother taught us the only words
she said we needed to know:

Yes. More.

I pressed my tongue to their shapes,
held their sounds like cigarette smoke.

On Ellis Island, she said *Please*
was a worthless word, throw it away
like an old love letter. Answer their questions
softly:

Are you well? *Yes.*
Why did you come? *More.*

In our apartment I pushed my cheek to the cool squares
of the kitchen's black and white floor.

In the building's basement, boys found me
folding laundry, their tongues wet
with America, their hands full

of its money. Down the street, I touched the glass
of the candy case. The boys' sweeping hands

meant *choose.* At home, I unfolded the chocolate
from its foil. The boys called from the street below.
Mother stood but meant, *Go close the window.*

The Magician's Assistant
Philip Memmer

The first night he sawed me in half
I expected a trick—another girl

huddled in the stage-left end
of the polished cabinet,

waiting to poke out her toes
while I smiled, unworried,

from the opposite side.
Once we both were clear, I imagined,

he'd lift the rhinestone-handled saw
and slice the air between us,

faking the work it would take
to cut through a body.

But then he opened the golden lid
and there wasn't a trick, wasn't

a girl. Just pine boards,
splintered and bare. All the same,

when he took my hand
I climbed in. I'd seen his act

over and over, other chicks
in the same short sequined dress,

smiling at their own feet
from across the stage. As tricks go

it's hardly rare—we've all cheered
a man who wouldn't be sated

with a single cut, who'd slice a woman
in half, then halve each half again.

How did I grin through that pain?
A wave of his wand

and I was whole again. Scarless.
I didn't ask how. Six nights a week

for two years, he broke me apart,
put me together. *Just like new,*

he bragged—never pausing
even once to look—then took his bow.

Melvin's Story
Susan Elbe

A curse on your marriage and your life
she spat out at our wedding dance
when we refused to grease the gypsy's palm.

Blowing in with raw November clinging
to her woolen shawl, old-country
metal circling her nail-chewed fingers,

she shoved her basket toward us and when
we laughed her off, the wicked words
flew from her tongue like bats and folded

sooty wings inside us. Our first child, jar-eyed,
ocean-eyed, born blind. Our second, born
dancing to the Devil's tune, convulsive

puppet swallowing the pink fish of his tongue.
And these past 20 years, my wife's muscles
jerking in betrayal, her body in decline.

My curse, to witness and attend. You're thinking,
in a lifetime, bad things visit everyone.
You're thinking, superstition, but I'm telling you

words can be a darkness you fall into, the stub
of a candle in your fist. You know
there's no way out, but you light it anyway.

My Name is Quinn Margaret

Jeanne E. Clark

My sister wore a peignoir
From the time she was three. She knew
All the names for froufrou nightgowns
And the time of night when any woman,
As she said, who was truly a woman,
Puts up her hair. Lucy Electa was nylon
On the move, hair spray and cherry-
Painted toes hitching roads
Named Bluelick and Slabtown.

When I was born, summer curled
Tomato leaves dead brown.
I was named Quoin, after a man,
My father's Indiana uncle who wasn't a man,
Really. He brought carnations
And pictures of his second house in Mexico,
Always the parrots and young boys
Whose names I couldn't say.

I was born with weevils in my stomach.
I was born with wooden feet,
Or, as my mother says, pronating arches.
My legs knocked. She says
My job is harder,
To be smart instead of beautiful,
To know men like Nietzsche,
Words in which women like my mother
Find inspiration: *that storm*
Which does not kill you makes you happier.

So each day I work harder,
My pink hands pulling
The strings that make my bottom half go.
I learn the names for my puppet parts:
Pelvis, a basin, *knee*, which is the joint
Between the thigh and lower leg. *Heel*,
Back part, despicable person.
The *foot*, a group of syllables
Serving as a unit of measure in verse.

I walk a slant board.
I pick up marbles with my toes.
My hands work faster. My legs faster,
Get strong, get hungry,
These parts below my stomach,
The sounds they make:
Wood against wood, Ohio Blue Tips,
And their harder job: *to burn*,
As in the verb, to be on fire.

Necessary Knives
Tara Betts

—for F.V.

We turn our silver serrated grins
toward light, hungry enough to glint,
knowing we do not need to be fed.
We should rest in sheaths or glass cases
like sharp butterflies, willing to cut air
in flight but pinned in place, quiet and safe.

Instead, we greet dark caverns of deep pockets.
We feel the rush of a grip snatching us out,
ticking our spines into a straight long snick,
startling eyes wide. The warm blanket of meat,
raw and salty, can hold a kiss or surround us.

We cannot forget the taste, no matter how much
we've been cleaned, despite polish. A vigilant
infantry ready to separate and save, hoping
to smile and reflect moon glow when we leer
into the dark. We only flick open if we have
to flutter, not because we want to, we must.

Our Chef is Delicious
David Welch

When we first found him,

he was a poor creature who couldn't handle a paring knife,
    but that year in Tuscany did him well.

      He returned a devout palate.

A man of peculiar desire.
    Please note, he must be garnished with mint;

        chop finely, so, when rare, the meat bathes
        the cut leaf.

It was a long day when our chef committed himself
    to the fineries of flesh—

        the first drop of blood crowned the shaved
        Parmesan;

the bouillabaisse thickened.
    Loving the body for the body alone is bitter.

        He knew this, yes. He always thought parsley

the sprig of amateurs. At high temperatures
    his flesh will emit a faint, distinguished odor,

        but this is common

for roasts of his nature. Add Chianti just after the boil.
  That his lips were cracked with salt is no cause for concern—

    thirst is
    the first measure of longing. Open this.

Breathe a short while before we eat.

Parable: A Training Exercise
Carolina Monsiváis

—The Trainer

A woman waits for her husband to leave for work. The night shift. Though no one is sure what he does, he always leaves at night then the woman sneaks out to meet her lover. Sometimes they reside on an island, sometimes in two different cities connected by a bridge, there is always a crossing. And it is always night. One night she and her lover fight. He either throws her keys into the water or into the bushes. Sometimes he slashes her tires. What is certain is that she has forgotten her purse, she always forgets her purse. She doesn't have any money for the pay phone or a cab. Perhaps they are no longer running. And she doesn't know anyone she can call collect. If the story has been updated then she forgot her cell phone. In all versions she attempts to walk home. A man comes out from behind a bush or he follows her on the bridge. Either way he kills her. Just like that. There is always a picture in either chalk or black marker to go along with the lesson.

You are asked whose fault was it?

Something Might Be Gaining on You

Steven D. Schroeder

That's not my name, I told the neighbors
When I fell and they found me calling

Happy, that's my Dachsie mix,
Gone up sixteen years this Sunday.

Are you my son? If so, which one?
No, I named my sons James and Jacob

And James, the oldest, who stole my mail
Except the bills, so we're not speaking.

Though Doctor Blake made me promise
To take those pills, I flushed them because

He's a black. I looked back but couldn't see
The voice who whispered *Hello, Crazy Lee.*
Anyway, that's not my name.

The Tilted Knot
Carol Guess

Widowed both, when we finished sitting shiva we shared shy glances at Central Synagogue. I thought of her more than I should have, I know. They say the guilty return to the scene, but what of the innocent? For a time I stood accused because of my access to Rose Fishman's room. For thirty years I've cleaned apartments on Hester and Essex. Now all I see is that fishbowl room, bottles of perfume, pink towels askew. I found her strangled with her bathrobe belt. Thought I'd go to jail until a cop paused at the knot. Tilted up, as if she'd hung. Threads on the door where her garment was torn.

Waiting

Christopher S. Soden

> *…but in a sieve I'll thither sail…*
> —Shakespeare's *Macbeth*

I loathe the perpetual cycles of returning
to the tables every ten minutes measuring
water, coffee, carefully and endlessly
brewed tea, the miracle of steeping
and suffusion wasted on them. I loathe
the bloated stock traders and doctors
forever reaching for a glory beyond
their dreaming, crones I am obliged
to supplicate and revere. I cannot bear
the insult of feeding them, bringing
plates of herbs and lamb to provincial
dolts and bumpkins in three piece silks
and weaves older, more cunning
than their temples. How ridiculous they are.
The callas and jonquils drinking
from their crystal sleeves, carry the history
of procreation and destruction, breath
and transmutation in every cell, intuition
sharper than what passes for understanding.
Now a shoe store manager pretends
I am somehow derelict because I scratch
the hand that will not leave my thigh.
A receptionist shrieks because she has no
butter left on her plate. My mother gave me
the wry smile from all her mothers
before her, giving birth below
a tainted moon. It serves me well.
Gato no longer hesitates when I insist

on bussing a table myself. A trace of lipstick
or spittle on a napkin. An eyelash
or whisker floating in rosehip sorbet is all
I require. No portal is shut to me. No stream
inaccessible. You will sleep in ashes, awake
in a glacier. The goddess I serve is rapacious
and without peer. She will pilfer your spirit
with tallow and a thread of smoke.

What Happened at Work
Caki Wilkinson

When the door
swings open,
he's inside
smelling like
gasoline and hot
grass just cut,
and I smack
my rag
on the counter,
say, "Can I get
you something
or what?"

I'm already
sweating down
the back
of my blouse,
but I flick
my chin above
the muscle
of his cigarette
smoke, and blink
like Cleopatra,
or someone else,
someone ancient
and brave.

He says, "How's
your car,
does it idle, still?"

I say, "Buddy,
you're dodging
the problem,"
and I can see
his brains rattle
in his head
like loose change.

"I think I'll take
the special," he says.
I say, "It's liver;
you hate liver,"
then slide
a piece, brown
and dripping,
on the plate
in front of him.

Maybe he chews it;
I don't know.
I am turned
around, wiping grease
from my elbow
and trying
to smooth my hair
in the chrome
of the ice machine.

He knocks his fork
against his cup;
I can hear
it plink like
he wants me
to spin back, so
I don't. "Listen,"

he says, "I'm fryin'
catfish at the dock
and you should go."

"I got bad bug
bites as it is," I say,
looking over
my shoulder,
tightening
my apron strings,
and he says, "Jesus,
stop it will you,"
so I am quick
this time, glaring,
"Give me one
good reason."
"Because I dreamed
about two things
last night," he says,
"boiled peanuts
and your eyes,"

and it's funny
what's enough
sometimes.

Contextual Notes

Liz Ahl: "Submariner" was inspired by a news item about a letter (to his wife) recovered with the body of a Russian sailor who was trapped and died in the submarine Kursk in 2000. It led me to imagine submarine life and the question of how someone faces death.

Dan Albergotti: I was miserable at the time. I loved her, and she didn't love me. Waking up every day seemed like torment. I thought of Prometheus, chained to his rock, his liver pecked out by an eagle every day. Back then, I thought I'd never find a better metaphor for love.

Kazim Ali: When I think of Icarus, I always thought of him plummeting, wings on fire. Icarus had dared too much, dared to break the rules of his father, to seek for the sun, and would pay for the crime with his life. But what about Icarus the brave? The soaring and brilliant?

Maureen Alsop: "Leda's Flashback," written as a post-traumatic response, amplifies a mythic figure, Leda, underscoring the animal/supernatural power deriving from experience of shock. In the Greek myth the god Zeus disguises himself as a swan and rapes or seduces Leda. The poem grapples with Leda's anxiety following the encounter.

Ivy Alvarez: "Holes" forms part of a novel-length sequence of poems about a man who shoots his wife, his son and then himself, leaving a daughter as the sole survivor. The speaker in this prose poem is the mother, who has just witnessed her son getting shot.

Francisco Aragón: On September 9, 2001, *The New York Times* featured a front page article describing the plight of Liu Minghe, wrongfully convicted to face death in China. His story inspired this poem. I wanted to challenge myself to combine my own language, language from the news, and some French poetry in translation. My strategy was collage.

Cynthia Arrieu-King: Setsuko Hara spent years as Japan's most beloved leading actress. Never married, she was nicknamed "The Eternal Virgin." In 1963, after the death of the director who made her famous, she called a press conference, declared she had never liked acting, then promptly withdrew from public life to the small village of Kamakura. She has not been interviewed or photographed since.

Rane Arroyo wrote the following note in his original submission of this poem: "I'm well known for using persona—from a grieving sister to a drag queen to historical figures like Ponce de Leon to car thieves."

Elizabeth Austen: I grew up Catholic, and as a child I absorbed the idea of Eve as trouble-maker. Reimagining this story from another point of view—one in which the apple wants to be eaten ("known"), and Eve is hungry for awareness—was part of a larger inquiry into the place of women in society.

Corrina Bain: Medusa is a mythological figure who allows us to think about heroism, gender, and beauty. I am drawn to her story as a way to conceptualize the defilement of the sexual object. The origin story given here is my own invention.

Sally Ball: "Memory" departs from notes Isaac Newton kept as a student under the heading *Some Philosophical Questions*. Often in these notes, you can see the empiricist grappling with the intuitionist.

Tony Barnstone: "The Werewolf of Green Knolls" was inspired by case studies of women who thought they were werewolves and became violently hypersexual. I was interested in the internalized fear of female agency that would make a woman need to imagine she was demon-possessed in order to be able to express her sexuality.

Curtis Bauer: I'm interested in the image. I found this photo reproduction from the '50s in the *New York Times* and wanted to write a sort of ekphrastic poem. This one, a dwarf sitting in the middle of a diner, everyone looking at him, seemed to need to voice for the man being watched.

Shaindel Beers: Calypso is a goddess in *The Odyssey* who imprisoned Odysseus on Ogygia. She promises him immortality if he stays with her, yet he longs to return home to Penelope. There are many poems from Penelope's point of view, but I wanted to tell Calypso's story as I imagined it.

Carol Berg: When Ophelia and Hamlet meet in scene three, the tension between them is high. Hamlet tells Ophelia he did love her, and then he tells her he did not. Ophelia goes mad and drowns in the river. Perhaps I wanted Ophelia to feel an intimacy or love one last time.

Tara Betts: "Necessary Knives" was inspired by a knife collection. I wondered what the knives might say about potentially being used for violence, much like guns in Nas' "I Gave You Power" and Organized Konfusion's "Stray Bullet." I imagined that they might crave cutting, but would feel remorse or anxiety.

Tamiko Beyer: Keshav Jiwani left Pakistan to escape religious and anti-gay persecution. In the U.S. for 17 years without papers, he received deportation orders after 9/11 when men from Muslim and Arab countries were forced to register with the government. He applied for asylum; I never found out whether his application was ever accepted.

Joelle Biele: Cupid fell in love with a beautiful girl named Psyche. Making her promise never to light a lamp and look at him, Cupid marries her and visits her every night. Psyche's jealous sisters tell her she married a snake. Psyche lights a lamp and looks at him. He awakens and flies away.

Paula Bohince: My poems are situated within a collection that concerns itself with a murder. Though three men conspired and committed the crime together, these persona poems illustrate each man's specific point of view. The poems allude to the New Testament gospels in which the apostles recount Christ's death.

Shane Book: The persona in this poem is a figure newly arrived in a nation undergoing a moment of historical change. He/she is an observer, who may be construed as watching and noting unfolding political events, on behalf of a larger powerful nation whose motives are, to say the least, impure. Or not.

Ash Bowen: "Lexicons" is a poem born out of an experience I had when teaching a student who had come from China to study in the U.S. She recounted how she'd felt like a child because she felt as though she had to learn everything all over again.

Traci Brimhall & Brynn Saito: The speaker in "The Watchtower" is a fabricated persona, which we imagine to be a ruined city. At one time we were both writing about ruins, so we started a collaborative project. Each poem begins with a place in the abandoned city that speaks to a girl who is wandering through the ruins.

Meghan Brinson: The persona was inspired by the Alphonse Mucha painting referenced in the title. I wrote the poem the summer before I moved cross-country from my family. Sensing that part of my life was over, I finally sympathized with Hamlet's story, particularly the blonde, female version Mucha painted.

Jericho Brown: Diana Ross and the Supremes were accused of not being "black enough" in the 1960s. By the time of the riots that followed the assassination of Dr. Martin Luther King, Jr., their hit "Reflections" had made it to #2 on the pop chart.

Derrick Weston Brown: This poem is part of a larger series that explores the voices and stories of The Sweet Home Men from Toni Morrison's novel, *Beloved*. I used the haiku to capture Paul D's tenderness during a revealing moment when Sethe uncovers just how deep slavery has wounded her.

John Canaday: Robert Oppenheimer was the scientific director of the Los Alamos Laboratory, where the first nuclear weapons were designed. Before the war he once said, "My two great loves are physics and desert country. It's a pity they can't be combined." The poem is set shortly after the bombings of Japan.

Kara Candito: Federico García Lorca was a Spanish poet, dramatist, and friend of the Surrealist painter Salvador Dalí. When Franco's forces took over Spain in 1936, Dalí swore allegiance to the fascist government. Lorca did not and was executed by Nationalist militia on August 19, 1936. His body has never been found.

James Caroline: While working on a manuscript of poems and prose based on rock and blues culture, a friend handed me a biography on Chet Baker. I was mesmerized. Already familiar with his beauty, voice, and skill as a musician, I felt I had to look at his death to go back through his life.

Tina Chang: The Empress Dowager, who was also known as *Tzu Hsi, Cixi,* and the *Empress Dowager of the West,* was the last empress of China, and ruled from 1861 until her death in 1908. Issues of femininity and power were at the heart of my interest in inhabiting her voice.

Ching-In Chen: I had been searching for the right metaphor while writing a choreopoem about coolies—Asian indentured laborers sent around the world after the slave trade was abolished. I found it walking by two men cooking in a food truck in Queens, New York.

Jeanne E. Clark: Quinn Margaret's persona took over as narrator for *Ohio Blue Tips,* my first collection. I needed a character through which I could shape some autobiographical material—growing up in a Midwestern prison town or was it an imprisoning Midwestern town—and through which I could imagine others' stories inside the prison walls.

Kevin Clark: At the non-violent 1977 Seabrook nuclear plant protests, the guardsmen wanted to split the men from the women. My wife often describes how "Elizabeth" suggested the protestors strip and sit in concentric circles, women on the outside. The guardsmen retreated because they couldn't bring themselves to touch naked women.

Allison Adelle Hedge Coke: "Memory" is a repetitive persona character in the verse-play *Blood Run* written in portrayal of historical memory of the Indigenous mound city the poems are in testament to. These persona poems were originally used in actual testimony in hearings petitioning to preserve the world history site. The case was successful.

Don Colburn: This poem began—and ends—with the *New York Times* photo of a jetliner's emergency landing in the Hudson River. Assuming a passenger's persona was liberating to me as a longtime newspaper reporter; it allowed me to discover an imagined but accurate truth, based on facts in *The Times.*

Elizabeth J. Colen: General Edwin Walker was a right-wing, once-candidate for Texas governor (1962) and the target of a foiled assassination attempt that took place April 10, 1963, at Walker's home in Dallas. The shooter was eventually alleged to be Lee Harvey Oswald. This poem is told from Oswald's point of view.

Steven Cordova: In "Confessions," invisibility is the mask through which I worry about getting older, about standards of beauty, etc. Thus I reference *The Invisible Man* loosely.

In his novel, H. G. Wells dares to imagine a monster—a protagonist of great cruelty and selfishness—long before he renders himself invisible.

Eduardo C. Corral: During the California Gold Rush (1848–1855), as many as 25,000 Mexicans migrated to mining regions in California. Some of these migrants possessed superior expertise and mining skills, which provoked envy and anger from Anglo miners. Envy and anger soon turned to violence. At least 170 Mexicans were lynched in California between 1848 and 1860.

Nina Corwin: In the New Testament, Salome is depicted as a dangerous seductress who asks for John the Baptist's head after her "Dance of the Seven Veils" before King Herod, her step-father, and his court. Varied accounts depict Salome as an innocent pawn for a scheming mother, a victim of Herod's illicit appetites, a femme fatale whose affections the prophet has spurned.

Barbara Crooker: I have long admired the work of Frida Kahlo, so seeing her retrospective at the Philadelphia Art Museum moved me enormously, especially since I'd seen the Julie Taymor movie not too long before. This poem wanted to be written in her voice, not mine, and I was happy to oblige.

Rachelle Cruz: "Anthropologist Dreams" is located in my reimagined version of the 1904 St. Louis World's Fair. Here, the anthropologist seeks to capture the Philippine mythological creature, the aswang, in order to name her "otherness." This poem is part of a larger project. I'm drawn to the psychological landscape of constructed spaces of spectacle, especially the World's Fair.

Kevin Cutrer: I see this speaker as a middle-aged woman in a small town in southeast Louisiana. Growing up there, I noticed that whenever someone put another person down, there was invariably someone else to take up for the slighted. There was always someone encouraging us to love each other.

Chad Davidson: "The *Kama Sutra*'s Banished Illustrator" began as an exercise in which I tried to describe the movements of a friend as she sketched a female nude. I remember envying the ease with which her hands floated over the paper, wanting to render that dynamism in a "third-order" portrait: words illustrating hands illustrating the human form.

Nik De Dominic: George Maledon was a hangman who lived in Arkansas in the late nineteenth century. Although Maledon is a real historical figure, the voice and his son, Abbot, are creations. Through them, I wanted to explore the complexities of a relationship that hinges on a particular kind of work: killing men.

Madeline DeFrees: I learned about the whalers' wives on a whale watch in Truro, Massachusetts—how they were mostly left at home, hoping their husbands didn't drown. Later I found written accounts, and began writing poems in their voices. Sometimes I'd come across something so good, I'd have to use it verbatim.

Brian Komei Dempster: This poem imagines the voice of my grandmother, Chiyoko, after her husband, my grandfather Archbishop Nitten Ishida, was forcibly removed from their church home and imprisoned in various undisclosed internment camps. During their years of separation, letters censored by the U.S. government were their only means of communication.

Danielle Cadena Deulen: In *The Odyssey*, the Lotus-eaters give three of Odysseus' men "lotus plants to eat, whose fruit, / sweet as honey, made any man who tried it / lose his desire ever to journey home." This poem is spoken from the perspective of the forgotten wife of one of those men.

Gillian Devereux: The impetus for this poem came from the film *Nightmare Alley* starring Tyrone Power. Power plays a bitter con man who tries to seduce a carnival mentalist into revealing her trade secrets. My speaker finds the clairvoyant's secrets equally fascinating, but his obsession is fueled by love rather than greed.

T. M. De Vos: The speaker in this piece is one of the werewolves, a symbol for someone transformed by rage. I wrote it to document the moment when the claws retract, the teeth are unbared, and the warring creatures just want to be comfortable again.

LaTasha N. Nevada Diggs: "Today on Maury" was one of several poems I wrote about talk shows. Written in the voice of one young woman on *The Maury Show* requesting a paternity test, my goal was to explore self-esteem, loneliness, emotional abuse, discomfort, and body issues. I wanted the poem to speak about her position and how a show like such exploits rather than heals.

Liz Dolan: Elizabeth Barrett Browning was a very popular poet in the late nineteenth century. Forbidden by her father to wed, she eloped with the equally famous poet Robert Browning. As an adolescent I loved her poem, "How Do I Love Thee?" As I read a recent biography of her, I was intrigued by her interest in the occult, which my poem reflects.

Chris Dombrowski: The italicized passage that opens "Bill Monroe" is lifted from a live recording. Intrigued by The Father of Bluegrass' notion that a song played with skill and passion could do its listener some good, I wanted to hear more of what he might have said—so I listened.

Jehanne Dubrow: "In the fever-world, my dearest" comes from my book, *From the Fever-World*, a series of fragments written in the voice of an imaginary Yiddish poet. The character of Ida Lewin—a woman stranded between modernity and tradition—was born out of my research at the US Holocaust Memorial Museum, in Washington, DC.

Denise Duhamel: Born Vickie Lynn Hogan in 1967, Anna Nicole Smith rose to fame as a model for Guess? jeans and *Playboy* magazine. Her marriages, weight issues, addiction, and the death of her son served as tabloid fodder.

Camille T. Dungy: What a person says is often a distillation of feeling. I might feel something that pride, experience, or circumstance would prevent me from saying. "How

She Didn't Say It" draws on the jazz great Ella Fitzgerald's interviews and lyrics to create a collage that reflects the thoughts I imagine she must have felt but could not say.

Cornelius Eady: My good friend (and Till scholar) Harriett Polack sent me a newspaper article about the fate of Emmett Till's casket, and as I wrote, it became clear that the persona desired to be the casket, which held the aspects of a mother who has lost a child.

Carolina Ebeid: Abel is one of the most passive characters in literature, only being acted upon by Cain. Here I attempted a midrash, which is the Hebraic method of investigation into a dark passage in Scripture, one that would restore an active voice from beyond the grave to this young shepherd.

Susan Elbe: This is a childhood memory; Melvin is a relative who married in the mid-1950s. I vaguely remember the wedding, but I do remember the gypsy. Back then, gypsies were still thought of as exotic, and they were feared. Melvin and his wife did experience all the hardships stated in the poem.

Kelly Madigan Erlandson: In 1911, after the last of his family had died, and decades after his tribe was thought to be extinct, an aboriginal "wild man" walked out of the remote canyon where he had been living in northern California. He came to be called Ishi, which meant *man*, after refusing to say his own name.

John Olivares Espinoza: Orson Welles (1915–1985) was an American filmmaker who, at the age of 25, directed *Citizen Kane*, bringing movies to the modern age. In retaliation, William Randolph Hearst crippled Welles' nascent career. Welles never fully recovered from this topple. The idea of peaking early is the basis for this poem.

Kathy Fagan: *Lip* is primarily interested in exploring voices—through personae, monologues, portraits, and arias—that are subversively female. As poets know, Ovid provides a rich source of such characters in his *Metamorphoses*. In *Lip*, Medea joins St. Joan, Penelope, and other anonymous women in a little opera of anger.

Blas Falconer: This poem was inspired by the story of the first documented murder in Puerto Rico. The Taíno people killed Diego Salcedo to determine if the Spaniards were immortal. The story appealed to me because it captured both a sense of loss and empowerment one might feel in discovering that someone is human and fallible.

Jennifer Fandel: While listening to the Writer's Almanac, I heard the details that became the epigraph—and the dramatic situation—for this poem. I could sense so much emotion in the last moments of Andersen's life, and that led me to imagine the forever-waiting lover whose voice was frozen *for decades* on the page.

Annie Finch: I wrote "Coy Mistress" as a college student. I had been assigned by my poetry professor, John Hollander, to write an answer to a famous poem. When a boyfriend read Andrew Marvell's poem to me, I felt inspired to write my answer. I recall that it came to me very quickly.

Kathleen Flenniken: John Archibald Wheeler, eminent American theoretical physicist, interrupted his academic career to participate in the development of the atomic bomb at the Hanford site in southeastern Washington state. Even before the startup of B Reactor, Wheeler had anticipated the accumulation of "fission product poisons."

William Robert Flowers: The persona I chose was Rebecca, Isaac's wife from Genesis. I wanted in this poem to explore the notion of lasting trauma, of psychological damage in Isaac, to consider him as a man, rather than a figure, and found myself speaking from behind his wife's veil.

Vievee Francis: The Venerable Bogwang (Lee Sang-chul) was a monk with a tragic story to tell. His life, complicated by political violence, was a kind of "fish story." However, nothing whimsical rested in his account; he wanted only to be believed. Here, I explore veracity and memory as a haunting.

Gregory Fraser: Common assumptions typically situate scientists in sterile laboratories, cut off from social and domestic life. Persona poems, by giving voice to widely unrecognized facets of other people's lives, can wake us from our presumptive slumbers, and make interesting figures such as Galileo and his daughter come to life afresh.

Todd Fredson: Boris Pasternak wrote one of my favorite poetry collections, *My Sister— Life*. Its lush emotional tones extend from Pasternak's landscapes. His contemporary, Marina Tsvetaeva, explained, *. . . trees at a meeting. Over Pasternak's Square, it is they that are the ringleaders. Whatever Pasternak might write, it is always the elements, not the characters.*

Jeannine Hall Gailey: "When Red Becomes the Wolf" is a playful way of looking at the persona of Red Riding Hood. "Lupae" is old Roman slang for "prostitute" as well as the Latin for "female wolf." When Red puts on the grandmother's fur coat, she completes her transformation into ravenous wolf.

Martin Galvin: My interest in poetic voices led me to the role of the home-keeping wife of a Civil War soldier. The irony in the soldier's complaint and her response provide a wee bit of humor; the tone might throw some quiet light on women's role in historical wars.

Molly Gaudry: Someone once told me Picasso stole the *Mona Lisa* and, scared, threw it in the Seine and ran away. After reading the line "I can steal her heart like a bird's egg" (Jeannette Winterson, "The Poetics of Sex"), I began writing about a ruthless Picasso who steals young girls' hearts.

Frank Giampietro: "Like This" is part of a series written in the voices of world record holders in which I wholly imagine their biographies to explore the emotional upheavals that drive people to strive for seemingly trivial notoriety. Via characters like *Monsieur Mangetout*, my own humble artistic ambitions are reflected and revealed.

Rodney Gomez: The persona in this poem is a pocho who is observing the scene captured in the John Valadez painting *Car Show* (2001). I was trying to imagine how, being unable to speak the vernacular of the cholos in the painting, he would nevertheless be able to communicate.

Rigoberto González: "Gila" is a poem inspired by the undocumented border-crossings from Mexico to the U.S. There is at least one fatality a day because of the heat and very few stories of survival, though living through heat is an everyday victory for at least one desert dweller—the gila monster.

Henrietta Goodman: As my first marriage ended, I fell in love. My Gretel poems arose from my feeling that the new relationship was both illicit and innocent. The following year, at the Boyden Wilderness Writing Residency, I lived, like the witch, alone in a cabin deep in the woods. And so the lines between good and bad, vulnerability and threat, blurred.

Arielle Greenberg: Written, while pregnant, in the ghostly voice of Katie Smith, who lured Sarah Brady, nine months pregnant and found through an online baby shower registry, to her home, faking pregnancy, then attacked Sarah to keep the baby for her own. Sarah fought back and ended up killing Katie. True story.

Jennifer Gresham: The Biblical prophet Daniel was skilled in dream interpretation, most famously for his prophecy of the Babylonian King Nebuchadnezzar's descent into madness. Success brought him the love of kings but also a host of adversaries, ultimately leading to his imprisonment within a den of lions, though he was untouched.

Sarah Grieve: Martha Jane Cannary Burke, better known as Calamity Jane, was a frontierswoman in the second half of the nineteenth century. Pop culture texts tend to depict her as crass and uncouth. Calamity had a reputation for stretching the truth and so her "relationship" with Wild Bill Hickok is highly contested.

Gail Griffin: Hecuba was the wife of King Priam of Troy. The Greek attack on Troy, facilitated by the famous "Trojan Horse" ruse, destroyed the city and her family. Hecuba often appears as a figure of maternal devastation; I chose her to represent my own sense of (non-maternal) loss as I age.

Matthew Guenette: The busboy persona is both an *experience* (for I was an actual busboy once, for four years, way back when) and an attempt at an *achieved experience* (an ironic resistance to the indignities of unskilled labor and the zombie hordes/consumption of a deep-fried tourist economy).

Carol Guess: "The Tilted Knot" is part of a series responding to "The Nutshell Studies of Unexplained Death": crime scene dioramas created by Frances Glessner Lee and photographed by Corinne May Botz. In my forthcoming book, *Doll Studies: Forensics*, I give voice and music to Lee's silent creations.

Mary Hammerbeck: billy americana, the protagonist in a poetic script that aims to redefine what it means to be feminine and American, is a persona born out of the poet's obsessions with borderlands, hillbilly music, Bob Dylan, wandering, and Spanglish. billy's quest for redefinition incorporates border themes from musical and poetic traditions.

Jeremy Halinen: The speaker could be any young man who loved Matthew Shepard—it's more the locale of the poem, Laramie, Wyoming, where Shepard was murdered, that takes on a dramatically different persona in the poem. In this imagined Laramie, it's completely normal and safe for men to show affection in public.

Derrick Harriell: Aunt Rose undertakes the traditional "Big Mama" role that is present in most African-American families. She represents the voice of African-American women who migrated North during the early to mid stages of the twentieth century in hopes of greater opportunity.

Reginald Harris: I am obsessed with the multiple levels of meaning at play in the original *King Kong*. "Millionaires" asks to reader to consider what it feels like to be a commodity. One wonders if sports figures or human stars feel as Kong does: just an image to be sold by someone else.

Christopher Hennessy: "The Carriers" infuses the idea of the Ancient Greek muse with a modern day, Christian mythos—embodied in the poem's voice, an angel flying the earth with words (inspiration?) for humans. Inhabiting this voice enables one to imagine "tasting" language, to ponder our human capacity for creativity, from an outsider's perspective.

Matthew Hittinger: Aunt Eloe : Uncle Remus :: The Bird Woman : The Spider :: Goddess of fury : Trickster god. Eloe first spoke to me in a PBS documentary about ravens, reappeared in Neil Gaiman's novel *Anansi Boys*, and terrified me in the performance piece *Caw*. She is more than *nevermore*.

Lois Holub: In many traditions, the first humans were Adam and Lilith. Lilith resisted Adam's authority, was banished from Eden, and replaced with Eve. Here, Eve searches for someone she can only sense, and Lilith responds to her disempowered sister. I wanted to give voice to women's perspective in this old story.

John Hoppenthaler: I've always been attracted to bars. I've worked in them, and I've patronized them. The speaker in "Ice Jesus" is that guy who you, by chance, sit next to in a bar in some strange city, the one who can't help himself, who has to tell you his only story.

Randall Horton: The temporal setting for this poem is central Alabama, circa 1931. Elvie had been arrested for selling moonshine by the revenuers in 1930 during The Great Depression. The poem is in the voice of his wife Rosetta, who describes her husband's return from prison in 1932.

T. R. Hummer: Fernando Pessoa (1881-1935) was Portugal's premiere modernist poet, and one of the most mysterious and prodigious writers who ever lived. He wrote and published his poems under the aegis of at least 81 personae, or "heteronyms." Who better to be the subject of a persona poem?

Donald Illich: "Beetle Bailey" is a newspaper comic that started during the Korean War. In the strip, Private Bailey is often lazy, and he is verbally and physically abused by his sergeant. Their relationship in this poem was influenced by "Don't Ask, Don't Tell," and how military people had to hide their sexualities under this rule.

Major Jackson: "Leaving Saturn" is written in the voice of jazz pianist and big band leader Sun Ra, whose eccentricity in style and personality was only matched in intensity by his intergalactic visionary cosmic-reaching sound. He claimed to be from Saturn, sent here to save planet Earth. Listening to his music, I believe him, thus the power of art.

Charles Jensen: I imagined Dorothy Gale living when the film *The Wizard of Oz* was made—Kansas, 1939, on the cusp of the Dust Bowl that pushed poor farmers even deeper into poverty. The concept of Oz, with gold streets and jeweled buildings, then takes on more urgency.

Hershman John: The poem is based around the 1943 film *The Song of Bernadette*. In the grotto of Lourdes, in 1858, a young girl, Bernadette, spoke with the Virgin Mary. The film may portray "holiness," but the actors are still "human." The narrator is able to identify with flaws of innocence lost.

Luke Johnson: "Doomsayer" grew from a grad school assignment: to write a dramatic monologue in blank verse. I wrote this sonnet featuring a street-bum proclaiming the apocalypse to a crowd of passers-by. To me, there's a compelling friction to a homeless man speaking in iambic pentameter, albeit loosely.

Mary Kaiser: The persona in my poem is a young woman from Natchez, Mississippi, in the 1840s, a reformed spiritualist medium who joins the Shakers. However, while trying to learn one of the sect's complex dances, she is interrupted by a visitation from her former spiritualist "control," a long-dead Cherokee Indian.

Ilya Kaminsky: "Musica Humana" is the long poem written in voices of Osip and Nadezhda Mandelshtam. Osip Mandelshtam was a Russian poet who happened to write a poem against the government. It happened to be Joseph Stalin's government, the time happened to be 1930s, and the place was the former USSR. Mandelshtam was sent into Siberian camps, where he died. His wife was forced into internal exile, but she survived.

Ariana-Sophia Kartsonis: This is both the known Pinocchio, because of the ventriloquism possible and so that he might question all the trade-offs that come from becoming *real*. Themes of borrowed-voice are central to my collection *The Rub* and therein, too, is a bit of Hamlet, with his sea of troubles and mortal woes.

M. Nzadi Keita: "History" is part of a work-in-progress, *Brief Evidence of Heaven*, which imagines the world of Anna Murray Douglass (1813–1882). Her forty-four year marriage began after this free-born laundress met Frederick Douglass and helped him escape. "History" challenges her dismissal by many scholars, who read her illiteracy and domesticity as powerlessness.

Collin Kelley: The poem was inspired by David Lynch's film, *Mulholland Drive*. The voice is Diane, played by Naomi Watts, who wins a jitterbug contest in her Canadian town and comes to Hollywood to find fame. After being jilted by a movie star, Diane has a psychotic break and becomes lost in a bizarre fantasy world.

Jee Leong Koh: Studies #1 and 7 are inspired by particular artworks, Albrecht Dürer's *Self-Portrait* (1500) and Yasumasa Morimura's *Self-Portrait–After Marilyn Monroe* (1996). The other Studies are based on a corpus of the artist's self-presentation. The speakers are not simply the artists, nor purely the poet. They are, instead, the "double eye."

Jason Koo: The voice for this poem was inspired by a cartoon drawing by the Argentine artist Guillermo Mordillo. This tiny man was stranded on an island the size of a pitcher's mound, comforting himself by imagining it was the kneecap of a gigantic woman. I thought this was funny.

Keetje Kuipers: I enjoy poems by American men that celebrate the numerous positive features of masculinity or that grapple with the ethical, emotional, and psychological situation of being male. This poem is a critique of a different kind of voice popular in contemporary poetry, which performatively glorifies an egocentric, irresponsible, misogynistic masculinity.

Laurie Clements Lambeth: I feel a physical connection to Frankenstein's monster. When my multiple sclerosis flares, I walk like him. MS scars brain tissue and damages nerves, so I imagined an MS brain entering the monster's skull, poorly controlling the newly-constructed body. In the poem, I imbue the cinematic Frankenstein with MS symptoms: electric, disembodying, and ultimately uncontrollable.

Jacqueline Jones LaMon: "The Facial Reconstructionist has Cocktails with the Girls" is part of a sequence of poems from my collection, *Last Seen*, that deals with the silences left in our world by long-term missing African-American children overlooked by our national media.

Quraysh Ali Lansana: In *They Shall Run: Harriet Tubman Poems*, I employ dramatic narrative techniques to infuse the related, history-based poems with character, conflict, and forward action. The poems, which collectively dramatize the story of Harriet Tubman and the Underground Railroad, are a narrative, delivered in the voice of one of several characters.

Iris A. Law: Rachel Carson incited rabid controversy when she published *Silent Spring*, her 1962 account of DDT's deleterious effects on ecosystems. Carson argued, among other things, that DDT use had led to the disappearance of the bald eagle. The title of her book alludes to Keats' poem "La Belle Dame Sans Merci."

Anna Leahy: Lizzie Siddal (1829–1862) was an artist's model, a painter, and a poet. She modeled for renowned Victorian painters, including John Everett Millais and D. G. Rossetti, whom she married. She suffered intermittent ill health, and after a stillbirth and becoming pregnant again, she died of a laudanum overdose.

Sarah Lindsay: Constantinople was the capital of the Roman empire in the sixth century when it was struck by bubonic plague. I was struck some time later by a description of how people tried to live through it. The dancer is fictional; the supposed preventives are not.

Sandy Longhorn: Knowing that motherhood wasn't for me, when my body began insisting that I give birth in my early thirties, this internal strife came out in a series of persona poems, where both mother and child are imperfect and troubled. Readers are often distressed to learn that I have no children.

Peter Ludwin: I chose the persona of a woman from the East coming out to Kansas in the mid-nineteenth century based upon historical data and photographs, as well as upon my own familiarity with the singular atmosphere of the Great Plains. For some, their vast expanse was deeply alienating and destabilizing.

Alison Luterman: I first read about Greg Withrow in a *People* magazine article. In the photo, he was shown all bandaged up because he'd been attacked and literally crucified by the same band of neo-Nazis he had helped train before falling in love had opened his eyes to what he was doing. His story haunted me for years until I wrote it.

Alessandra Lynch: Frida Kahlo (twentieth century Mexican painter) stares at me from a small wooden replica of one of her self-portraits, which I've propped on my bookshelf for daily consultation. The emotional upheaval Kahlo suffered is beautifully rendered in her paintings. This poem is my humble vision of a "self-portrait" for Frida.

Angie Macri: Marianne was a Native-American slave to the Aubuchons of Illinois Country. I'd been taught to think of slavery and racism as events far from home. Having learned differently, I wanted Marianne to have a voice. My love for my sons was our common ground, the key.

Marie-Elizabeth Mali: In the painting that inspired this poem, "The Little Deer," by iconic Mexican painter Frida Kahlo (1907–1954), her face looks out from a deer's body pierced with arrows. I asked myself, "What would a woman with such a steady gaze in the face of pain and violence say?"

Marjorie Manwaring: In 1920, Zelda Sayre married American writer F. Scott Fitzgerald in New York, where they both became literary celebrities. It was a stormy relationship. Zelda had her own artistic aspirations and found it frustrating to live in her husband's shadow. Scott's alcoholism and Zelda's mental illness further complicated the marriage.

Diane K. Martin: Fernande Olivier was a model who became Pablo Picasso's mistress and muse from 1905–1912. After reading her memoir (at the Vermont Studio Center), I wrote this poem and eleven others in the voices of the women in Picasso's life, a portrait of him by the women he painted.

Cate Marvin: The persona from whose perspective the poem "All My Wives" speaks is not a dead or living person, but a figment of my imagination. He essentially represents the "ex-husband" in my book, *Fragment of the Head of a Queen* (Sarabande, 2007).

Sebastian Matthews: This voice starting telling me stories about Jack Benny while I was driving through western Ohio. The guy seemed to be a comic himself. I took notes at a rest stop then later did research on Benny and the comic clubs that thrived in the Midwest back in the day.

Marty McConnell: Tara Conner was named Miss USA in 2006 and nearly dethroned six months later after media reported that she had been seen drinking underage and frequenting Manhattan clubs. Entering rehab enabled her to keep her title; in an interview post-rehab, she hinted that her "demons" were linked to childhood abuse.

Jeffrey McDaniel: In 1995, Silvana Straw, a DC poet, suggested that I write a poem in the voice of an exceedingly sleazy man, which is how The Jerk was born.

Leslie McGrath: This poem honors those who work with their hands. My friend's grandmother, a Mexican immigrant, had supported the family by working as a maid. My friend took care of her grandmother during her last year, preparing her body for a pauper's funeral the morning she died. Love is wealth.

Claire McQuerry: Marc Chagall (1887–1985), one of the twentieth century's greatest artists, grew up in a poor Jewish family, the son of a herring merchant's assistant. Many of his paintings, such as "Blue Violinist," on which this poem is based, depict the village of Vitebsk, Russia, where he was born. Vitebsk was destroyed by the Nazis during WWII.

Philip Memmer: "The Magician's Assistant" was written as part of a sequence called *The Ventriloquist's Ex*, which used the voices of invented women to critique/examine the men with whom they were involved. To some degree, I am each of the men in the poems . . . using these voices allowed me to engage in self-critique without doing so from a first-person perspective.

Billy Merrell: The Russian-American novelist Vladimir Nabokov traveled frequently on butterfly-collecting trips while writing the novel *Lolita*, his most famous work. Nabokov's obsession with lepidoptery (butterfly observation) was so central to his life that he permanently impaired his eyesight by looking through a microscope for several hours each day.

Sarah Messer: "I am the Real Jesse James" is based on myths surrounding the outlaw Jesse James (1847–1882) who, while somewhat famous in life, became legendary after his death. Newspapers claimed James had escaped, and many claimed to be "The Real Jesse James." These "confessions" inspired the poem's elliptical form.

Philip Metres: "Installation / Occupation" is a double-sonnet based on the words of Vera Tamari, a Palestinian artist in Ramallah. During the early years of the Israeli occupation of the West Bank and Gaza Strip, strict controls were placed upon artists and writers; even the word Palestine—not to mention the flag colors (red, white, green and black)—were forbidden.

Seth Michelson: "Listen" honors the Turkish writer Nâzim Hikmet (1902–1963), who was persecuted and imprisoned throughout his adult life for his political beliefs and writing. An advocate of independence, egalitarianism, and peace, he opposed the Armenian genocide and railed against Franco and Hitler, for example. His honors include the International Peace Prize.

Jory M. Mickelson: Berenice was the wife of Ptolemy III of Egypt. Ptolemy waged a war against the Assyrians, and when he returned victorious from battle, he shaved his wife's head, offering her hair to Aphrodite. It is said her hair vanished from the temple and became a constellation in the night sky.

Tiffany Midge: "The Monster's Bride Questions the Motives of Her Creator" is a poem which innocently began as a love poem. It also speaks to the puzzling out of one's various aspects, which, as a mixed-race person, I've spent a fair amount of time attending to, most especially in my writing.

Thorpe Moeckel: My daughter and I made a snowman. This was years ago, a snowfall followed by warmth. The "first-person snowman" let me animate a frigid figure, which was fun. I don't normally worry a rhyme scheme, but this poem called for one, to shade the changes—the melting, refreezing.

Carolina Monsiváis: The series is based on a training exercise for new employees and volunteers in the field of domestic violence and sexual assault—a field I worked in for many years. Through the characters' imagined voices, I attempted to explore the tension the exercise has caused.

Juan J. Morales: In the early sixteenth century, a group of Spaniards sailing the South American coast brought an indigenous man on board to quiz him about this new land. I wrote this poem in varying personae to depict the legacy of miscommunication in first contact and one of history's naming stories for the country of Peru.

Tomás Q. Morín: Accounts of the Greek prophet Teiresias, who lived for seven years as a woman for offending the gods, are silent about this part of his life. We're told he was a prostitute, but little else. My aim was to give the female Teiresias a voice to tell her own story.

Andrew Mulvania: The poem included in this anthology is written in the voice of Robert Frost. The action of the poem takes place early in Frost's career when he was still fairly obscure and struggling with the loss of his first son. I wanted to explore how Frost dealt with feelings of self-doubt and grief.

Paul Nemser: "To the Stockyard Bulls" is from a book-length sequence called "Taurus," an epic phantasmagoria about a bronze bull-gargoyle who comes to life in St. Petersburg, Russia, and pursues a mysterious beauty named Europa across a sea of rhyme. Bull meets Girl—and all Hell breaks loose.

Laura P. Newton: The idea for "The Wife of Sisyphus" comes from an obsession with Sisyphus (aren't we all ceaselessly rolling a rock to the top of the mountain?) and a recent rereading of "The Myth of Sisyphus" by Camus, which encouraged me to rethink the story from the wife's point of view.

Aimee Nezhukumatathil: I was enchanted by the myth of Arachne, who was turned into a spider for boasting that she could create a tapestry better than even Athena, goddess of the arts. The myth silences Arachne forever, but I wanted to give her voice back, show a smidge of her pride once more.

Matthew Nienow: What can I say about Whitman that hasn't already been said? He was the grandfather of American poetry. I merely adopted the setting of his youth and had fun with the stance of his famous lines: "I Celebrate myself, and sing myself... / For every atom belonging to me as good belongs to you."

Gregory Pardlo: The main character of Richard Wright's novel, *Native Son*, is based in part on accounts of Robert Nixon, a murderer whom the journalist, Charles Leavell, described to readers of the *Chicago Tribune*. The playwright, Paul Green, was commissioned to adapt Wright's novel to the stage.

Diana Park: This persona was a gift from Norman Dubie, who called one winter day, saying that he had just misdialed and spoken to another woman. He envisioned her as the sole caretaker of an ailing father and a child in a rustic home. I wondered about her for days, soon imagining my own vision of her.

Ed Pavlić: Ornette Coleman (b. 1930) is an instrumentalist from Fort Worth, TX. An architect of the "free jazz" movement ca. early 1960s. Coleman's 1959 album, *The Shape of Jazz to Come,* announced a piano-less, thus "free," structure in jazz. Unlike "free" experiments such as those of John Cage, Coleman's evoked an unwritten history via a distilled, vernacular voice. His 2007 album, *Sound Grammar,* won the Pulitzer Prize.

Alison Pelegrin: "Homewrecker" was written after I saw an intact double wide wheeling down a bridge with curtains still in the windows, as though the house were being moved in anger or haste. I dreamed up a domestic drama and wrote the poem from a man's point of view.

Peter Pereira: Dr. Francisco Balmis led the 1803–1806 *Expedition of the Vaccine,* in which 22 Spanish orphan boys were used as live carriers to bring a small-pox vaccine to the

New World. This poem imagines Balmis at a key juncture in the expedition in which the vaccine was nearly lost.

Jennifer Perrine: In the early 1800s, the only legal source of cadavers for medical schools in the UK was capital punishment. However, as the study of anatomy expanded, more corpses were needed, and "resurrectionists"—men who secretly disinterred the recently deceased and sold them for dissection—arose to meet this increased demand.

Leigh Phillips: My persona is 74 year-old Daisy, writing to her estranged beloved, Eleanor, who lives in Florida with her husband. As Daisy begins to lose her memory, her letters to Eleanor are a means of remembering their affair. Through Daisy's perspective, I reclaim lesbian desire from the margins of history.

Kenneth Pobo: The speaker feels vitally connected with poets Li Po and Tu Fu, so much so that they seem to be living entities to him. The border between the living and the dead fades. Poetry offers that capacity. The poem's brevity happened mostly for two reasons: 1) in general, I work for economic language and 2) I didn't want the scene to be belabored. The tone is fairly light-hearted, and there was no need to belabor the images.

John Poch: Søren Kierkegaard (5 May 1813–11 November 1855) was a Danish philosopher and theologian. Kierkegaard's early work was written under various pseudonymous characters who present distinctive viewpoints and interact with each other in complex dialogue. Kierkegaard's life and writing were deeply affected by his broken engagement to Regine Olsen.

Iain Haley Pollock: Shotgun houses in New Orleans' unreconstructed neighborhoods still bear spray-painted Xs. In Katrina's aftermath, rescuers painted these marks to indicate which houses had been searched and what—survivors, corpses, pets—had been found therein. Riding to help build Musicians' Village, I found these Xs suggesting sets of fragmented, choral narratives.

R. Elena Prieto: Mary Ann Cotton was one of the first women in history to be called a black widow, and I find it difficult to understand her actions, but after attending a reading by Rigoberto González that included a poem about Lizzie Borden, I wanted to try.

Donna Prinzmetal: Several years ago I became obsessed with the Snow White fairy tale and began to write a book of persona poems. In researching, I also looked at other adaptations of the fairy tale. One of these was Alexander Pushkin's poem, "The Tale of the Dead Princess."

Stephanie M. Pruitt: The poem's speaker, Adelia, is a young woman living on a Middle Tennessee plantation in the 1840s. This piece is part of a manuscript exploring intimate, epiphanic moments in the lives of women who have been treated as public fodder. I'm drawn to her complex reckoning of desire, and dominion.

Shelley Puhak: Nadya Krupskaya was Lenin's wife. After Lenin's death, Stalin attempted to blackmail her with rumors of a long-term affair between Lenin and Inessa Armand, one of Nadya's friends and a fellow revolutionary. Despite her quarrels with Stalin, Nadya Krupskaya would avoid arrest and die naturally of old age.

Khadijah Queen: The persona in my poem haunted me when I heard the news story; I felt a parallel, having grown up in drug-ravaged South Central Los Angeles in the 1980s, where I lost friends and family to violence. I wanted to show how political/social strife directly affects lives, to say *enough*.

Rita Mae Reese: The sin-eater was most often a beggar who was shunned by the rest of the village. The villagers believed sin-eaters consorted with evil spirits. Though the practice of sin-eating allegedly survived until the late nineteenth or early twentieth century in Wales, there is very little information recorded about it.

Barbara Jane Reyes: "Black Jesus Speaks" is part of a series of persona poems inspired by "black" figures in Philippine history, the Black Nazarene statue in Quiapo, and the Buffalo Soldier, both of whom have North American origins, contrasted against the prevalence of skin whitening products in the Philippines.

Shelley Renée-Ruiz: Controversy swirls around the interpretation of Judges 11. In this poem, I decided to look at the story literally in order to examine the feelings of a girl about to lose her life. I wanted to emphasize how the names of unfortunates are often forgotten and their individual stories unexamined.

Jonathan B. Rice: "House of Galicia" refers to a point of pilgrimage mentioned in the 30th sonnet of Dante's *La Vita Nuova*. I imagined my poem's speaker as a modern day version of one of the weeping pilgrims encountered by Dante in the preamble to that poem.

Susan Rich: Sarah was the biblical matriarch, wife of Abraham. Information on her is from Genesis: 11–23. When Abraham was almost a hundred, God spoke to him promising that Sarah would have a child. When Sarah overheard this conversation, she laughed, as she was ninety years old. One year later, her son Isaac was born.

Kathleen Rooney: "If Robinson Came from the Heartland" is from a collection of poems based on the life and work of the poet and mysterious disappearee Weldon Kees (1914–1955?). Kees wrote four poems containing the character of Robinson, and this project uses him to tell a version of Kees' own life story.

Laurel Rust: In 1975, right out of high school, I hitchhiked through Northern Ireland, which was very much a war zone at that time. A woman stopped me, and we started talking. She invited me into her house and told me her story. I can still see the fence from which she helped the British soldier get unsnagged.

Natasha Sajé: This poem was prompted by a *New York Times* article about people who confess to crimes they didn't commit. Marcel, the narrator of Proust's *In Search of Lost*

Time, shares certain traits with the author Proust, including a repressed attraction to violence and a heightened aesthetic sensibility.

Greg Santos: Hulk is an odd superhero: his superpowers derive from anger management issues. I imagined him as a modern-day worker chasing the "American Dream," but I think that everyone can relate to his frustrations.

Kelly Scarff: In the Bible, Lazarus' resurrection was the final miracle performed by Jesus and the one that set the crucifixion into motion. We are taught to assume that Lazarus wanted to live, but I was intrigued to imagine him embracing death as something soothing, perhaps even preferring it to life.

Steven D. Schroeder: The persona of "Something Might Be Gaining on You" is someone aging into dementia, based partially on my grandmother and my girlfriend's grandmother. I felt a poem from within this character would be more sympathetic and nuanced than if I simply spoke about aging using my own inexperienced perspective.

Anne Shaw: The speaker is Dido, from Virgil's epic, *The Aenid.* Throughout *The Aenid,* Dido is associated with flames: first in her passion for Aeneis, and later when she is so heart-broken over losing him that she has herself burned alive. Here she is speaking to the Little Matchgirl from Hans Christian Andersen's fairytale.

Matthew Shenoda: This poem is rooted in my engagement with the debate over the repatriation of ancient artifacts. It appears in the persona of King Tutankhamen in an effort to humanize the remains of ancient Egypt and shift our purely archaeological understanding to one that recognizes culture as a living continuum.

Evie Shockley: Frederick Douglass was an abolitionist, writer, suffragist, and statesman whose masterful account of his journey from slavery to freedom led him to international renown. Paul Laurence Dunbar and Robert Hayden, among others, have commemorated his invaluable contributions in poetry, but I was inspired to imagine the personal costs to him and his family of his celebrity and political commitments.

Martha Silano: After spending weeks researching the Milky Way galaxy—size, composition, myths surrounding its origin—I wrote this poem in the voice of Mother Earth. Much to my surprise, "she" is quite a bit like my maternal grandmother, Victoria Pickarski Katrosh; they both champion a relaxed syntax, hold firm opinions regarding "shapewear," and are blissfully content right where they are.

Sean Singer: Larry Fine was in *The Three Stooges.* He started in show business as a violinist. I tried to create a persona who, on the surface, is a clown, but beneath that is a sensitive and tragic one. The persona in this poem is a distorted figure.

Susan Slaviero: As a writer, I am interested in the concept of hybridity and the straddling of multiple identities. I think the Chimera, an amalgam of lion, goat and snake, which appears as an omen in early mythologies, makes for a compelling subject, especially when (dis)placed in a contemporary setting.

Erin Elizabeth Smith: Cammi Granato is considered the "female Wayne Gretsky." She broke nearly every scoring record in women's college hockey, and for fifteen years, Granato played for the Women's National Team, earning gold in the Nagano Olympics. In 2008, she became the first woman to be enshrined in the U.S. Hockey Hall of Fame.

Patricia Smith: Someone painted a swastika on Plymouth Rock. Really. The incident was traced to a group called the White Youth League; a representative spewed the usual hatred of blacks, Jews, gays. I needed to explore how our lives could have veered so crazily in different directions.

Christopher S. Soden: I'm uneasy discussing the poem's inception, fearing enigmas intrinsic to its strategy. The narrator here shares key characteristics with Medea. Though powerful and skilled, she is at the mercy of mere mortals. My protagonist's power lies in her secret capacity to achieve revenge, with ingredients easily accessible to any waitress.

Alison Stine: Several years ago, a murder trial in Germany made the news: the accused had answered a personal ad where the writer was looking for a man to murder and consume him. I had to imagine the point of view of someone who would want such a thing. In my story, it's a young abused girl.

Adam Tavel: "The Apostle's Wife" is set in the first century CE and attempts to render an intimate, though fictional, account of a female missionary amid the turbulent period documented in the Book of Acts.

Molly Tenenbaum: Julia Child (1912–2004), an American chef, was known for introducing Americans to French cooking, with her book *Mastering the Art of French Cooking*; for hosting the first television cooking show, *The French Chef*; and for being a positive, enthusiastic character. Her kitchen is on display at the National Museum of American History in Washington, D.C.

Maria Terrone: "His Cassandra," first published as "Pilate's Wife," was inspired by my hearing the Gospel of St. Matthew read aloud in church before Easter. I was struck by the strong voice of this woman, who appears nowhere else in the New Testament, and began to imagine her more fully in my poem.

Jeffrey Thomson: Forneus is one of a group of fallen angels whom God casts into exile for different reasons. Their sins were among the infractions that incited God to inflict the Great Flood upon the Earth. The poem is a cento made up from the collected sayings of President George W. Bush.

Matthew Thorburn: "Graciela and the Song of One Hundred Names" was inspired by Compay Segundo's rendition of "Linda Graciela," recorded when the great Cuban musician was nearly 90. Hearing Segundo's song, I imagined the speaker of this poem, another man whose romantic feelings had only been heightened by many years of living.

Angela Narciso Torres: Beethoven's bust was a fixture in my childhood home, as was his thunderous, passionate music, which my father played long into the night. This poem imagines the voice of someone privy to Beethoven's life while his hearing deteriorated around the time he wrote the Pastoral Symphony, my father's—and my—favorite.

Tony Trigilio: In a biographical note to his unpublished manuscript, "The Kollective," Lee Harvey Oswald, alleged assassin of John F. Kennedy, described himself as "the son of an insurance salesman whose early death left a far mean streak of independence brought on by neglect." My poem attempts to explore what lies between the lines of Oswald's statement.

Brian Turner: This poem rises out of my experiences in Iraq as a soldier in the U.S. Army (as well as with an event in my own personal life back home in America). It is an attempt to better understand some of the intimate losses which occur in our lives.

Kristine Uyeda: Some of the most interesting moments occur between the big events. The small, unreported episodes in history or myth offer a space in which persona can emerge and redefine motive or character. These moments create a window into new aspects of the individual's personality.

Susan Varnot: Re-reading Ovid's *Metamorphoses*, I was struck by how few lines record-ed Medusa's transformation from a lovely young woman to the hideous gorgon. Since she is often regarded as a victimizer, I wanted instead to present her as a sympathetic character, one who was a victim of the gods.

R. A. Villanueva: On 23 January 1960, accompanied by Lt. Don Walsh of the U.S. Navy, Jacques Piccard survived a prolonged descent into the Challenger Deep, the deepest trench in the ocean floor. Their submersible, the Trieste, incorporated the life's work of Auguste Piccard, famed physicist, stratospheric balloonist, and Jacques' father.

Adam Vines: In "Hamlet Beside the Stream," Shakespeare's Hamlet imagines himself at the stream where Ophelia drowned. In the play, Hamlet's self-consumed reactions to Gertrude and Laertes about Ophelia's death are disconcerting. My persona poem is by no means an apologia; however, I try to assume a more contemplative and guilt-ridden Hamlet.

Elizabeth Volpe: Homer creates the quintessential male in Odysseus, yet his Penelope is woman as man might have preferred her: faithful, patient, essentially helpless, incomplete without her man. This poem allows Penelope a voice that's perhaps more realistic: impatient, brimming with inner life, more fully female in her reactions and her longings.

Donna Vorreyer: Strong. Fiercely independent. Unmarried when this was unthinkable. Maudie Atkinson in *To Kill A Mockingbird* is a favorite character of mine. Her loyalty to those she cared for showed her large heart and capacity for love. In this poem, I was able to give her love in return.

Davi Walders: Noah's wife is not named in Genesis; however, she is given the name "Na'amah" (*pleasantness* in Hebrew, so named because her conduct was pleasing to God) in rabbinic literature such as the Talmud.

Valerie Wallace: Jezebel was a Phoenician princess, and then a queen, in ancient Israel. She's often thought of as a powerful, evil, promiscuous person, and I was interested in how she might act in the modern world. I wanted to write about Jezebel as a woman of action who makes no excuses for her behavior.

Nagueyalti Warren: The poem using voices of three personae derives mainly from my imagination, although the events involve a close friend who died from contracting the AIDS. The forms selected for the voices, free verse for the child's voice and sonnet for the mother's, help to structure the emotions of the voices.

Israel Wasserstein: Irish legend tells of Fergus mac Róich, king in Ulster, who gave up his kingship and lived in exile. In "Who Goes with Fergus," William Butler Yeats imagines Fergus as one who "rules the shadows of the wood, / and the white breast of the dim sea[.]"

David Welch: "Our Chef Is Delicious" takes its title from a (poorly, I assume) translated menu I saw at a restaurant in Spain where I once ate. When drafting the poem, I began to wonder about a world in which the claim was literal and attempted to insert realist sentiment into an otherworldly situation.

Gabriel Welsch: "Granola Jones Cooks for the Potluck" is from a longer narrative collection of poems. The speaker works at a women's shelter and is a broken spirit, of sorts, regaining her strength through a friendship with a neighbor. I am drawn to her work, her compassion, and her anger.

Carolyn Beard Whitlow: During the Civil War, husbands and sons abandoned Southern plantations to fight for the Confederacy, and slaves escaped. Scarcity reigned, accompanied by loneliness for women. Here the mistress—who raised as her own her husband's daughter by a slave woman—now wants the child to convert to slave status.

Caki Wilkinson: When I wrote this poem, I was in college and working as a waitress, so I definitely drew from my own experience. The voice, though, evolved from imagining a younger version of my grandmother, who ran a diner for many years.

Eliot Khalil Wilson: The Spanish explorer Francisco Vázquez de Coronado was something of a screw-up—remarkable mostly for the shocking depths of his rapaciousness and bad judgment. Who else would quest for the mythical golden city of Quivira only to end up outside of Wichita, Kansas? (I've been to Wichita, and the only gold there is wheat.)

L. Lamar Wilson: The name Bobby McFerrin immediately brings "Don't Worry, Be Happy" to mind. This poem aims not only to capture the spirit of the man who sired and inspired the pop and jazz great who sang that award-winning song but to herald the graceful defiance of our underappreciated African-American opera giants.

Laura Madeline Wiseman: This poem is based on the life of the nineteenth century suffragist and lecturer Matilda Fletcher (1842–1909). After the death of her one and only child, Matilda joined the lecture circuit, authored several books, and wrote and published poems, including "The Heart of a Man." She is also my great-great-great-grandmother.

Carolyne L. Wright: From 1927–1928, Pablo Neruda lived in Rangoon with a Burmese woman who called herself "Josie Bliss." According to Neruda's memoir, she suffered from jealous rage. He finally departed for Ceylon, abandoning her, and never saw her again. In 1971, Neruda won the Nobel Prize. Did Josie Bliss see the announcement?

Erica Wright: The speaker of this poem is an alternate version of Hans Christian Andersen's little mermaid—one who marries and lives in rural Tennessee. As an old woman, she is looking back on her life and longing for the ocean.

Jake Adam York: I grew up in Alabama, but spent my professional life elsewhere. Often I'm asked to "explain" Alabama, its racial history. Wallace represents that clearly. Crossing his story with Robert Johnson's and letting the devil speak, maybe the poem gives voice to evil, which, I think, is what people ask for.

Contributors

Liz Ahl is the author of *Luck* (Pecan Grove Press, 2010) and *A Thirst That's Partly Mine* (Slapering Hol Press, 2008). She has been awarded residencies at the Vermont Studio Center, the Kimmel Nelson Harding Center for the Arts, and Jentel. She lives in New Hampshire.

Dan Albergotti is the author of *The Boatloads* (BOA Editions, 2008). His poems have appeared in *The Cincinnati Review, The Southern Review, The Virginia Quarterly Review, Pushcart Prize XXXIII: Best of the Small Presses,* and elsewhere. He teaches at Coastal Carolina University in Conway, South Carolina.

Kazim Ali's books include three volumes of poetry, *The Far Mosque, The Fortieth Day* and *Bright Felon,* two novels, *Quinn's Passage* and *The Disappearance of Seth,* and most recently, *Orange Alert: Essays on Poetry, Art and the Architecture of Silence.* A new book of essays, *Fasting for Ramadan,* was published in 2011.

Maureen Alsop is the author of *Apparition Wren, The Diction of Moths,* and several chapbooks, most recently *Luminal Equation* in the collection *Narwhal,* and *the dream and the dream you spoke.* She is the winner of *Harpur Palate's* Milton Kessler Memorial Prize for Poetry and *The Bitter Oleander's* Frances Locke Memorial Poetry Award.

Ivy Alvarez is the author of *Mortal* (Red Morning Press, 2006). A recipient of fellowships from MacDowell (USA), Hawthornden Castle (UK) and Fundación Valparaiso (Spain), her poetry appears in journals and anthologies in many countries and online. She was poet-in-residence at the Museum of Welsh Life, Cardiff, during 2010.

Francisco Aragón is the author of *Puerta del Sol* and *Glow of Our Sweat,* as well as editor of *The Wind Shifts: New Latino Poetry.* His poems have appeared in various anthologies and journals. He directs Letras Latinas—the literary program of the Institute for Latino Studies at the University of Notre Dame.

Cynthia Arrieu-King is an assistant professor of creative writing at Stockton College. Her book *People are Tiny in Paintings of China* is available from Octopus Books. Her reviews and poems have appeared in *Boston Review, Jacket, Prairie Schooner, Black Warrior Review, New Orleans Review* and other journals. She lives on Absecon Island and in Philadelphia.

Rane Arroyo (1954–2010) was a poet, playwright, and fiction writer whose ten collections of poetry included *The Buried Sea: New & Selected Poems* (University of Arizona Press, 2008) and *The Sky's Weight* (Turning Point Press, 2009). At the time of his death in 2010, he was a Distinguished Professor of English and Creative Writing at the University of Toledo.

Elizabeth Austen is the author of two poetry chapbooks, *The Girl Who Goes Alone* (Floating Bridge Press, 2010) and *Where Currents Meet*, part of the Toadlily Press quartet *Sightline*. Her full-length poetry collection, *Every Dress a Decision*, was published by Blue Begonia Press in 2011.

Corrina Bain is a writer-performer living in Brooklyn. She was showcased on Final Stage at the National Poetry Slam in 2004. She has performed with such legends as Jim Carroll and Patricia Smith. Her work appears in the *November 3rd Club, decomP* literary magazine, *killauthor* and others.

Sally Ball is the author of *Annus Mirabilis* (Barrow Street, 2005). She is also the associate director of Four Way Books and an assistant professor of English at Arizona State University. *Annus Mirabilis* centers on the lives and theories of Newton and Leibniz, rival inventors of calculus.

Tony Barnstone is The Albert Upton Professor of English Language and Literature at Whittier College and the author of twelve books. His third book of poems, *The Golem of Los Angeles* (Red Hen Press), won the Benjamin Saltman Award in Poetry, and his fourth, *Tongue of War: From Pearl Harbor to Nagasaki* (BKMK Press), won the John Ciardi Prize in Poetry.

Curtis Bauer's poems and translations have been published widely. A finalist for numerous poetry and translation prizes, he won the John Ciardi Poetry Prize for his collection, *Fence Line* (BkMk, 2004). He teaches Creative Writing and Translation at Texas Tech University and is the publisher of Q Ave Press Chapbooks.

Shaindel Beers' first poetry collection, *A Brief History of Time*, was published by Salt Publishing in 2009. She is the Poetry Editor of *Contrary* and lives in Pendleton, Oregon.

Carol Berg has poems forthcoming or in *Artifice, Fifth Wednesday Journal, Pebble Lake Review, Rhino, qarrtsiluni, Melusine*, and elsewhere. She has an MFA from Stonecoast and an MA in English Literature. She lives in Massachusetts with her husband and son.

Tara Betts is the author of *Arc & Hue* (Aquarius Press-Willow Books, 2009). She is a Cave Canem fellow, and she teaches creative writing at Rutgers University. Her work appears in several journals and anthologies, including *Gathering Ground, Black Nature Poetry*, and *Bum Rush the Page*.

Tamiko Beyer is the author of *bough breaks* (Meritage Press). Her poems have appeared in *Sonora Review, h_ngm_m, Copper Nickel Review,* and elsewhere. She leads community writing workshops and is the poetry editor of *Drunken Boat.* She is a founding member of the queer, multi-racial writing collective Agent 409, and a Kundiman fellow.

Joelle Biele is the author of *White Summer* and the editor of *Elizabeth Bishop and The New Yorker: The Complete Correspondence.* A Fulbright scholar in Germany and Poland, she has received awards from the Poetry Society of America and the Maryland State Arts Council.

Paula Bohince is the author of *Incident at the Edge of Bayonet Woods* (2008) and *The Children* (2012). Her poems have appeared in *The New Yorker, The Nation,* and *Ploughshares.* She has received a fellowship from the National Endowment for the Arts and the Amy Lowell Poetry Travelling Scholarship.

Shane Book recently directed a film based on his first poetry collection, *Ceiling of Sticks,* winner of the 2009 Prairie Schooner Book Prize. A graduate of the Iowa Writer's Workshop, his honors include a Wallace Stegner Fellowship, an Academy of American Poets Prize, a *New York Times* Fellowship, and a National Magazine Award.

Ash Bowen's poetry has appeared in *New England Review, Black Warrior Review, Rattle* and elsewhere. He co-edits the online poetry journal *Linebreak,* which presents original poetry in a dynamic and innovative multimedia platform.

Traci Brimhall is the author of *Rookery* (SIU Press), winner of the Crab Orchard Series First Book Award. Her poems have appeared in *Kenyon Review, Slate, Virginia Quarterly Review,* and elsewhere. She was the 2008–09 Halls Poetry Fellow at the Wisconsin Institute for Creative Writing and is a current Kings/Chavez/Parks Fellow at Western Michigan University.

Meghan Brinson is the author of two chapbooks, *Fragrant Inferno* and *Broken Plums on the Sidewalk.* She has had poems published in *Gulf Coast, Puerto del Sol, The Greensboro Review,* and *Copper Nickel,* among others. She edits the journal *MisFit.*

Jericho Brown received his Ph.D. in Creative Writing from the University of Houston. The recipient of the Whiting Writers Award and the Bunting Fellowship from the Radcliffe Institute at Harvard University, Brown teaches at the University of San Diego. His first book, *Please* (New Issues), won the American Book Award.

Derrick Weston Brown First born. Only child. Buddhist-In-Training. Son o' the South. Published poet. Cave Canem. VONA. Lives, works, and loves in D.C. MFA. American University. Middle School Creative Writing Teacher. Poet-In-Residence, Busboys and Poets. Debut Book: *Wisdom Teeth.* Out now.

John Canaday's first book of poems, *The Invisible World,* won a Walt Whitman Award from the Academy of American Poets; he is also the author of a critical study, *The Nuclear Muse: Literature, Physics, and the First Atomic Bombs.*

Kara Candito is the author of *Taste of Cherry* (University of Nebraska Press), winner of the 2008 Prairie Schooner Book Prize. Her work has appeared in such journals as *AGNI*, *The Kenyon Review*, and *Gulf Coast*. She is an Assistant Professor of Creative Writing at the University of Wisconsin, Platteville.

James Caroline is a Boston-based poet and musician. He has taught and performed at The Saints and Sinners Literary Festival in New Orleans as well as the Atlanta Queer Literary Festival. He is working on a novel in verse retelling the myth of Dionysus.

Tina Chang was the poet laureate of Brooklyn and is the author of *Half-Lit Houses* and co-editor of the anthology *Language for a New Century: Contemporary Poetry from the Middle East, Asia, and Beyond*. She teaches poetry at Sarah Lawrence College. Her new collection of poetry, *Of Gods & Strangers*, was published in 2011 by Four Way Books.

Ching-In Chen is a Kundiman, Macondo, and Lambda Fellow and the author of *The Heart's Traffic*. She has worked in San Francisco, Oakland, Riverside, and Boston Asian-American communities and is a co-editor of *The Revolution Starts at Home: Confronting Intimate Violence Within Activist Communities*.

Jeanne E. Clark teaches at California State University, Chico. She is the author of *Ohio Blue Tips* (University of Akron Press, 1999), which was the winner of the 1997 Akron Poetry Prize. Her second poetry collection, *Gorrill's Orchard* (Bear Star Press), was released in spring 2010.

Kevin Clark's *Self-Portrait with Expletives* won the Pleiades Press contest. His first, *In the Evening of No Warning*, earned a grant from the Academy of American Poets. Clark's writing appears in such places as the *Georgia*, *Iowa*, and *Southern Reviews*. He teaches at Cal Poly and The Rainier Writing Workshop.

Allison Adelle Hedge Coke's authored books include *Dog Road Woman* (American Book Award) and *Off-Season City Pipe*, poetry; *Rock Ghost, Willow, Deer*, a memoir; and *Blood Run*, a verse-play. Hedge Coke has edited eight additional collections. She came of age cropping tobacco, working fields and waters, and working in factories.

Don Colburn is a poet and journalist in Portland, Oregon. His new poetry collection is *Because You Might Not Remember*. His previous chapbook, *Another Way to Begin*, won the Finishing Line Press Prize, and his full collection, *As If Gravity Were a Theory*, won the Cider Press Review Book Award.

Elizabeth J. Colen is the author of the prose poetry collection *Money for Sunsets* (Steel Toe Books, 2010) and fiction chapbook *Dear Mother Monster, Dear Daughter Mistake* (Rose Metal Press, 2011).

Steven Cordova's collection, *Long Distance*, was published early in 2010 by Bilingual Review Press, and his poems have appeared in many journals and anthologies. He also has a story in *Ambientes: New Queer Latino Fiction* (University of Wisconsin Press) and an essay in *The Other Latino* (University of Arizona Press). He lives in Brooklyn, New York.

Eduardo C. Corral is a CantoMundo fellow and recipient of a "Discovery" / *The Nation* award and residencies from the MacDowell Colony and Yaddo. He was the Olive B. O'Connor Fellow in Creative Writing at Colgate University and Philip Roth Resident in Creative Writing at Bucknell University. His first collection, *Slow Lightning*, won the 2011 Yale Series of Younger Poets Competition.

Nina Corwin's second collection is *The Uncertainty of Maps* (Wordtech, 2011). A 2008 Pushcart nominee, her poetry appears in *ACM, Forklift, Hotel Amerika, New Ohio Review/ nor, Poetry East, Southern Poetry Review,* and *Verse.* Corwin is an Advisory Editor for *Fifth Wednesday Journal.* By day, she is a psychotherapist in Chicago.

Barbara Crooker's books are *Radiance,* winner of the 2005 Word Press First Book Award and finalist for the 2006 Paterson Poetry Prize; *Line Dance* (Word Press, 2008), winner of the 2009 Paterson Award for Excellence in Literature; and *More* (C&R Press, 2010). Her poems appear in a variety of literary journals and anthologies, including *Good Poems for Hard Times* (Garrison Keillor, editor) and the *Bedford Introduction to Literature.*

Rachelle Cruz is a Kundiman Fellow and a 2009 Emerging Voices Fellow. Her poems appear in several literary journals, most recently *Lantern Review* and *TAYO Magazine.* She hosts an online radio show called "The Blood-Jet Writing Hour." She is working toward her first collection of poems.

Kevin Cutrer was raised in Kentwood, Louisiana, and has lived in Boston and northeast Brazil. His poetry appears widely in such publications as *The Hudson Review, The Dark Horse, Texas Review, Louisiana Literature, Connecticut Review, The Raintown Review, Unsplendid,* and elsewhere.

Chad Davidson is the author of *The Last Predicta* (2008) and *Consolation Miracle* (2003), both on Southern Illinois University Press, as well as co-author, with Gregory Fraser, of *Writing Poetry: Creative and Critical Approaches* (Palgrave Macmillan, 2009). He teaches literature and creative writing at the University of West Georgia.

Nik De Dominic lives in New Orleans. His work has appeared in *DIAGRAM, Los Angeles Review, Fairy Tale Review,* and elsewhere. He is an editor of *The Offending Adam* and a regular contributor to the *Michigan Quarterly Review*'s blog.

Madeline DeFrees has published eight poetry collections, most recently *Spectral Waves* (2006). *Blue Dusk: New and Selected Poems, 1951–2001* was awarded the 2002 Lenore Marshall Poetry Prize. She has received fellowships from the Guggenheim Foundation and the NEA. In 2008, UW Libraries awarded her the Maxine Cushing Gray Visiting Writers Fellowship.

Brian Komei Dempster's poems have appeared in such journals as *New England Review, North American Review,* and *Ploughshares* as well as the anthologies *Language for a New Century: Contemporary Poetry from the Middle East, Asia, & Beyond* (Norton, 2008) and *Asian American Poetry: The Next Generation* (Illinois, 2004).

Danielle Cadena Deulen is the author of two books: *Lovely Asunder,* winner of the Miller Williams Arkansas Poetry Prize, and *The Riots,* winner of the AWP Prize in Creative Nonfiction. Formerly, she was a Jay C. and Ruth Halls Poetry Fellow at the University of Wisconsin-Madison.

Gillian Devereux received her MFA in Poetry from Old Dominion University in Norfolk, Virginia. She lives in Cambridge, Massachusetts, where she teaches English as a Second Language and Media Culture. Her poems have appeared in *FOURSQUARE, H_NGM_N, apt, Open Letters, Gargoyle, 32 Poems, Wicked Alice,* and other journals.

T. M. De Vos is the recipient of a Summer Literary Seminars fellowship, an MFA from New York University, and a Hopwood Award from the University of Michigan. She is a staff member of *Many Mountains Moving,* a performer with the Poetry Brothel, and a contributor to *Fiction Writers Review.*

LaTasha N. Nevada Diggs is the author of three chapbooks, including *Manuel is destroying my bathroom* (Belladonna Press), and the album *Television.* Her work has been published in *Ploughshares, Tea Party Magazine, Jubilat, Gathering Ground, Rattapallax, P.M.S., Black Renaissance Noir,* and *Nocturnes.* She is a native of Harlem.

Liz Dolan's second poetry manuscript, *A Secret of Long Life,* was nominated for the Robert McGrath Prize. A five-time Pushcart nominee, she won an established artist fellowship from the Delaware Division of the Arts in 2009. Her first poetry collection, *They Abide,* was published by March Street Press.

Chris Dombrowski is the author of a collection of poems, *By Cold Water,* and a chapbook, *Fragments with Dusk in Them.* His poems have appeared in *Colorado Review, Crazyhorse, Denver Quarterly, Poetry,* and others. He has taught creative writing at The University of Montana and Interlochen Center for the Arts.

Jehanne Dubrow is the author of three poetry collections, most recently *Stateside* (Northwestern University Press, 2010). Her work has appeared in *Poetry, The New England Review, Ploughshares,* and *The New Republic.*

Denise Duhamel's most recent poetry titles are *Ka-Ching!* (University of Pittsburgh Press, 2009); *Two and Two* (Pittsburgh, 2005); *Mille et un Sentiments* (Firewheel, 2005); *Queen for a Day: Selected and New Poems* (Pittsburgh, 2001); and *The Star-Spangled Banner* (Southern Illinois University Press, 1999). She is a professor at Florida International University in Miami.

Camille T. Dungy is author of *Suck on the Marrow, Smith Blue,* and *What to Eat, What to Drink, What to Leave for Poison.* She has edited *Black Nature: Four Centuries of African American Nature Poetry* and the *From the Fishouse* poetry anthology. Dungy teaches creative writing at San Francisco State University.

Cornelius Eady is the author of *Kartunes; Victims of the Latest Dance Craze; The Gathering of My Name; You Don't Miss Your Water; The Autobiography of a Jukebox; Brutal*

Imagination; and most recently, *Hardheaded Weather*. He is the co-founder of Cave Canem and is currently The Miller Family Endowed Chair in Literature and Writing and Professor in English at The University of Missouri-Columbia.

Carolina Ebeid's poems appear widely in journals such as *Poetry, Gulf Coast, Fugue* and *Memorious*. She has been both a McNair Scholar and a fellow at the Michener Center for Writers. She is originally from West New York, NJ.

Susan Elbe is the author of *Eden in the Rearview Mirror* (Word Press) and a chapbook, *Light Made from Nothing* (Parallel Press). Her work has been widely anthologized and has appeared in many journals, including *Ascent, Blackbird, MARGIE*, and *North American Review*. She lives in Madison, Wisconsin.

Kelly Madigan Erlandson is the author of *Getting Sober* (McGraw-Hill). Her poems and essays have appeared in *Best New Poets 2007, Crazyhorse, The Massachusetts Review,* and *Prairie Schooner*. She has received the Distinguished Artist Award in Literature from the Nebraska Arts Council and a National Endowment for the Arts Fellowship.

John Olivares Espinoza is the author of *The Date Fruit Elegies* (Bilingual Press, 2008), plus two chapbooks. Born and raised in Southern California, he holds degrees in creative writing from UC Riverside (BA) and Arizona State University (MFA). He lives, teaches, and writes in San Jose, California.

Kathy Fagan is the author of four collections, most recently *Lip*. Her work has appeared in *The Paris Review, The New Republic, Field*, and *The Kenyon Review*, among other magazines. She teaches at The Ohio State University, where she also co-edits *The Journal*.

Blas Falconer is the author of *A Question of Gravity and Light* (University of Arizona Press, 2007) and the co-editor of *Mentor and Muse: Essays from Poets to Poets* (Southern Illinois University Press, 2010). He coordinates the Creative Writing Program at Austin Peay State University.

Jennifer Fandel's poetry has appeared in *The Laurel Review, Relief, The Chiron Review,* and the Prentice-Hall textbook *Higher Education: A Reader for College Lives*. She lives in St. Louis, works in the publishing industry, and is a volunteer for the literary magazine *River Styx*.

Annie Finch is author of numerous works of poetry, poetic translation, music, art, and theater collaboration, and poetics. Her most recent books include the audio CD of the poetry collection *Calendars* and *Among the Goddesses: An Epic Libretto in Seven Dreams*. She is Director of the Stonecoast MFA Program.

Kathleen Flenniken's first book is *Famous* (University of Nebraska, 2006), named a Notable Book by the American Library Association. Her poems have appeared in *The Iowa Review, Prairie Schooner,* and *New Poets of the American West*, and she is a recipient of fellowships from the NEA and Artist Trust.

William Robert Flowers earned an MFA in Poetry from The University of North Carolina Wilmington, and his work has appeared in journals such as *Hunger Mountain, The Apple Valley Review,* and *Great River Review.*

Vievee Francis is the author of two poetry collections *Blue-Tail Fly* (2006) and *Horse in the Dark* (Northwestern Press, 2011). Her work is also forthcoming or has appeared in numerous journals and anthologies, including *Callaloo, Indiana Review, Best American Poetry 2010,* and *Angles of Ascent: A Norton Anthology of Contemporary African American Poetry.*

Gregory Fraser is the author of two poetry collections, *Strange Pietà* (Texas Tech, 2003) and *Answering the Ruins* (Northwestern, 2009), as well as the co-author, with Chad Davidson, of two textbooks, *Writing Poetry* (Palgrave-Macmillan, 2008) and *Analyze Anything: A Guide to Critical Reading and Writing* (Continuum, forthcoming in 2012).

Todd Fredson's poetry and non-fiction appears in journals such as *Blackbird, Puerto del Sol, Gulf Coast, The American Poetry Review, Poetry International* and *42 Opus.* He is Director of Programming at the McReavy House Museum of Hood Canal in Union, WA.

Jeannine Hall Gailey is the author of *Becoming the Villainess,* published by Steel Toe Books. Her poems were featured on The Writer's Almanac and Verse Daily. She teaches in the MFA program at National University. Her new book, *She Returns to the Floating World,* was published by Kitsune Books in 2011.

Martin Galvin's *Sounding the Atlantic (2010)* is his new poetry collection. His first book, *Wild Card* (Washington Writers' Publishing House), won the 1989 Columbia Prize, judged by Howard Nemerov. In the last ten years, he has published over 170 more poems in journals and magazines, including *Poetry, The New Republic, The Atlantic Monthly,* and *Commonweal.*

Molly Gaudry is the author of the verse novel *We Take Me Apart* (Mud Luscious, 2009) and the editor of *Tell: An Anthology of Expository Narrative* (Flatmancrooked, 2010).

Frank Giampietro's first book of poems, *Begin Anywhere,* was published by Alice James Books in 2008. He is the editor and designer of the online poetry journal *La Fovea.* Awards include a Florida Book Award, an Academy of American Poets Prize, and fellowships from The Virginia Center for Creative Arts and the Sewanee Writers' Conference.

Rodney Gomez works as a transportation planner in Weslaco, Texas. He holds a BA from Yale and an MFA from UT-Pan American. A recent associate artist at the Atlantic Center for the Arts, his poetry appears in *Denver Quarterly, Borderlands, Barrow Street, Salt Hill, The Pinch,* and *NANO Fiction.*

Rigoberto González is the author of eight books and the editor of *Camino del Sol: Fifteen Years of Latina and Latino Writing.* The recipient of Guggenheim and NEA fellowships, the American Book Award, and The Poetry Center Book Award, he is an Associate Professor of English at Rutgers-Newark, State University of New Jersey.

Henrietta Goodman is the author of *Take What You Want* (Alice James Books, 2007). Her poems have recently appeared in *Massachusetts Review, Guernica, Valparaiso Poetry Review,* and *Field,* and can be read and heard online at *From the Fishouse: An Audio Archive of Emerging Poets.*

Arielle Greenberg is co-author, with Rachel Zucker, of *Home/Birth: A Poemic,* and author of *My Kafka Century, Given,* and several chapbooks. She is co-editor of three anthologies, most recently *Gurlesque* with Lara Glenum. She is the founder-moderator of the poet-moms listserv and is an Associate Professor at Columbia College Chicago.

Jennifer Gresham is a scientist and author of the blog Everyday Bright. Her poems have appeared in journals such as *Prairie Schooner, Crab Orchard Review,* and *Rattle,* among others. Her book, *Diary of a Cell,* won the 2004 Steel Toe Books Poetry Prize.

Sarah Grieve is currently a Ph.D. student at Arizona State. She holds degrees from Florida State (MFA) and Cal Poly, SLO (BA and MA). Her work has appeared in *Apalachee Review, New Ohio Review, New Madrid, Salamander, Sow's Ear Poetry Review,* and *The Mind's Eye: A Guide to Writing Poetry.*

Gail Griffin is the author of three nonfiction books, including *"The Events of October": Murder-Suicide on a Small Campus* (Wayne State University Press). Her poetry has appeared widely in journals and anthologies, and she won the Cranston poetry prize from *Calyx* in 2006. She teaches at Kalamazoo College in Michigan.

Matthew Guenette is the author of *Sudden Anthem,* winner of the 2007 American Poetry Journal Prize from Dream Horse Press, and *American Busboy,* a Finalist and Editor's Choice in the 2010 Akron Poetry Prize. He lives and works in Madison, WI.

Carol Guess is the author of six books of poetry and prose, including *Switch* and *Tinderbox Lawn.* Forthcoming books include a novel, *Homeschooling,* and a prose poetry collection, *Doll Studies: Forensics.* She is an Associate Professor of English at Western Washington University.

Mary Hammerbeck teaches writing at Whatcom Community College in Bellingham, WA. Her poems have appeared in *The Talking Stick* literary journal and *The Lucky Dumpster* writer's workshop publication. She is currently working on her poetic script, *billy americana's Poesía de la Frontera*—a long poem about physical and metaphorical borderlands.

Jeremy Halinen co-edits *Knockout Literary Magazine.* His first full-length collection of poems, *What Other Choice,* won the 2010 Exquisite Disarray First Book Poetry Contest. His poems have also appeared in *Best Gay Poetry 2008, The Los Angeles Review, Poet Lore, Sentence,* and elsewhere. He resides in Seattle.

Derrick Harriell holds an MFA in Creative Writing from Chicago State University and is currently a dissertator in UW-Milwaukee's English Ph.D. program, where he also teaches Creative Writing. *Cotton* (Aquarius Press/Willow Books, 2010) is his first collection of poems.

Reginald Harris is a Pushcart Prize Nominee and the author of *10 Tongues: Poems*. He is also Poetry in the Branches Coordinator for Poets House. His work has appeared in a variety of publications, including *African American Review, MELUS Journal, smartish pace, Sou'wester,* and the *Best Gay Poetry 2008, Gathering Ground,* and *The Ringing Ear* anthologies.

Christopher Hennessy is the author of *Outside the Lines: Talking with Contemporary Gay Poets.* He is a Ph.D. candidate in English at the University of Massachusetts-Amherst. His poetry appeared in *Ploughshares'* "Emerging Writers" edition, and work appears in *American Poetry Review, Verse, Cimarron Review, Court Green, The Writer's Chronicle* and elsewhere.

Matthew Hittinger is the author of the chapbooks *Platos de Sal* (Seven Kitchens Press, 2009), *Narcissus Resists* (GOSS183/MiPOesias, 2009), and *Pear Slip* (Spire Press, 2007), which won the Spire 2006 Chapbook Award. Matthew lives and works in New York City.

Lois Holub lives in Deming, WA, and has done many public readings of her poetry. A CD of "Her Voice," a live performance with Mockingbird, is available.

John Hoppenthaler's books of poetry are *Lives of Water* and *Anticipate the Coming Reservoir,* both from Carnegie Mellon University Press. For *Connotation Press: An Online Artifact,* he edits "A Poetry Congeries," and he teaches creative writing and literature at East Carolina University.

Randall Horton is the author of *The Definition of Place* and *The Lingua Franca of Ninth Street,* both from Main Street Rag. He has an MFA from Chicago State University and a Ph.D. from SUNY Albany. Randall is a Cave Canem Fellow and Assistant Professor of English at the University of New Haven.

T. R. Hummer has altogether too few heteronyms, but he has published ten books of poetry; the most recent, *Ephemeron,* appeared from LSU Press in November of 2011. His second book of essays, *Available Surfaces,* will be published in 2012 in the University of Michigan Press' *Poets on Poetry* series.

Donald Illich has published poetry in *The Iowa Review, LIT, Fourteen Hills,* and many other journals. He won Honorable Mention in the Washington Prize book contest and was a "Discovery"/Boston Review 2008 Poetry Contest semifinalist. Additionally, he was a semifinalist in the Elixir Press Poetry Book Award Contest.

Major Jackson is the author of *Holding Company* (W. W. Norton, 2010), *Hoops* (W. W. Norton, 2006), and *Leaving Saturn* (University of Georgia, 2002), winner of the 2001 Cave Canem Poetry Prize and finalist for the National Book Critics Circle Award. He is the poetry editor for *Harvard Review* and teaches at the University of Vermont and for the Bennington College Writers Seminars.

Charles Jensen was a finalist for the 2010 Lambda Literary Award for his book *The First Risk*. His poems have previously appeared in *The Journal, New England Review, Willow Springs,* and *West Branch*.

Hershman John is a full-time faculty member at Phoenix College. His works have been widely published in journals including *Arizona Highways, Hayden's Ferry Review, Puerto del Sol, Wicazo* and *Sa Review*. The University of Arizona Press published his first poetry collection, *I Swallow Turquoise for Courage*.

Luke Johnson is the author of *After the Ark* (New York Quarterly Books, 2011). His poems have appeared in *Beloit Poetry Journal, Epoch, New England Review, Greensboro Review,* and have twice been featured in the *Best New Poets* anthology. He currently lives in Seattle, Washington.

Mary Kaiser's chapbook, *Falling into Velázquez,* was awarded the 2006 Slapering Hol Chapbook Prize from the Hudson Valley Writer's Center. Her poems have appeared in *The Cincinnati Review, New Orleans Review* and *The Portland Review*, among others. She is the recipient of an Individual Artist Fellowship from the Alabama State Council on the Arts.

Ilya Kaminsky was born in Odessa, former USSR, and arrived in the USA in 1993, when his family was granted asylum by the American government. He is the author of *Dancing in Odessa,* which won a Ruth Lilly Fellowship from *Poetry,* the Whiting Writers Award, the Dorset Prize, and the Metcalf Award from the American Academy of Arts and Letters. In 2010, his anthology, *Ecco Anthology of International Poetry,* was published by Harper Collins.

Ariana-Sophia Kartsonis' poems, stories, and essays have appeared or are forthcoming in *Cafe Review, Fine Madness, Glimmer Train, Hayden's Ferry Review, Southern Review* and *Third Coast*. Her book of poetry, *Intaglio,* was published in 2006 by Kent State University Press.

M. Nzadi Keita's poems appear in anthologies, including *The Ringing Ear: Black Poets Lean South*. Some of her most fruitful research has taken place on the porch of Anna Murray Douglass' Washington, D.C., home and while walking along the Baltimore harbor. Keita, a Cave Canem alumna, teaches at Ursinus College.

Collin Kelley is a poet and novelist from Atlanta, GA. He is the author of the novels *Conquering Venus* and *Remain in Light* and three poetry collections: *Better to Travel, Slow to Burn,* and *After the Poison*. Winner of a 2007 Georgia Author of the Year Award, Kelley's poetry has been published in literary magazines and journals around the world.

Jee Leong Koh is the author of three books of poems, *Payday Loans, Equal to the Earth,* and *Seven Studies for a Self-Portrait* (Bench Press, 2011). Born and raised in Singapore, he lives in New York City.

Jason Koo is the author of *Man on Extremely Small Island*, winner of the 2008 De Novo Poetry Prize. The recipient of fellowships from the National Endowment for the Arts and the Vermont Studio Center, he teaches at Lehman College, where he serves as Director of Graduate Studies in English. He lives in Brooklyn.

Keetje Kuipers is a former Stegner Fellow at Stanford University. She was the Margery Davis Boyden Wilderness Writing Resident, and her book, *Beautiful in the Mouth*, won the 2009 A. Poulin, Jr. Poetry Prize and was published by BOA Editions. She is the Emerging Writer Lecturer at Gettysburg College and splits her time between Gettysburg and Missoula.

Laurie Clements Lambeth is the author of *Veil and Burn*, selected by Maxine Kumin for the National Poetry Series. Her poems and essays have appeared in *The Paris Review*, *Mid-American Review*, *The Iowa Review*, *Crazyhorse*, and elsewhere. She currently teaches at the University of Houston.

Jacqueline Jones LaMon's first collection, *Gravity, U.S.A.*, received the Quercus Review Press Poetry Series Book Award. Her second collection, *Last Seen*, received the 2011 Felix Pollak Prize in Poetry. She is Director of the MFA Program in Creative Writing at Adelphi University, where she teaches poetry, literature, and pedagogy.

Quraysh Ali Lansana, author of five poetry books and a children's book, and editor of eight anthologies, is Director of the Gwendolyn Brooks Center for Black Literature and Creative Writing and Associate Professor of English/Creative Writing at Chicago State University. *Our Difficult Sunlight: A Guide to Poetry, Literacy & Social Justice in Classroom & Community* (Teachers & Writers Collaborative) was published in 2011.

Iris A. Law received her MFA from the University of Notre Dame and her BA from Stanford. Her work has been published in a number of small magazines and has been reprinted in the 2010 *Best of the Net Anthology*. She edits *Lantern Review: A Journal of Asian American Poetry*.

Anna Leahy won the Wick Poetry Prize for her book *Constituents of Matter* and has published two chapbooks. She edited *Power and Identity in the Creative Writing Classroom* and publishes widely about pedagogy. She teaches in the MFA and BFA programs at Chapman University and directs *Tabula Poetica*, including its reading series.

Sarah Lindsay, a recipient of a Lannan Literary Fellowship, is the author of *Primate Behavior*, *Mount Clutter*, and *Twigs and Kucklebones*. She works as a copy editor and plays the cello; she and her husband are testing how many books will fit in their house.

Sandy Longhorn is the author of *Blood Almanac*, winner of the 2005 Anhinga Prize for Poetry. Recent poems appear in *Spillway*, *New Madrid*, *Connotation Press*, *Passages North*, and elsewhere. Longhorn lives in Little Rock and is an Arkansas Arts Council fellow.

Peter Ludwin is the recipient of a literary fellowship from Artist Trust. His first collection, *A Guest in All Your Houses*, was published in 2009 by Word Walker Press. His work has appeared in journals such as *The Bitter Oleander*, *The Comstock Review*, *Midwest Quarterly*, and *South Dakota Review*.

Alison Luterman has written two collections of poetry, *The Largest Possible Life* (Cleveland State University Press) and *See How We Almost Fly* (Pearl Editions). She teaches creative writing and performs with the dance theatre improvisation troupe Wing It! in Oakland, California.

Alessandra Lynch is the author of *Sails the Wind Left Behind* and *It was a terrible cloud at twilight*. Her poems have appeared in *The American Poetry Review*, *jubilat*, *The Massachusetts Review*, *Ploughshares*, *The Virginia Quarterly Review*, and other journals. Alessandra lives near an Indianapolisian canal and teaches at Butler University.

Angie Macri was born and raised in southern Illinois. Her work has been featured in *Spoon River Poetry Review* and appears in *Best New Poets 2010*. A recipient of an individual artist fellowship from the Arkansas Arts Council, she teaches in Little Rock, where she lives with her husband and children.

Marie-Elizabeth Mali is the author of *Steady, My Gaze* (Tebot Bach, 2011). She is a co-curator of louderARTS: the Reading Series and Page Meets Stage, both in New York City. Her work has appeared in *Calyx*, *Poet Lore*, and *Rattle*, among others.

Marjorie Manwaring lives in Seattle, where she is a freelance writer and an editor for the online poetry and art journal the *DMQ Review*. Her work has appeared in *5 AM*, *Crab Orchard Review*, *Sentence*, and other journals, and her chapbook *Magic Word* was published in 2007.

Diane K. Martin's work has appeared in *Field*, *New England Review*, *Poetry Daily*, *Harvard Review*, *Narrative*, and was included in *Best New Poets 2005*. She received a Pushcart Special Mention and won the Erskine J. Poetry Prize from *Smartish Pace*. Her collection, *Conjugated Visits*, was published in May 2010 by Dream Horse Press.

Cate Marvin is the author of *World's Tallest Disaster* (2001) and *Fragment of the Head of a Queen* (2007), both from Sarabande. A Whiting Award recipient, she is an Associate Professor in English at the College of Staten Island, CUNY, and co-directs, with poet Erin Belieu, VIDA: Women in Literary Arts.

Sebastian Matthews is the author of *We Generous* (poems) and *In My Father's Footsteps* (memoir). He lives with his family in Asheville, North Carolina, where he teaches at Warren Wilson College. He also serves on the faculty of the low-residency MFA at Queens University in Charlotte.

Marty McConnell is the director of Vox Ferus and a co-founder of the louderARTS Project. Her work has been published in magazines including *Crab Orchard Review*,

Booth, Salt Hill Review, Rattle, Ratapallax, and *Fourteen Hills,* as well as anthologies including *Women of the Bowery, Spoken Word Revolution Redux,* and *Women.Period.*

Jeffrey McDaniel is the author of four books of poetry: *The Endarkenment* (University of Pittsburgh Press, 2008), *The Splinter Factory* (Manic D, 2002), *The Forgiveness Parade* (Manic D, 1998), and *Alibi School* (Manic D, 1995). He is the recipient of a creative writing fellowship from the National Endowment for the Arts and teaches creative writing at Sarah Lawrence College.

Leslie McGrath's poems have appeared widely. Winner of the 2004 Pablo Neruda Prize for poetry, McGrath edited Reetika Vazirani's posthumous poetry collection, *Radha Says.* McGrath's first collection, *Opulent Hunger, Opulent Rage* (2009), was a finalist for the Connecticut Book Award in poetry. She is the former managing editor of *Drunken Boat.*

Claire McQuerry teaches literature and writing at the University of Missouri and works as an editor at *The Missouri Review.* Her first book of poetry, *Lacemakers,* was published by Southern Illinois University Press in 2011.

Philip Memmer is the author of three collections of poems, including *Lucifer: A Hagiography* (Lost Horse Press, 2009), winner of the 2008 Idaho Prize for Poetry; *Threat of Pleasure* (Word Press, 2008), winner of the 2008 Adirondack Literary Award for Poetry; and *Sweetheart, Baby, Darling* (Word Press, 2004).

Billy Merrell is the author of *Talking in the Dark* (Scholastic, 2003) and a co-editor for *The Full Spectrum* (Knopf Books for Young Readers), which received a 2006 Lambda Literary Award. He currently serves as Web Developer of the website of the Academy of American Poets.

Sarah Messer has received fellowships from the Fine Arts Work Center in Provincetown, the NEA, the Radcliffe Institute for Advanced Study, and others. Her hybrid history/memoir *Red House* was published in 2004. A poetry collection, *Bandit Letters,* was published in 2001. She teaches at the University of North Carolina-Wilmington.

Philip Metres is the author of numerous books, including *To See the Earth* (poetry, 2008), *Come Together: Imagine Peace* (2008), *Behind the Lines: War Resistance Poetry on the American Homefront since 1941* (criticism, 2007), and *Catalogue of Comedic Novelties: Selected Poems of Lev Rubinstein* (2004). He lives in Cleveland.

Seth Michelson is the author of *Maestro of Brutal Splendor* (Jeanne Duval Editions), *House in a Hurricane* (Big Table Publishing), and *Kaddish for My Unborn Son* (Pudding House Publications), as well as the translator of *El ghetto,* by Tamara Kamenszain, into English as *The Ghetto* (Point of Contact).

Jory M. Mickelson's poems have appeared in *Oranges & Sardines, Gertrude, Knockout, New Mexico Poetry Review,* and *Free Verse.* He is the nonfiction editor of the literary magazine *5x5.* He is currently pursuing an MFA at the University of Idaho.

Tiffany Midge is an enrolled member of the Standing Rock Sioux. She is the recipient of the Diane Decorah Poetry Award for *Outlaws, Renegades and Saints: Diary of a Mixed-Up Halfbreed* (Greenfield Review Press). Her chapbook is *Guiding the Stars to Their Campfire, Driving the Salmon to Their Beds* (Gazoobi Tales). She holds an MFA in poetry from the University of Idaho.

Thorpe Moeckel is the author of *Venison: a poem* (Etruscan Press, 2010), *Making a Map of the River* (Iris Press, 2008), and *Odd Botany* (Silverfish Review Press, 2002). He teaches at Hollins University and farms with his family near Buchanan, VA.

Carolina Monsiváis is a recipient of the Premio Poesia Tejana for her book *Somewhere Between Houston and El Paso*. Most recently, Mouthfeel Press published her chapbook, *Elisa's Hunger*. She completed her MFA in poetry at New Mexico State University, and she currently teaches at El Paso Community College.

Juan J. Morales is the author of *Friday and the Year that Followed* (Bedbug Press). His poems have most recently appeared or are forthcoming in *Pilgrimage, Washington Square, Zone 3*, and other journals. He is the Director of Creative Writing at Colorado State University-Pueblo.

Tomás Q. Morín's poems have appeared in *Ploughshares, Slate, Threepenny Review, Poetry International, Boulevard, The Southern Review*, and *Narrative* magazine. He has received scholarships from the Bread Loaf Writers' Conference, the New York State Writers Institute, and the Fine Arts Work Center. He teaches writing and literature at Texas State University.

Andrew Mulvania is an assistant professor of English at Washington & Jefferson College. His first book, *Also in Arcadia*, was published by The Backwaters Press in 2008. His poems have appeared in *Poetry, North American Review, Southern Poetry Review*, and elsewhere. He was the recipient of a 2008 Pennsylvania Council on the Arts Grant.

Paul Nemser co-translated two books of Ukrainian poetry during the '70s. Visits to St. Petersburg in 2005 and 2006 triggered a return to his poetic and cultural roots and an outpouring of poetry culminating in "Taurus." Recent poems have appeared or are forthocming in *Arion, Blackbird, Columbia, Pequod, Raritan*, and *Redivider*.

Laura P. Newton's poems have appeared in *Snake Nation Review, Green Mountains Review, Naugatuck River Review* and *Redheaded Stepchild*. She was nominated for a Pushcart prize in 2010. She is co-editor of *Between Two Rivers: Stories From the Red Hills to the Gulf* and *My Last Door*, poems by Wendy Bishop.

Aimee Nezhukumatathil is the author of three books of poetry, most recently *Lucky Fish*, from Tupelo Press. Awards for her writing include an NEA Fellowship and the Pushcart Prize. She is an Associate Professor of English at SUNY-Fredonia.

Matthew Nienow is the author of two chapbooks: *The Smallest Working Pieces* (2009) and *Two Sides of the Same Thing* (2007). His work has appeared in *Best New Poets, Cincin-*

nati Review, Indiana Review, Prairie Schooner and *Willow Springs*. He is currently attending the Northwest School of Wooden Boatbuilding.

Gregory Pardlo, the author of *Totem* (APR, 2007), has received grants from the New York Foundation for the Arts and the National Endowment for the Arts. His work has appeared in *Callaloo, Ploughshares, The American Poetry Review,* and *Best American Poetry,* among other publications. Pardlo teaches at George Washington University.

Diana Park is the 2010-2011 Emerging Writer Fellow at the Stadler Center for Poetry at Bucknell University. She is also the recipient of fellowships from Kundiman, the MacDowell Colony, and the Fulbright Program. Her work has appeared in *Tin House, Indiana Review,* and elsewhere.

Ed Pavlić's most recent book is '. . .*but here are small clear refractions'* (Achebe Center, 2009). Others include *Winners Have Yet to be Announced: A Song for Donny Hathaway, Labors Lost Left Unfinished,* and *Paraph of Bone & Other Kinds of Blue.*

Alison Pelegrin is the recipient of a fellowship from the National Endowment for the Arts. Her two most recent collections are *Big Muddy River of Stars* (2007) and *Hurricane Party* (2011), both from The University of Akron Press.

Peter Pereira is a family physician in Seattle. His books include *What's Written on the Body* (Copper Canyon, 2007) and *Saying the World* (Copper Canyon, 2003). His poetry has been featured on Garrison Keillor's *The Writer's Almanac* and was included in the 2007 *Best American Poetry.*

Jennifer Perrine's first book of poetry, *The Body is No Machine,* was published by New Issues in 2007 and won the 2008 Devil's Kitchen Reading Award in Poetry. Her recent work received the *Bellingham Review* 49th Parallel Award. She teaches creative writing and gender studies at Drake University in Iowa.

Leigh Phillips is an Assistant Professor of English at Hostos Community College with the City University of New York. Her works most recently appear in *Mad Hatters Review, So To Speak: A Feminist Journal of Language and Art, Rhino, The Prose Poetry Project* and *Paterson Literary Review.*

Kenneth Pobo's book *Glass Garden* was published in 2008 by WordTech Press. In 2009, he won *Main Street Rag*'s chapbook contest with *Trina and the Sky,* which was published that year. *Tea on Burning Glass,* a chapbook from Tandava Poetry Press, was published in 2010. He teaches Creative Writing and English at Widener University in Pennsylvania.

John Poch is the author of three poetry collections, most recently *Dolls* (Orchises Press, 2009). His poems have appeared in *Agni, Poetry, Paris Review, The New Republic,* and other journals. He is the editor of *32 Poems Magazine* and teaches in the English Department at Texas Tech University.

Iain Haley Pollock's first poetry collection, *Spit Back a Boy*, won the 2010 Cave Canem Poetry Prize and was published in 2011 by The University of Georgia Press. He lives in Philadelphia and teaches English at Chestnut Hill Academy.

R. Elena Prieto is a graduate of the MFA creative writing program at Southern Illinois University-Carbondale. Her work has appeared in *Compass Rose Literary Magazine* both online and in print, and she received an honorable mention from the Rondeau Roundup's 2009 Love Rondeau Contest.

Donna Prinzmetal has taught creative writing for over twenty years. She is also a licensed psychotherapist. Her work has appeared in numerous small press publications including *The Cincinnati Review* and *The Journal*. Her manuscript, *Snow White, When No One Was Looking*, has been a finalist in many contests and hopes to find a home soon.

Stephanie M. Pruitt teaches in the Department of English at Vanderbilt University and is the Poet-in-Residence at The Curb Center for Art, Enterprise, and Public Policy. The Cave Canem Fellow and Affrilachian Poet lives in Nashville, TN, with her husband, 10-year-old daughter, and two furry, tail-wagging kids.

Shelley Puhak's first collection, *Stalin in Aruba* (Black Lawrence Press, 2009), was awarded the 2010 Towson University Prize for Literature. Her poems have appeared in *Alaska Quarterly Review, Beloit Poetry Journal, New South, Southeast Review*, and many other journals.

Khadijah Queen is the author of two poetry collections: *Conduit* (Black Goat/Akashic Books 2008), and the forthcoming *Black Peculiar*, which won the 2010 Noemi Press Book Award. She is a Cave Canem fellow and three-time Pushcart Prize nominee; individual poems appear widely in journals and anthologies.

Rita Mae Reese has received a Rona Jaffe Foundation Writers' Award, a Stegner fellowship, and a "Discovery"/*The Nation* award. Her work has been nominated for a Pushcart Prize and has appeared in numerous journals and anthologies. Her first book, *The Alphabet Conspiracy*, was published by Arktoi Books/Red Hen Press in 2011.

Barbara Jane Reyes is the author of *Diwata* (BOA Editions, Ltd.). She was born in Manila, Philippines, raised in the San Francisco Bay Area, and has authored two previous poetry collections, *Gravities of Center* (Arkipelago Books) and *Poeta en San Francisco* (Tinfish Press), which received the Academy of American Poets' James Laughlin Award.

Shelley Renée-Ruiz is a writer and illustrator living in Austin, Texas. She received her MFA from Antioch University in Los Angeles. Her work has been published in *Poetry Midwest, The Cortland Review, DMQ Review, Eclipse Literary Journal, The Coe Review, So to Speak* and *Crab Orchard Review*.

Jonathan B. Rice's poems have been published in *AGNI Online, Colorado Review*, and *Sycamore Review*, among others, and received the 2010 Indiana Review Poetry Prize and

Crab Orchard Review's 2010 Richard Peterson Poetry Prize. He is pursuing a Ph.D. at Western Michigan University and is the Associate Editor for New Issues Press.

Susan Rich is the author of three collections of poetry, *The Alchemist's Kitchen* (2010), *Cures Include Travel* (2006), and *The Cartographer's Tongue* (2000), which won the PEN Award for Poetry. Her work appears in journals such as *The Antioch Review, Harvard Review*, and *New England Review*.

Kathleen Rooney is a founding editor of Rose Metal Press and the author of the essay collection *For You, For You I Am Trilling These Songs*. With Elisa Gabbert, she co-authored the poetry collection *That Tiny Insane Voluptuousness*, and her solo collection, *Oneiromance (an epithalamion)*, was published by Switchback Books.

Laurel Rust's first collection was *What Is Given* (Brooding Heron Press), and her poems have appeared in many magazines. She earned a degree from the University of Washington and lives off the coast of northwest Washington on Orcas Island, where she works for the state ferry system.

Brynn Saito's poetry has been anthologized in Helen Vendler's *Poems, Poets, Poetry: An Introduction and Anthology*, 3rd ed., and *From Totems to Hip-Hop: A Multicultural Anthology of Poetry Across the Americas 1900-2002*, by Ishmael Reed. Her work has also appeared in *Pleiades, Harpur Palate*, and *Copper Nickel*. In 2008, she was awarded a Kundiman Asian American Poetry Fellowship.

Natasha Sajé is the author of two books of poems, *Red Under the Skin* (Pittsburgh, 1994) and *Bend* (Tupelo, 2004), as well as many essays. She teaches at Westminster College in Salt Lake City and in the Vermont College MFA in Writing Program.

Greg Santos was born and raised in Montreal. He is the poetry editor of *pax americana* and lives in New Haven, Connecticut, with his wife and daughter. His first book, *The Emperor's Sofa*, was published by DC Books in 2010.

Kelly Scarff holds an MFA in Creative Writing from Chatham University. Her poems have appeared in *5 AM, LABOR, Nerve Cowboy*, and elsewhere. She currently resides in Greensburg, PA.

Steven D. Schroeder's first book of poetry is *Torched Verse Ends* (BlazeVOX [Books]). His poems are available or forthcoming from *New England Review, Pleiades, The Journal, Indiana Review*, and *Verse Daily*. He edits the online poetry journal *Anti-* and works as a Certified Professional Résumé Writer.

Anne Shaw is the author of *Undertow* (Persea Books), winner of the Lexi Rudnitsky Poetry Prize. Her work has appeared or is forthcoming in *Black Warrior Review, Beloit Poetry Journal*, and *Harvard Review*.

Matthew Shenoda is the author of the poetry collections *Seasons of Lotus, Seasons of Bone* and *Somewhere Else*, winner of the American Book Award. He is Assistant Provost for Equity & Diversity and Professor in the School of Critical Studies at California Institute of the Arts.

Evie Shockley is the author of *the new black* (Wesleyan, 2011), *a half-red sea* (Carolina Wren Press, 2006), and two chapbooks. She co-edits the journal *jubilat*. Her poetry criticism and scholarship appear in *African American Review, Callaloo, Indiana Review,* and elsewhere. Shockley teaches African-American literature and creative writing at Rutgers University, New Brunswick.

Martha Silano's most recent books are *The Little Office of the Immaculate Conception* (Saturnalia, 2011) and *Blue Positive* (Steel Toe Books, 2006). Her work has also appeared in *AGNI, Paris Review, TriQuarterly,* and *The Best American Poetry 2009,* among others. Silano teaches at Bellevue College, near her home in Seattle, WA.

Sean Singer's first book, *Discography,* won the 2001 Yale Series of Younger Poets Prize, selected by W. S. Merwin, and the Norma Farber First Book Award from the Poetry Society of America. He is the recipient of a Fellowship from the National Endowment for the Arts.

Susan Slaviero's first full-length collection of poetry, *CYBORGIA,* is available from Mayapple Press. Her work has appeared in journals *RHINO, Flyway, Fourteen Hills, Artifice Magazine, Oyez Review,* and elsewhere. She lives just outside of Chicago, where she edits *blossombones* (an online literary journal) and performs with the Chicago Poetry Brothel.

Erin Elizabeth Smith is the author of *The Fear of Being Found* (Three Candles Press, 2008) and managing editor of *Stirring* and the *Best of the Net Anthology*. Her poems have appeared in *32 Poems, New Delta Review, Yalobusha Review, Water~Stone,* and *RHINO.* She currently teaches at the University of Tennessee.

Patricia Smith is the author of five books of poetry, including *Blood Dazzler,* a finalist for the 2008 National Book Award. She is a professor of creative writing at the City University of New York and a faculty member of Cave Canem and the Stonecoast MFA program.

Christopher S. Soden received his MFA in Writing from Vermont College in 2005. His work appears in *Ganymede, Poetic Voices Without Borders 2, The Texas Observer, Sentence, Borderlands, Cafe Review, Off the Rocks, The James White Review, The New Writer, Windy City Times, ArLiJo,* and *Best Texas Writing 2.*

Alison Stine is the author of *Wait,* winner of the Brittingham Prize (The University of Wisconsin Press, 2011), and *Ohio Violence,* winner of the Vassar Miller Prize in Poetry (The University of North Texas Press, 2009). Her awards include a Wallace Stegner Fellowship and the Ruth Lilly Fellowship from the Poetry Foundation.

Adam Tavel won the 2010 Frost Award from the Robert Frost Foundation. His poems have appeared or are forthcoming in *Indiana Review, Redivider, Portland Review, South Carolina Review, Poet Lore, New South,* and *Cave Wall,* among others. He lives and teaches on Maryland's Eastern Shore.

Molly Tenenbaum is the author of *Now* (Bear Star Press, 2007) and *By a Thread* (Van West & Co, 2000). A recipient of a 2009 Artist Trust Fellowship, she also plays Appalachian music and has two CDs: *Instead of a Pony* and *Goose and Gander*. She teaches English at North Seattle Community College.

Maria Terrone is the author of two poetry collections, *A Secret Room in Fall*, co-winner of the McGovern Prize (Ashland Poetry Press), and *The Bodies We Were Loaned*, and a chapbook, *American Gothic, Take 2*. Her work has appeared in magazines including *Poetry* and *Hudson Review* and in more than a dozen anthologies.

Jeffrey Thomson is the author of four books of poems, including *Birdwatching in Wartime* and *Renovation*. He also co-edited an anthology of emerging poets: *From the Fishouse: An Anthology of Poems that Sing, Rhyme, Resound, Syncopate, Alliterate, and Just Plain Sound Great* (Persea, 2009).

Matthew Thorburn is the author of a book of poems, *Subject to Change* (New Issues, 2004), and a chapbook, the long poem *Disappears in the Rain* (Parlor City, 2009). He lives in New York City, where he manages the creative services team at an international law firm.

Angela Narciso Torres was born in Brooklyn, New York, and grew up in Manila, Philippines. Her poems have appeared in *Collagist, Crab Orchard Review, North American Review,* and *Rattle*, among others. A graduate of the Warren Wilson MFA Program for Writers, she co-edits *RHINO* and received a Ragdale Foundation fellowship in 2010.

Tony Trigilio's recent books include *Historic Diary* (BlazeVOX [Books]) and *The Lama's English Lessons* (Three Candles Press). With Tim Prchal, he co-edited *Visions and Divisions: American Immigration Literature, 1870-1930* (Rutgers University Press). He teaches at Columbia College Chicago and co-edits *Court Green*.

Brian Turner is the author of two collections of poetry: *Here, Bullet* and *Phantom Noise* (both available from Alice James Books). He has received a USA Hillcrest Fellowship in Literature, an NEA Literature Fellowship in Poetry, the Amy Lowell Traveling Fellowship, the Poets' Prize, and a Fellowship from the Lannan Foundation.

Kristine Uyeda is a Kundiman Fellow and works as a writer-in-the-schools for InsideOut Literary Arts. Her work has appeared in *Asian Pacific American Journal, Cyphers, Rattle,* and *The Lantern Review*, among others.

Susan Varnot's poems have appeared in a number of journals, including *Arts & Letters, Beloit Poetry Journal, Cimarron Review, Crab Orchard Review,* and *Southern Poetry Review*. She lives in California, where she teaches at University of California, Merced.

R. A. Villanueva's writing has appeared or is forthcoming in *Virginia Quarterly Review, AGNI, McSweeney's Internet Tendency, Indiana Review, DIAGRAM, The Collagist, Bellevue Literary Review,* and elsewhere. A Kundiman fellow, he lives in Brooklyn.

Adam Vines is an assistant professor of English at the University of Alabama at Birmingham, where he co-edits *Birmingham Poetry Review*. During the summers, he is on staff at The Sewanee Writers' Conference. He has published poetry in *North American Review, Greensboro Review, Cincinnati Review, Barrow Street, New Orleans Review,* and *Tampa Review,* among others.

Elizabeth Volpe is the author of *Brewing in Eden,* winner of the 2007 Robert Watson Poetry Award from Greensboro Review/Spring Garden Press. Her poems have appeared in many journals and on Verse Daily and From the Fishouse. She won The Briarcliff Review 2004 Poetry Contest, the 2006 Metro Detroit Writers Contest, and the 2008 Juniper Prize from *Alligator Juniper.*

Donna Vorreyer's poetry has appeared in many journals, including *New York Quarterly, Cider Press Review, Apparatus, Boxcar Poetry Review, qarrtsiluni,* and *After Hours.* Her chapbook *Womb/Seed/Fruit* is available from Finishing Line Press. She teaches middle school and tries to convince teenagers that words matter.

Davi Walders' poetry and prose have appeared in more than 200 journals and anthologies, been read by Garrison Keillor on Writer's Almanac, and nominated for Pushcart Prizes. Her collection, *ReSisters: Poems of Women's World War II Resistance,* was published by Clemson University Digital Press in 2011.

Valerie Wallace is an award-winning poet whose work has appeared in *Waccamaw, Potomac, RHINO, Maize, Court Green, Valparaiso Poetry Review, Santa Clara Review,* and others. She leads writing workshops in Chicago and with the Afghan Women's Writing Project.

Nagueyalti Warren is the author of *Margaret Circa 1834-1857,* a persona poem about the life of historical figure Margaret Garner, which won the Naomi Long Madgett poetry Prize in 2008. She is the editor of *Temba Tupu! (Walking Naked) Africana Women's Poetic Self-Portrait.* Her works have also appeared in anthologies and magazines.

Israel Wasserstein is lecturer in English at Washburn University in Topeka, KS. His poetry and prose have appeared in *Flint Hills Review, Blue Mesa Review, Coal City Review, Fickle Muses,* and elsewhere.

David Welch has published poems in journals including *Subtropics, Massachusetts Review,* and *Indiana Review,* and in the anthologies *Best New Poets 2007, Best of the Web 2010,* and *Helen Burns Poetry Anthology: New Voices from the Academy of American Poets' University and College Prizes: 1999-2008.* He lives in Chicago.

Gabriel Welsch is the author of the collection of poetry, *Dirt and All Its Dense Labor* (2006) and the chapbook *An Eye Fluent in Gray* (2010). He works as vice president of advancement and marketing at Juniata College, in Huntingdon, PA, where he lives with his wife and daughters.

Carolyn Beard Whitlow, Dana Professor of English at Guilford College in NC, won the 2006 Naomi Long Madgett Poetry Award for *Vanished* and has poems and essays in *African American Review, The Kenyon Review, The Massachusetts Review, Indiana Review, Callaloo, Crab Orchard Review, Cold Mountain Review, 5 A.M.*, and the anthologies *After New Formalism* and *Gathering Ground.*

Caki Wilkinson's poems have appeared in *The Atlantic, Poetry, Yale Review*, and other journals. Her first collection of poems, *Circles Where the Head Should Be*, won the 2010 Vassar Miller Prize and was published in 2011.

Eliot Khalil Wilson's first book of poems, *The Saint of Letting Small Fish Go*, won the Cleveland State Poetry Prize. His second book, *This Island of Dogs*, will be published by Margie/Intuit Press.

L. Lamar Wilson, a Cave Canem Fellow and English Ph.D. student at UNC-Chapel Hill, has poetry in *Callaloo, Rattle, Crab Orchard Review, Obsidian, Mythium* and the *100 Best African American Poems.* Like Robert McFerrin, Sr., he was born in a Southern town called Marianna and writes from and about it often.

Laura Madeline Wiseman is a doctoral candidate at the University of Nebraska-Lincoln, where she teaches English. She is the author of *My Imaginary* (Dancing Girl Press, 2010), *Ghost Girl* (Pudding House, 2010), and *Branding Girls* (Finishing Line Press, 2011). Her work has appeared in *Margie, Blackbird*, and *Prairie Schooner.*

Carolyne L. Wright's eight books and chapbooks of poetry include *A Change of Maps* (Lost Horse Press, 2006), and *Seasons of Mangoes and Brainfire* (EWUP/Lynx House Books, 2nd edition 2005), winner of the Blue Lynx Prize and American Book Award. *Mania Klepto: the Book of Eulene* was published by WordTech in 2011.

Erica Wright is the author of the collection of poems *Instructions for Killing the Jackal* (Black Lawrence Press/Dzanc Books) and the chapbook *Silt* (Dancing Girl Press). She is the Poetry Editor at *Guernica Magazine.*

Jake Adam York is the author of three books of poems: *Persons Unknown* (Southern Illinois University Press, 2010), *A Murmuration of Starlings* (Southern Illinois University Press, 2008, co-winner of the Crab Orchard Open Competition in Poetry) and *Murder Ballads* (Elixir, 2005). He is a professor at the University of Colorado Denver and an editor for *Copper Nickel.*

Credits

For their assistance and support, we would like to thank Adrian Matejka, Meredith Josey, Gabriel Fried, Howard Rambsy II, and Matt O'Donnell.

We'd also like to thank our colleagues and students at Southern Illinois University Edwardsville and Western Washington University. Additional thanks to Western Washington University for the Manuscript Preparation Grant that assisted in the preparation of this book and to the SIUE Undergraduate Research and Creative Assistants—Abby Souza, Bridget Nelson, Jeremiah Driver, and Denise Clamors—whose help with this project was invaluable.

Our gratitude to everyone at The University of Akron Press, especially Mary Biddinger, Thomas Bacher, Carol Slatter, and Amy Freels.

Finally, grateful acknowledgment is made to the following rights-holders for their permission to print and/or reprint the poems in this anthology:

Dan Albergotti: "Still Bound" appears in *The Boatloads* by Dan Albergotti. Copyright © 2008. Reprinted by permission of BOA Editions.

Maureen Alsop: "Leda's Flashback" appears in *Apparition Wren* by Maureen Alsop. Copyright © 2007. Reprinted by permission of Main Street Rag.

Francisco Aragón: "Liu Minghe Speaks" first appeared in *The Journal*. Copyright © 2003. Reprinted by permission of the author.

Cynthia Arrieu-King: "Setsuko Hara" first appeared in *Fogged Clarity*. Copyright © 2009. Reprinted by permission of the author.

Elizabeth Austen: "It Didn't Happen that Way" first appeared in the anthology *The Moment Witnessed*, published by the Skagit River Poetry Festival. Copyright © 2008. Reprinted by permission of the author.

Hershman John: "I am the Immaculate Conception" first appeared in *Yellow Medicine Review*. Copyright © 2007. Reprinted by permission of the author.

Mary Kaiser: "A Medium Rehearses the Square Order Shuffle" first appeared in *PMS poem/memoir/story*. Copyright © 2010. Reprinted by permission of the author.

Ilya Kaminsky: "Musica Humana" appears in *Dancing in Odessa* by Ilya Kaminsky. Copyright © 2004. Reprinted by permission of Tupelo Press.

Ariana-Sophia Kartsonis: "Pinocchio's Elegy for the Unreal" first appeared in *Bellevue Literary Review*. Copyright © 2001. Reprinted by permission of the author.

Collin Kelley: "Go Somewhere with Me" appears in *We Don't Stop Here* by Collin Kelley. Copyright © 2008. Reprinted by permission of The Private Press.

Jee Leong Koh: "Seven Studies for a Self-Portrait" first appeared in *Ganymede* (2009) and appears in *Self Studies for a Self Portrait* by Jee Leong Koh. Copyright © 2011. Reprinted by permission of Bench Press.

Jason Koo: "Man on Extremely Small Island" appears in *Man on Extremely Small Island*, by Jason Koo. Copyright © 2009. Reprinted by permission of C&R Press.

Keetje Kuipers: "Speaking as the Male Poet" first appeared in *Painted Bride Quarterly*. Copyright © 2010. Reprinted by permission of the author.

Laurie Clements Lambeth: "Case History: Frankenstein's Lesions" appears in *Veil and Burn* by Laurie Clements Lambeth. Copyright © 2008. Reprinted by permission of the University of Illinois Press.

Quraysh Ali Lansana: "fodderhouse" appears in *They Shall Run: Harriet Tubman Poems* by Quraysh Ali Lansana. Copyright © 2004. Reprinted by permission of Third World Press.

Sarah Lindsay: "Constantinople, Plague Summer" appears in *Primate Behavior* by Sarah Lindsay. Copyright © 1997. Reprinted by permission of Grove/Atlantic, Inc.

Sandy Longhorn: "Etude" appears in *Blood Almanac* by Sandy Longhorn. Copyright © 2006. Reprinted by permission of Anhinga Press.

Peter Ludwin: "Notes from a Sodbuster's Wife, Kansas, 1868" first appeared in *South Dakota Review* and appears in *A Guest in All Your Houses*. Copyright © 2009. Reprinted by permission of Word Walker Press.

Alison Luterman: "The Ballad of Greg Withrow" appears in *The Largest Possible Life* by Alison Luterman. Copyright © 2001. Reprinted by permission of Cleveland State University Press.

Marie-Elizabeth Mali: "Steady, My Gaze" appears in *Steady, My Gaze* by Marie-Elizabeth Mali. Copyright © 2011. Reprinted by permission of Tebot Bach.

Index